5 Ideas from Global Diplomacy

System-wide Transformation Methods to
Close the Compliance Gap and
Advance the 2030 Sustainable Development Goals

Marvin Cheung

GROUND ZERO BOOKS LLC
New York, NY

2024 Summer Preprint

First published 2024
by Ground Zero Books LLC
New York, NY

Disclaimer: The ideas and opinions expressed in this book
are those of the author's and can in no way be taken to
reflect the official views of the United Nations, UNITAR,
or affiliated organizations. The designations employed and
the presentation of the material in this publication do not
imply the expression of any opinion whatsoever concerning
the legal status of any country, territory, city or area or of
its authorities, or concerning delimitation of its frontiers or
boundaries. Trade names or commercial processes cited do
not constitute endorsement.

Trademark notice: Product or corporate names may be
trademarks or registered trademarks, and are used only for
identification and explanation without intent to infringe.

Library of Congress Control Number: 2024909204

ISBN: 979-8-218-41883-0 (paperback)
ISBN: 979-8-218-42843-3 (hardcover)

Doi: https://doi.org/10.17613/xzxt-7567

Cover illustration and design by Marvin Cheung
Typeset in Times New Roman

Dedicated to all

who create space

for dialogue and change

About the Author

Marvin Cheung

Marvin Cheung is a business executive and global governance scholar. He co-directs the Center for Global Agenda (CGA) and directs the Venture Strategy Group (VSG) at Unbuilt Labs, where he serves as a special advisor to individuals, boards, and research organizations. He advises on the ideas, methods, and organizations that have the potential to change global dynamics. He is a Global Diplomacy Fellow at the United Nations Institute for Training and Research (UNITAR), a UNESCO Inclusive Policy Lab Expert on the 2030 Sustainable Development Goals and Strategic Planning, and a member of different groups, including the Harvard Business Review Advisory Council, Planetary Health Alliance, Boards Impact Forum, and Chairman's Network, where he regularly shares research and perspectives to private and public Boards of Directors. In 2022, he succeeded the advisor to four successive Directors General at the International Institute for Applied Systems Analysis (IIASA) as Chair of the Global Consortium for Systems Research (GCSR). In 2023, he began serving on the Advisory Board of the Lifeboat Foundation, dedicated to mitigating existential risks, alongside four Nobel Laureates. He was a featured speaker at the United Nations General Assembly Science Summit.

Marvin holds an MA from the Johns Hopkins School of Advanced International Studies, and a BFA from the Parsons School of Design. He was also a Departmental Visiting Student at the University of Oxford.

Contents

Part 1 Theoretical Perspectives

Part 2 Findings & Discussions

Part 3 Conclusion & Recommendations

Table of Contents

Part 1 Theoretical Perspectives

Chapter 1   *Foundational Concepts*: Systems, Systems Research, and Transdisciplinary Research

Part 2 Findings and Discussions

Chapter 4 *Effecting Global Change*: **Navigating and Altering Constraints**

Chapter 5   Global Stakeholder Consultation Process

Part 3 Conclusion and Recommendations

Chapter 6   System-wide Transformation Guidance

List of Illustrations

Tables

Preface

As Co-Directors of the Center for Global Agenda (CGA) at Unbuilt Labs, we, Marguerite and Marvin, have worked with a lot of people across the private and public sectors. We began working together as we share a common background in the arts. As creatives, we were disheartened by the slow progress towards the 2030 Sustainable Development Goals, and we felt that there could be alternative ways of thinking about the methods to reach those Goals. To that end, Unbuilt Labs brought together thinkers and creatives to lead research, conferences, engagements, and publications.

This book is the culmination of a 3-year investigation. We are delighted to share our findings with you, and hope to hear from you.

Marvin Cheung
Dr. Marguerite Van Cook

Co-Directors, Center for Global Agenda (CGA) at Unbuilt Labs
New York 2024

Acknowledgements

This was an undeniably tremendous undertaking, made possible by all those who shared their time, expertise, and resources. Many researchers you find on this list like myself work behind-the-scenes: we build arguments and proofs to make recommendations on complex global challenges, and we always exercise caution because initiatives have the potential to do harm just as they have the potential to do good. Some days we feel like we have things together, then there are others when we wish we could have done more. In many respects we are ordinary people doing our jobs as meticulously as we can with the time that we have. Thank you to everyone who contributed to this publication though all errors are my own. This section is for everyone who made this project possible by sheer force of will, creativity, and dedication. Thank you!

This project would not be possible without the support of the United Nations Institute for Training and Research (UNITAR) during my time as a Global Diplomacy Fellow. I would like to offer a heartfelt thank you to my advisor H.E. Ambassador Dr. Yuriy Sergeyev (Visiting Lecturer, UNITAR) who was the first to support the project. I would also like to thank Mr. Nikhil Seth (Executive Director, UNITAR), and H.E. Ambassador Mr Marco A. Suazo (Head of New York Office, UNITAR). Thank you to my reader Ms. Larisa Schelkin (Professor of Practice, UNITAR) for her expertise on science diplomacy, and Mr. Pelayo Alvarez (Programme Coordinator, UNITAR) for his continued support.

I am grateful for the support of the Center for Global Agenda (CGA) at Unbuilt Labs, and in particular my Co-Director, Dr. Marguerite Van Cook (Adjunct Professor, Columbia University), for going on this journey with me. Thank you to the universities that provided research support. The breadth and depth of this publication was staggering. I received additional research training for this publication from the University of Oxford Dept. of Politics and International Relations and the Dept. of Continuing Education Graduate School. I have also attended many research seminars at the MIT Sloan School of Management, the University of Oxford Faculty of Law, and the Oxford Centre for Economic and Social History. They provided an understanding of different disciplinary logics that were critical to this transdisciplinary research project.

A sincere thank you goes to SDG16 Hub, a practitioner's platform hosted by the UNDP Oslo Governance Centre, for providing the space for our public forum, and the UN General Assembly Science Summit for hosting the Future of Global Governance Series Workshops. Thank you goes to the SDG16 Hub, the Network for Transdisciplinary Research of the Swiss Academies of Arts and Sciences (Td-Net), and the Academic Council on the United Nations System (ACUNS) for supporting our outreach. Thank you to the Planetary Health Alliance (PHA) at Johns Hopkins University, the Global Mental Health Action Network (GMHAN), Act4SDGs by the UN Sustainable Development Goals Action Campaign, and JISCMail for providing a platform for outreach. I would also like to recognize the value of the public archives provided by the Secretary-General's High-Level Advisory Board on Effective Multilateralism, the UNESCO Inclusive Policy Lab, the WHO Council on the Economics of Health For All, and the Internet Archive.

Thank you to everyone who took time out of their already busy lives to contribute to the Global Stakeholder Consultation Process. Special thanks goes to Benjamin Hanussek (Director, Polish-Japanese Academy of Information Technology Game Lab), Brent M. Shea, Ph.D. (Professor of Sociology, Emeritus & Adjunct, Sweet Briar College), Christina Ntulo (Country Director, StrongMinds Uganda), Damian Pattinson (Executive Director, eLife, UK), Dennis Larsen (Co-Founder and Director, Initiative for Global Sustainable Economies (IGSE); University Lecturer, BI Norwegian Business School), Domenico Dentoni (Full Professor and Co-Director of the Chair COAST (Communication and OrgAnizing for Sustainable Transformations), Montpellier Business School), Emma Leiken (Chief of Programs, Omidyar Network), Inez Harker-Schuch, Ph.D. (Co-founder, The Planet Academy; Researcher and Environmental Scientist), Ivy Kwan Arce (President, Treatment Action Group (TAG)), Jerome Glenn (CEO, The Millennium Project), Jim Hall, FREng (Professor of Climate and Environmental Risks; Director of Research, School of Geography and the Environment, University of Oxford), Joachim Nijs (Founder, 自然をつくる国日本 (Japan: Nation Building Nature)), Julien Isoré (Alan Tod, Forest Artist), Lowell Clare (Independent Researcher); Peggy Cyphers (Professor of Painting, Pratt Institute), Peter Kennard (Professor of Political Art, Royal College of Art), Rachele Hendricks-Sturrup, DHSc, MSc, MA (Research Director, Real World Evidence, Duke-Margolis Institute for Health

Policy), Shady El Damaty, Ph.D. (President, OpSci; Co-Founder, Holonym), Steve MacFeely (Director of Data and Analytics, World Health Organization (WHO)), Stuart RF King (Research Culture Manager, eLife, UK), Umberto Fracassi (Research Scientist, Istituto Nazionale di Geofisica e Vulcanologia (INGV)), and others.

Thank you to the Global Consortium for Systems Research (GCSR) for coordinating the collaborative peer review process. Special thanks goes to collaborative peer reviewers especially Andrzej Klimczuk, Ph.D. (Sociologist and public policy expert; Assistant Professor in the Department of Social Policy of the Collegium of Socio-Economics at the SGH Warsaw School of Economics, Poland), Annabel Pretty (Senior Lecturer, Te Pūkenga, Aotearoa), Brent M. Shea, Ph.D. (Professor of Sociology, Emeritus & Adjunct, Sweet Briar College), Jacqueline Mitchell (Professor Emeritus in Health, Futurist, and Community Advocate), Roni Kay M. O'Dell, Ph.D. (Associate Professor of Political Science, Coordinator of the Political Science and Global Studies Program, Seton Hill University), Dr. Marguerite Van Cook (Adjunct Professor, Columbia University), Umberto Fracassi (Research Scientist, Istituto Nazionale di Geofisica e Vulcanologia (INGV)), and others.

Thank you goes to the participants of our Global Stakeholder Consultation Process as well. Special thanks to Arthur Wandzel (Founder, Delta Capture), Cathleen Zeippen (Independent), James Romberger (Artist and Professor, School of Visual Arts), Lee Cherry (NC State University College of Design), Louise O'Boyle (Associate Dean (Academic Quality & Student Experience), Ulster University), Martina De Sole (Director, European Network of Living Labs (ENoLL)), Nabiha Miskini (Chief Service, National Institute of Statistics), Sarah Johnson (PhD Candidate, Kingston School of Art), Dr. Swati Bute (Associate Professor, Jagran Lakecity University, Bhopal-India), and others.

Thank you to the many people who supported this project off the record.

Thank you to my friends and family in every sense of the word, and thank you to my Airedale Terrier Frederic.

List of Abbreviations

ACUNS	Academic Council on the United Nations System
A/Res/70/1	Resolution of the United Nations General Assembly: 1st Resolution of the 70th session in 2015
CAS	complex adaptive systems
CDT	United Nations Institute for Training and Research Core Diplomatic Training
CERI	Organisation for Economic Co-operation and Development Centre for Educational Research and Innovation
CGA	Center for Global Agenda at Unbuilt Labs
CPRP	Collaborative Peer Review Process
CST	Critical Systems Thinking
DESA	United Nations Department of Economic and Social Affairs
DPPA	United Nations Department of Political and Peacebuilding Affairs
DSG	United Nations Deputy Secretary-General
DSG/SM/	United Nations Deputy Secretary-General statements and messages
ESG	Environmental, Social, and Governance
EU	European Union
GC	grand challenges
GCSR	Global Consortium for Systems Research
GDI	United Nations Institute for Training and Research Global Diplomacy Initiative
Goals	2030 Sustainable Development Goals
GPG	Global Public Goods
GSDR	United Nations Global Sustainable Development Report
HST	Hard Systems Thinking
IIASA	International Institute for Applied Systems Analysis
IIR	Venture Strategy Group at Unbuilt Labs, Innovator in Residence Program
INGO	international non-governmental organization
IO	international organization

IPCC	Intergovernmental Panel on Climate Change, the United Nations body for assessing the science related to climate change
IPE	international political economy
IR	international relations
ISC	International Science Council
ISSS	International Society for the Systems Sciences
MNC(s)	Multinational corporation(s)
MSMEs	micro-, small and medium enterprises
NGO	non-governmental organization
NHS	National Health Service
OECD	Organisation for Economic Co-operation and Development
OICT	United Nations Office of Information and Communications Technology
PAR	participatory action research
Pilcrow (¶)	paragraph
Q&A(s)	Question and Answer(s)
R&D	research and development
SDGs	2030 Sustainable Development Goals
SDPAR	Sustainable Development and Participatory Action Research
SDSN	Sustainable Development Solutions Network
SFDR	Sustainable Finance Disclosure Requirements
SG	United Nations Secretary-General
SG/SM/	United Nations Secretary-General statements and messages
SST	Soft Systems Thinking
SSUNGA	United Nations General Assembly Science Summit
Td-Net	Network for Transdisciplinary Research of the Swiss Academies of Arts and Sciences
TDR	transdisciplinary research
TSG	Transdisciplinary Systems Guidance
TSR	Transdisciplinary Systems Research
TSR RQ	Transdisciplinary Systems Research, Research Questions
TST	Transdisciplinary Systems Thinking
UN	United Nations
UNCTAD	United Nations Conference on Trade and Development
UNDP	United Nations Development Programme
UNESCO	United Nations Educational, Scientific and Cultural Organization

UNESCO	United Nations Educational, Scientific and Cultural
IBE	Organization International Bureau of Education
UNFCCC	United Nations Framework Convention on Climate Change
UNGP	United Nations Global Pulse
UNITAR	United Nations Institute for Training and Research
UNU	United Nations University
UNU CPR	United Nations University Centre for Policy Research
VSG	Venture Strategy Group at Unbuilt Labs
WBA	World Benchmarking Alliance
WBCSD	World Business Council for Sustainable Development
WHO	World Health Organization

Part 1

Theoretical Perspectives

1

Foundational Concepts: Systems, Systems Research, and Transdisciplinary Research

1.0 Outline

Reaching the 2030 Sustainable Development Goals is a challenge – if the solutions were simple or obvious, we would have already reached the Goals. Despite increasing awareness globally that the Goals are a systems problem and a system-wide transformation is necessary, guidance on *methods* have been extremely lacking. Given the Goals' interconnectedness, this book does not seek to target one Goal but rather the contemporary global governance network in which we all participate. However, as I show in *Section 1.2.3*, past efforts to devise guidance for a system-wide transformation have been inconsistent in their understanding of systems, and tend to offer imperatives despite *operationally* and *managerially independent*[1] actors within the contemporary global governance network. As a response, I develop a novel approach known as Transdisciplinary Systems Research to provide actionable recommendations.

---

[1] See *Table 1.1.*

To offer some definitions:
- *global diplomacy* describes the set of principles, methods, and actions to achieve the common goals of the global community within the contemporary global governance network[2]
- a *compliance gap* in international law occurs when action falls short of commitments to international agreements e.g. progress towards the 2030 Sustainable Development Goals (the Goals) in A/Res/70/1
- the *contemporary global governance network* refers to the complex global processes post-1990s that enable stakeholders to commit to and act upon shared goals, with managerially and operationally independent stakeholders[3]

It is also important to recognize the subtle distinction between a system-wide transformation from systems research in *Part I*, its methods from neo-institutionalist theory in *Part II*, and guidance based on the theory and practice of global diplomacy in *Part III*:
- *System-wide transformation* describes large scale, longer term changes to close the compliance gap and advance the 2030 Sustainable Development Goals[4]
- *System-wide transformation methods* provide stakeholders[5] with the means to navigate and alter the formal (i.e. laws and policies) and informal (i.e. cultural) constraints that limit progress towards closing the compliance gap and advancing the 2030 Sustainable Development Goals[6]
- *System-wide transformation guidance* refers to advice that is grounded in implementation knowledge, and formulated to help stakeholders achieve a *system-wide transformation*[7]

Guidance to reach the Goals is challenging to formulate, but I have done my best to ensure this publication is engaging despite the subject's complexity. As a transdisciplinary research project, this study sought to create knowledge collaboratively with academic and non-academic stakeholders. The final written output presents not just the research, but also the interactions I had with diverse voices. *Chapter 1* is relatively conversational. It introduces core systems

---

[2] Sergeyev, Yuriy. "Sergeyev's Letter," November 9, 2021. p. 1.

[3] See *Section 4.1*.

[4] See *Section 1.2.1*.

[5] *Stakeholder* refers to all individuals, social groups, or organizations, that possess an interest, a legal obligation, a moral right, or other concern in the decisions or outcomes of the 2030 Sustainable Development Goals (adapted from Britannica)

[6] See *Section 4.2*.

[7] See *Section 6.2*.

research concepts through a series of deidentified Question and Answers (Q&As). It is my hope that these editorial decisions will increase the readability and relevance of the book to a wide audience.

This chapter frames a system-wide transformation as a grand challenge with properties of wicked problems. It establishes definitions and offers conceptual clarity in some challenging areas. This is particularly important in transdisciplinary research as multiple paradigms are synthesized, then put forward for workshop and consultation with a wide range of stakeholders. To be more specific, Chapter 1 reviews the literature on *systems, complex adaptive systems, systems change, system-wide transformation, grand challenges, wicked problems, systems research*, and *transdisciplinary research* to identify literature gaps. In so doing, it lays the foundation for the next chapter on Transdisciplinary Systems Research (TSR). *Figure 1.1* describes how this chapter is structured.

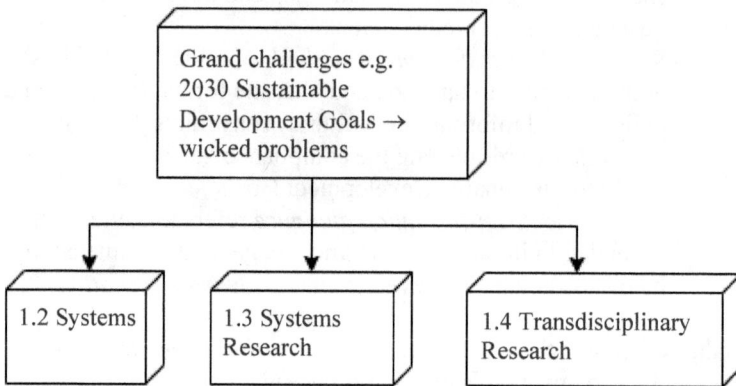

Grand challenges e.g. 2030 Sustainable Development Goals → wicked problems

1.2 Systems

1.3 Systems Research

1.4 Transdisciplinary Research

Figure 1.1. Outline for *Chapter 1*

1.1 *The Business of Doing Good*: A Workplace Anecdote

"Marvin, what is the right thing to do here?"
— The Starting Question

As a researcher and an advisor, I receive this question often. I offer an anecdote in this section to discuss the nuances and challenges of addressing this question in relation to the 2030 Sustainable Development Goals. I began my career as an architecture researcher at an EU-funded program on Hong Kong's public housing crisis, and later intrigued by the intersections of data and design I worked in Tech. I specialize in delivering actionable recommendations in high risk, high uncertainty environments. I have done so for multimillion dollar products and continue to advise private and public Board of Directors today. After the Cambridge Analytica incident broke news in 2018, I looked for perspectives on technology outside the industry and moved to the field of sustainable development in late 2019.

From the early 2000s to the mid-2010s, almost anything from Tech was "good": there was excitement, opportunity, and optimism in the air. There was a reliable process of answering what was the right thing to do: prioritize profitability or growth, optimize for engagement or transactions, evaluate macroeconomic or industry trends, segment the data, conduct user research, redesign the product, restructure the team, and *voila* — the right thing to do. It is not lost on me that many companies still follow that process today. By mid-2010s however, the deleterious effects of misinformation and disinformation cast a dark shadow over the industry. What was once a relatively straight forward question became fraught with peril.

Of the many conversations I had in the private sector on sustainable development, there is one I remember particularly well. It was with an early-stage startup's founder in 2020. The founder's startup, which was a leader in the space then, had little evidence to demonstrate its potential positive impact but a high potential for causing significant harm at a country-level scale. The answer ought to be straightforward: shut it down. However, multiple versions of that startup had already been funded by different investors and venture capital funds. Even if this startup had shut down, others would still grow. The startup's founder demonstrated the desire to curtail harm through organization policies, but a startup with no guardrails could overtake its market leader position. Oftentimes, there will be no outside intervention, e.g. regulations, until there is clear evidence of harm. This is reasonable to allow for innovation and to avoid government overreach, but it leaves a large grey area with little guidance.

In 2020, the guidance adopted by business communities was limited. On one hand, there are some things we know to be good, such as equal opportunity (e.g. gender equality and anti-discrimination) and climate action, but that is a very short list. Most people's work does not fall within this scope. It is one of the problems when we focus so narrowly on *sustainability* which is typically associated with climate action, instead of *sustainable development* which has a critical peace component. On the other hand, there are macro-level (e.g. country-level, regional-level, and global-level) indicators for the 2030 Sustainable Development Goals to guide action. Between the narrow scope and macro-level indicators, and taking into account that there is still little consensus on how to reach these goals, the advice I could offer then was minimal.

To offer more context, the subject of sustainable development was still new to the business community in early 2020. The 2030 Sustainable Development Goals were only enacted in 2015. Sustainability and sustainable development entered mainstream business lexicon in mid-2020 after Environmental, Social, and Governance (ESG) reporting requirements entered into law: the Hong Kong Stock Exchange (HKEX) began ESG disclosure requirements in July 2020 (HKEX A27 Version 3), the European Union Sustainable Finance Disclosure Requirements (SFDR) entered into force in March 2021 (Regulation (EU) 2019/2088), and the U.S. SEC's Climate and ESG Task Force created in March 2021 (SEC Press Release 2021-42) issued its first enforcement action in April 2022 (SEC Press Release 2022-72).

The options I laid out for the startup were: (1) shut down the startup and work on another project knowing that other people may still pursue the idea, (2) put in guardrails even though other companies may overtake the company's market leader position, (3) try to outlast competitors by putting in guardrails later, but before investors install a different CEO as the founders' shares get diluted from multiple funding rounds. Each of the options carried its own risks and benefits to the founders personally, the leadership team, the organization, and the broader community. Executives from startups to multinational companies face these options on a range of very contentious issues.

There is a tendency to question the integrity of individual actors without addressing systemic problems. Stories like this seem to make great headlines: CEO or President sent to jail for some years after a scandal. However, these headlines give the false impression that the problem is resolved once the rogue actor is caught and mask structural problems. A systems approach asks questions like: *Why are we stuck here? Why are we presented with this narrow list of unsatisfactory options in the first place?* Most of the time, the already narrow list of options gets even narrower because of our positions: who we are, who we have to support, who we represent, who is around us, and so forth.

This book is about creating options. It is about stepping back and identifying a broad range of methods to support a system-wide transformation for the 2030 Sustainable Development Goals. Everyone will be able to find at least one or two methods in global diplomacy they can contribute to at their workplace or in their everyday lives. Some of the methods have a track record of success while others have gained traction more recently. I outline clear recommended action in the last chapter, but I hope the chapters leading up to the guidance will inspire your own conclusions. The complexity of the solution parallels the complexity of the challenge, but the simple answer is: *a system-wide transformation can be achieved only when everyone takes a step forward together, like a puzzle that will be solved only when we turn all the keys at the same time.*

If I were talking to the same founder again today, I would recommend shutting down the initiative when there is reason to believe that it is likely to do more harm than good, and directing his energy elsewhere. This raises some tough questions: *What is next? Where should we direct commercial activities and creative energy to support sustainable development if nothing other than reducing consumption is sustainable? How do we deliver a system-wide transformation to achieve the 2030 Sustainable Development Goals?* I began my affiliation with the United Nations in search of answers, and this book documents my findings.

1.2 Systems

1.2.1 Definition of "System-wide Transformation" and Properties of Complex Adaptive Systems (CAS)

> *"Marvin, how would you even begin to answer the*
> *question about system-wide transformation for the*
> *2030 Sustainable Development Goals?" — In a car*
> *with an investigator for multinational companies*

The phrase "we need a system-wide transformation" is often used to explain why we struggle to close the compliance gap and advance the 2030 Sustainable Development Goals. The challenge with the phrase is that it *seems* all-encompassing especially given the prevalence of "systems" e.g. the legal system, the climate system, and the education system. In 1980, systems researchers Boulding, Boulding, and Burgess argued that a system is "anything that is not chaos"[8]: there is a system anytime there is a pattern, order, or structure[9]. Contemporary systems research however can offer more clarity on "system" and "system-wide transformation".

At its simplest level, a *system* is a collection of parts that interact to form a whole, whose characteristics depend both on the characteristics of the parts and their interconnections[10]. However, a *system-wide transformation* actually references a specific type of system known as complex adaptive systems (CAS)[11]. CAS are complex and adaptive. *Complexity* lies at the edge of chaos: there is insufficient agreement and certainty, but not so much disagreement that the system is

---

[8] Kenneth Boulding, Elise Boulding, and Guy Burgess, *The Social System of the Planet Earth* (Massachusetts: Addison-Wesley Publishing Company, 1980). p. IX.
[9] *ibid.*
[10] Evandro Agazzi, "Systemic Thinking: An Introduction," in *The Systemic Turn in Human and Natural Sciences: A Rock in The Pond*, ed. Lucia Urbani Ulivi, Contemporary Systems Thinking (Switzerland: Springer Nature, 2019), IX–XVII. p. X.
[11] Sobia Khan et al., "Embracing Uncertainty, Managing Complexity: Applying Complexity Thinking Principles to Transformation Efforts in Healthcare Systems," *BMC Health Services Research*, March 21, 2018, https://doi.org/10.1186/s12913-018-2994-0.

considered completely random or chaotic[12]. This idea can be understood intuitively: "coherent life on this planet is possible for us because the world outside ourselves does appear to be regular, not capricious."[13] Something is *adaptive* if it responds to input[14]. Consequently, *complex adaptive systems* can be understood as a collection of deeply interwoven parts and wholes that (1) cannot be understood in isolation, and (2) respond unpredictably to input. *Table 1.1* shows the defining characteristics of CAS in greater detail.

System concepts offer some clarity to the term *system-wide*. *System-wide* is used to specify changes at a system level as opposed to changes at a parts level, since systems can behave in similar ways despite changes at a parts level[15]. Whereas *change* can mean small or large-scale, short or long-term alterations, *transformation* is used to specify large-scale, longer-term changes[16]. The term "longer-term" here is used to recognize the *dynamic*[17] nature of CAS. Therefore, system-wide transformation *generally* refer to large-scale, longer-term changes within a complex adaptive system.

---

[12] Paul E Plsek and Trisha Greenhalgh, "Complexity Science: The Challenge of Complexity in Health Care," *BMJ* 323 (September 15, 2001). p. 627.
[13] Peter Checkland, *Systems Thinking, Systems Practice* (Chichester and New York: John Wiley & Sons, 1981). p. 3.
[14] Bob Williams and Richard Hummelbrunner, *Systems Concepts in Action: A Practitioner's Toolkit* (California: Stanford Business Books, 2011). p. 93.
[15] Pamela Buckle Henning, "Competencies Necessary for Systems Research," in *A Guide to Systems Research: Philosophy, Processes and Practice*, ed. Mary C. Edson, Pamela Buckle Henning, and Shankar Sankaran, vol. 10, Traditional Systems Sciences (Singapore: Springer Nature, 2017), 177–98. p. 182.
[16] Sandra Waddock, "Thinking Transformational System Change," *Journal of Change Management*, March 5, 2020, https://doi.org/10.1080/14697017.2020.1737179. p. 1.
[17] See *Table 1.1*.

Table 1.1 Properties of complex adaptive systems (CAS)

Property	Description
1. Starting condition-dependency	System behavior is highly dependent on starting conditions. Different starting conditions result in different behaviors.
2. Tightly coupled	System behavior is highly dependent upon interactions between a complex adaptive system's parts and its external environment.
3. Path dependency	System history influences current behavior and future events.
4. Feedback loops	Continuous feedback can either amplify or diminish the effects of an event.
5. Prescence of trade-offs	Time delays in feedback create different long-run and short-run responses, which may result in worse-before-better behavior or vice versa.
6. Self-organize	Parts continuously renew, resulting in new relationships, forms, or patterns of behavior (natural selection).
7. Evolve	Parts are influenced by and mutually adapt to changes.
8. Intentionality	CAS adapt towards some ends depending on what the system prioritizes or values, survival is an example of such.
9. Dynamic	Even systems that appear to be unchanging vary over a longer time horizon.
10. Emergence	New properties or "emergent behaviors" appear during the process of self-organization, which may come about suddenly.
11. Non-linearity	CAS respond unpredictably to input: the effects of an event cannot be predetermined or reduced to original intentions, and it is difficult if not impossible to establish clear relations of cause and effect.
12. System of systems	CAS are characterized by decentralized, distributed, and networked compositions of heterogeneous (diverse) and (semi)autonomous parts.

12A. Operationally independent parts	(*Property of system of systems*) The parts within the system fulfill purposes of their own and continue to operate for those purposes even when removed from the overall system.
12B. Managerially independent parts	(*Property of system of systems*) The parts within the system are not managed only for the purposes of the overall system.

Sources: Bob Williams and Richard Hummelbrunner, *Systems Concepts in Action: A Practitioner's Toolkit* (California: Stanford Business Books, 2011). p. 24, 25, 99, 167; Francesco Lamperti, Irene Monasterolo, and Andrea Roventini, "Climate Risks, Economics and Finance: Insights from Complex Systems," in *The Systemic Turn in Human and Natural Sciences: A Rock in The Pond*, ed. Lucia Urbani Ulivi, Contemporary Systems Thinking (Switzerland: Springer Nature, 2019), 97–119. p. 101; John D. Sterman, *Business Dynamics: Systems Thinking and Modeling for a Complex World* (McGraw-Hill Higher Education, 2000). p. 22; Claire Gear, Elizabeth Eppel, and Jane Koziol-Mclain, "Advancing Complexity Theory as a Qualitative Research Methodology," *International Journal of Qualitative Methods* 17, no. 1 (December 1, 2018): 1609406918782557, https://doi.org/10.1177/1609406918782557; Tim Gomersall, "Complex Adaptive Systems: A New Approach for Understanding Health Practices," *Health Psychology Review* 12, no. 4 (December 2018): 405–18, https://doi.org/10.1080/17437199.2018.1488603; Tariq Samad and Anuradha Annaswamy, "The Impact of Control Technology" (Institute of Electrical and Electronics Engineers Control Systems Society, 2011). p. 175; Raghav Rajagopalan, *Immersive Systemic Knowing: Advancing Systems Thinking Beyond Rational Analysis*, Contemporary Systems Thinking (Switzerland: Springer Nature, 2020). p. 13-24; Ervin Laszlo, *The Systems View of the World: The Natural Philosophy of the New Developments in the Sciences* (New York: George Braziller, 1972). p. 105-106.

To be more specific, the system described in "system-wide transformation" is determined by the goal "to close the compliance gap and advance the 2030 Sustainable Development Goals", which applies to "all countries and all stakeholders" (A/Res/70/1). The system that is most able to encompass such a scope and identifies the 2030 Sustainable Development Goals as a priority is the contemporary global governance *network*, the complex global processes post-1990s that enable stakeholders to commit to and act upon shared goals[18]. It is important to differentiate between a *system* and a *network*. This publication adopts the phrase contemporary global governance *network*, to reflect the United Nations Secretary-General's call for inclusive, networked multilateralism in 2020 (SG/SM/20264). The use of the word *network* to describe contemporary global governance highlights its complex nature characterized by low centrality and high density[19], in contrast to *system* which may be misinterpreted as high in centrality[20]. This can also be observed through the way the contemporary global governance network has operationally and managerially independent stakeholders. Companies and universities, for example, would continue to operate even if they were outside of the network, and they are managed not only for the purposes of the network.

Technically speaking, *a system-wide transformation* for the purpose of this publication describes large-scale, longer-term changes within the system of systems that is the contemporary global governance network, towards closing the compliance gap and advancing the 2030 Sustainable Development Goals.

---

[18] See *Section 4.1*.

[19] Bob Williams and Richard Hummelbrunner, *Systems Concepts in Action: A Practitioner's Toolkit* (California: Stanford Business Books, 2011). p. 73.

[20] *Centrality* describes the degree of centralization i.e. the extent to which a system is organized by a single, central authority. The opposite of centralization is decentralization. These topics are discussed in further detail in *Sections 4.2.3* and *4.2.4*.

Box 1-1: System-wide Transformation is a
Normative Endeavor

A system-wide transformation is a normative endeavor, because
some outcomes are desirable and some are not[21]. A normative
claim involves value and moral judgments: some standard ought
to prevail or some course of action would be considered good[22].
To quote Laszlo: "Nothing that pursues an end is value free"[23].
This is the fundamental challenge: certain outcomes of a complex
adaptive system are highly desirable, but initiatives' effects
cannot be fully anticipated. Strategies to address these challenges
are discussed in greater detail over the next chapters.

1.2.2 System-wide Transformation as a Grand Challenge: Properties of Grand Challenges and Wicked Problems

"Marvin, why are we not further along?" – one of
the most frequently asked questions

A system-wide transformation is a type of particularly challenging
problem known as grand challenges (GC). GC's properties include
(1) global scope, (2) high significance, (3) potential to be solvable, and
(4) "wickedness"[24].

Potential to be solvable is an important component in grand
challenges' definition. Despite the "grandness" of grand challenges, it
is possible to solve them. In 1968, Churchman made a clear case for
GC's potential to be solvable: "In principle, we have the technological

---

[21] Waddock, "Thinking Transformational System Change." p. 2.

[22] Marcus George Singer, *The Ideal of a Rational Morality: Philosophical Compositions* (Oxford: Oxford University Press, 2003). p. 123.

[23] Laszlo, *The Systems View of the World: The Natural Philosophy of the New Developments in the Sciences.* p. 105-106; see also *Table 1.1*

[24] Wojciech Czakon, "Grand Challenges: A Way Out of the Ivory Tower for Management Academic Discipline," *Management Issues* 17, no. 4 (October 17, 2019), https://doi.org/10.7172/1644-9584.84.1. p. 12-13.

capability of adequately feeding, sheltering and clothing every inhabitant of the world [...] In principle, we have the technological capability of providing adequate medical care for every inhabitant of the world [...] In principle, we have the technological capability of providing sufficient education for every inhabitant of the world"[25].

Wickedness or *wicked problems* describes problems associated with intervening in CAS. They were defined by urban design professors Rittel and Webber in 1973[26]. The term "wicked problems" have become increasingly prevalent among scholars, but Lönngren and Van Poeck's review suggest it is often used gratuitously[27]. The term wicked problems suffer from similar problems as many other systems concepts:

1. *It concerns implementation*: as *Sections 1.2.3, 1.4.2* and *2.3* will discuss, implementation knowledge is not robustly gathered in academia and can at times lack rigor.
2. *It comes intuitively once articulated*: some scholars argue that the concept of wicked problems lack a theoretical basis. In *Table 1.2*, I describe Rittel and Webber's ten properties of wicked problems in relation to the latest developments on the properties of complex adaptive systems (CAS) in *Table 1.1*.
3. *It is highly prevalent*: being a common feature across most if not all social and environmental problems is a strength of the theory, not a weakness. I reflect on the properties of wicked problems explicitly in *Section 6.4*.

---

[25] Charles Churchman, *The Systems Approach* (New York: A Delta Book, 1968). p. 3.
[26] Horst W. J. Rittel and Melvin M. Webber, "Dilemmas in a General Theory of Planning," *Policy Sciences, Springer* 4, no. 2 (June 1973), https://doi.org/10.1007/BF01405730. p. 155.
[27] Johanna Lönngren and Katrien Van Poeck, "Wicked Problems: A Mapping Review of the Literature," *International Journal of Sustainable Development & World Ecology* 28, no. 6 (August 18, 2021): 481–502, https://doi.org/10.1080/13504509.2020.1859415. p. 481.

Table 1.2 Revised properties of wicked problems

Property	Revised description
1. No definitive formulation	There are many theories on the cause and urgency of a wicked problem, and the framing determines the preferred actions[28].
2. No stopping rule	A better solution may always exist, because there are multiple formulations of the same problem (1. No definitive formulation) and the *dynamic* CAS will continue to *self organize* and *evolve*[29].
3. No true-or-false solutions	There is no true-or-false solutions, only "good", "good enough", or "bad" solutions. This is because each initiative will affect stakeholders differently with the *presence of trade-offs* in CAS[30].
4. No immediate tests	The short term impacts of an initiative may be unreliable due to CAS' *path-dependency*. Simultaneously, it is not possible to isolate the long-term impact of individual initiatives as the *dynamic* CAS *self-organizes* and *evolves*[31].
5. No redo-s	Every implemented solution changes the CAS irreversibly and it cannot be returned to its previous state due to its *starting condition-dependency, path dependency*, and *non-linearity*. Attempts to change, reverse a decision, or correct for the undesired consequences pose another set of wicked problems[32].

---

[28] See Rittel and Webber 1973: "Every specification of the problem is a specification of the direction in which a treatment is considered"

[29] See Rittel and Webber 1973: "Because (according to Proposition 1) the process of solving the problem is identical with the process of understanding its nature, because there are no criteria for sufficient understanding and because they are no ends to the causal chains that link interacting open systems, the would-be planner can always try to do better"

[30] See Rittel and Webber 1973: "Their assessments of proposed solutions are expressed as 'good' or 'bad' or, more likely, as 'better or worse' or 'satisfying' or 'good enough'"

[31] See Rittel and Webber 1973: "The full consequences cannot be appraised until the waves of repercussions have completely run out, and we have no way of tracing *all* the waves through *all* the affected lives ahead of time or within a limited time span."

[32] See Rittel and Webber 1973: "every implemented solution is consequential. It leaves 'traces' that cannot be undone. [...] Many people's lives will have been irreversibly influenced, and large amounts of money will have been spent"

6. No exhaustive list of solutions or permissible operations	There is no way to prove that all solutions and permissible operations have been identified, especially considering CAS is a *dynamic* system that continues to *self-organize* and *evolve*. It is as such a matter of judgment whether the search for solutions is sufficient, and whether to pilot test or implement the solutions[33].
7. Every wicked problem is essentially unique	Even when a current problem is substantially similar to a previous one, there will always be uncertainty over whether there is a distinguishing property of overriding importance (if such a property has not already been identified) due to CAS' *starting condition-dependency*, *path dependency*, and *non-linearity*[34].
8. Every wicked problem is a symptom of another problem	The level at which a problem is considered solved depends on the judgment and perspective of the solver[35].
9. Conflicting theories	There are conflicting theories but insufficient evidence as a result of wicked problems' uniqueness (7. No identical reference) and lack of opportunity for rigorous experimentation (5. No redo-s). This results in the importance of judgment and perspective when intervening[36].
10. Real world consequences	Every initiative has real world consequences and affects the lives of others, given the *presence of trade-offs* in CAS[37].

---

[33] See Rittel and Webber 1973: "There are no criteria which enable one to prove that all solutions to a wicked problem have been identified and considered. [...] It is then a matter of *judgment* [...] which of these solutions should be pursued"

[34] See Rittel and Webber 1973: "by '*essentially* unique' we mean that, despite long lists of similarities between a current problem and a previous one, there always might be an additional distinguishing property that is of overriding importance."

[35] See Rittel and Webber 1973: "The process of resolving the problem starts with the search for causal explanation of the discrepancy. Removal of that cause poses another problem of which the original problem is a 'symptom.' In turn, it can be considered the symptom of still another, 'higher level' problem."

[36] See Rittel and Webber 1973: "Because of the essential uniqueness of the problem (see Proposition 7) and lacking opportunity for rigorous experimentation (see Proposition 5) [...] The analyst's 'world view' is the strongest determining factor in explaining a discrepancy and, therefore, in resolving a wicked problem."

[37] See Rittel and Webber 1973: "Planners are liable for the consequences of the actions they generate; the effects can matter a great deal to those people that are touched by those actions"

Sources: Horst W. J. Rittel and Melvin M. Webber, "Dilemmas in a General Theory of Planning," *Policy Sciences, Springer* 4, no. 2 (June 1973), https://doi.org/10.1007/BF01405730. p. 161; Brian W. Head, *Wicked Problems in Public Policy: Understanding and Responding to Complex Challenges* (Switzerland: Palgrave Macmillan, 2022). p. 10.

1.2.3 Review of Notable System-wide Transformation Publications for the 2030 Sustainable Development Goals

"This sounds like a good idea, are you sure
nobody has done it before?" — On a Whatsapp
call with a long-time friend and marketing
executive

There have been notable transformation publications for the 2030 Sustainable Development Goals since their enactment in 2015:

1. "Six Transformations to Achieve the Sustainable Development Goals" by the Sustainable Development Solutions Network (SDSN) in 2019
2. Global Sustainable Development Report 2019 (GSDR 2019) by an independent group of scientists appointed by the United Nations Secretary-General
3. "Transformations within Reach: Pathways to a Sustainable and Resilient world, Synthesis Report" by the International Institute for Applied Systems Analysis (IIASA) and the International Science Council (ISC) in 2020
4. "Unlocking systems transformation: Vision 2050 issue brief" by the World Business Council for Sustainable Development (WBCSD) in 2020
5. "Set a system to change a system: Seven systems transformations for benchmarking companies on the SDGs" by the World Benchmarking Alliance (WBA) in 2021

WBCSD 2020 offers the clearest and most coherent view towards systems and system-wide transformation among the five publications:

> A system is a configuration of interdependent parts connected by a web of relationships. [...] In most modern social and economic systems, the parts, or actors, have at least a degree of autonomy. But the opportunities available to them, and the choices they make, are determined in relation to what others are doing. [...] Boundaries can be drawn around systems at many levels. At the same time, systems are often nested and interlinked.[38]

Some of the publications contain inconsistencies in their approaches to systems. For example, SDSN 2019 acknowledges that "SDG outcomes [...] are interdependent with complex coupling between human, technical, and natural systems"[39], but advocates for a "modular building-blocks" approach[40]. Because each person participates in multiple systems such as the food system, the financial system, *and* the cultural system, this modular approach would struggle to capture the amplifying or diminishing effects of *feedback loops[41]*. The IIASA & ISC 2020 Synthesis Report would benefit from a *system-of-systems[42]* approach with a keen awareness of how the individual systems interact. This is in contrast to the method of synthesis which summarized reports from separate systems[43]. More generally, there is an insufficient awareness of recommendations' limitations as a result of complex adaptive system's *dynamic[44]* nature. All recommendations are context-dependent as a result of CAS' *starting condition-dependency* and *path dependency[45]*, which means the window to act is time-sensitive. When a recommended action successfully creates a longer-term system change, it will by definition alter the CAS and recommendations will have to be re-evaluated and re-aligned.

---

[38] World Business Council for Sustainable Development (WBCSD), "Unlocking Systems Transformation: Vision 2050 Issue Brief" (Geneva, June 2020). p. 7.
[39] Jeffrey D. Sachs et al., "Six Transformations to Achieve the Sustainable Development Goals," *Nature Sustainability* 2, no. 9 (September 2019): 805–14, https://doi.org/10.1038/s41893-019-0352-9. p. 805.
[40] *ibid.*
[41] See *Table 1.1.*
[42] *ibid.*
[43] Leena Srivastava, Luis Gomez Echeverri, and Flavia Schlegel, "Transformations within Reach: Pathways to a Sustainable and Resilient World, Synthesis Report" (Laxenburg, Paris: International Institute for Applied Systems Analysis (IIASA), International Science Council (ISC), January 2021). p. 10.
[44] See *Table 1.1.*
[45] *ibid.*

Another problem of note is the overuse of imperatives in the publications. It is easy to sidestep a strong understanding of context or goals when an imperative is issued. For example, WBA 2021 recommends that "transparency, leadership and accountability *must* be front and center for business to positively impact people and the planet [emphasis added]"[46]. In another example, SDSN 2019 recommends that the "scientific community *should* take on the challenge of developing tools and methods for multi-stakeholder engagement and co-design [emphasis added]"[47]. How do these recommendations encourage people to change their practices? Who would finance these activities? What is the pathway-to-impact?

While there is certainly a moral imperative to act in situations involving the 2030 Sustainable Development Goals, it is not necessarily effective to merely offer an imperative (i.e. through the use of the words "should", "must", "require", or "need") when stakeholders are *operationally* and *managerially independent*[48]. People can choose whether or not to follow a recommendation, and they have to balance other priorities. Recommendations in this context are distinct from memos which outline legal requirements, speeches which employ imperatives as a rhetoric device, and position statements which express a matter of law or condemn a violation of rights.

It would be helpful to shift from an imperative-based approach to a goal-based approach when writing recommendations. A goal-based approach involves a more careful framing of recommendations to include how recommendations align with stakeholders' goals. This can also be understood intuitively: offering reasons and compelling arguments are foundational to writing persuasively. I demonstrate this further in *Table 1.3*, which shows the same recommendation (i.e. to use fewer imperatives) with and without imperatives.

---

[46] L. Urlings, "Set a System to Change a System: Seven Systems Transformations for Benchmarking Companies on the SDGs" (Amsterdam: World Benchmarking Alliance, 2021). p. 9.
[47] Sachs et al., "Six Transformations to Achieve the Sustainable Development Goals." p. 812.
[48] See *Table 1.1*.

Table 1.3 Reframing recommendations without imperatives

Note: The table shows the benefits of reframing recommendations without imperatives (i.e. "should", "must", "require", "need").

Recommendation with imperatives	Recommendation without imperatives
As 2030 draws near, now more than ever, we *need* science-based and evidence-based recommendations. To do so, scientists and researchers, and especially systems researchers, *must* communicate effectively.	This publication offers a new recommendation to help people and organizations within the fields of research, policy, and activism communicate better. There is an overuse of imperatives – the written equivalent to yelling, in system-wide transformation recommendations.
To communicate effectively, scientists and researchers *should* use fewer imperatives – the written equivalent of yelling, in their recommendations. They *need* to start thinking like consultants or advisors to the stakeholders whose behaviors they intend to change.	Reframing recommendations with fewer imperatives can amplify our collective impact: (1) our *guidance* is more likely to be heard – nobody likes being yelled at – imagine being yelled at for 150 pages, (2) it helps us think like an advisor and offer persuasive guidance, and (3) it offers breathing room for deep thought and careful reasoning.
Many stakeholders are looking for and *require* leadership. Scientists and researchers *need* to step up to the challenge. They have demonstrated the ability to make influential recommendations in the past, and they *should* act in the interests of the global community.	We hope you will join us today in growing the space for dialogue by using fewer imperatives in your recommendations. We know this is desirable and doable – there has not been a single imperative in this recommendation! We also know that some conversations will be difficult. Is there an audience who is already listening we can mobilize? Together, we can deliver more incisive and impactful guidance for positive change. Thank you for your incredible contributions to the global community.
The importance of better communication and taking more care when using imperatives – when yelling on paper, *should* be advocated by all. Policymakers, changemakers, and activists *need* to take note of this recommendation as well. The yelling *must* stop now!	
Imperatives = **10**	Imperatives = **0**

By conducting a manifest content analysis, I calculated the estimated average imperatives per page for the five system-wide transformation publications through a simple "Find" function (Ctrl+F) for imperatives (i.e. "should", "must", "require", and "need") on a modified pdf: pages before the main contents (e.g. cover page, author list, contents, acknowledgements, foreword, preface, prologue) and after (eg. afterword, notes, bibliography, references, endnotes, appendix) are not included in the calculations. The search shows that SDSN 2019 has the highest frequency of imperatives per page, with a score of 12.4. This is followed by IIASA & ISC 2020 at 4.9, GSDR 2019 at 4.6, WBCSD 2020 at 2.6, and WBA 2021 at 2.5.

This content analysis method does not account for diagrams, images, or blank pages' contributions to the page count. It also does not account for layout or font sizes. While a more sophisticated method of analysis such as natural language processing can be used, this method provides the most accessible and user-friendly method of assessment as it is low-tech and easily replicable. It also enables authors to easily and quickly gauge the persuasiveness of their recommendations during the writing process and make revisions or reframe recommendations as necessary. There are some possible explanations for the prevalence of imperatives in system-wide transformation recommendations:

1. Authors may not have the operational expertise to offer guidance, and may benefit from industry experience or collaborations.
2. Authors have not engaged sufficiently with the people they seek to provide guidance to understand their challenges or perspectives.
3. Authors may be able to revise and reframe recommendations with time and resources where appropriate.

In short, while there has been past attempts to design a system-wide transformation, they tend to contain inconsistencies in their approaches to systems, and offer imperatives rather than guidance despite *operationally* and *managerially independent stakeholders*[49]. This publication seeks to remediate these concerns.

---

[49] See *Table 1.1.*

1.2.4 Recommendations on Applying Foundational Concepts in Systems Research to Research and Practice

"How might we use these systems research concepts
in research and practice?" – In conversation with a
management researcher on Zoom

I offer guidance on research and practice based on foundational concepts in systems research in this section.

I.   *A Normative Philosophy for a Normative Endeavor*

A system-wide transformation is an inherently normative endeavor because some outcomes are desirable while others are not[50]. This highlights the tensions between a positivist paradigm (the value-free view) and the normative paradigm (the value-based view), as well as the limits of "scientific planning" [51] and "value-free science" [52]. This has been discussed since the 1970s:

- In 1978, Webber argued that while science continues to play a critical role in elucidating the paths forward, models and equations alone cannot tell us whether the means to the end are just: "Selecting among alternative ends is among the toughest planning tasks we face, and yet there is nothing in the apparatus of science – or of engineering – that can make those valuative choices for us"[53].
- In 1979, Churchman found that morality is often a strong but hidden theme even within "objective", "value-free" items

---

[50] Waddock, "Thinking Transformational System Change." p. 2.
[51] Melvin M. Webber, "A Difference Paradigm for Planning," in *Planning Theory in the 1980's: A Search for Future Directions*, ed. Robert W. Burchell and George Sternlieb (New Brunswick, N.J.: Center for Urban Policy Research, Rutgers University, 1978), 151–62. p. 152.
[52] Philip Mirowski, "How Positivism Made a Pact with the Postwar Social Sciences in the United States," in *The Politics of Method in the Human Sciences: Positivism and Its Epistemological Others*, ed. George Steinmetz (Durham, London: Duke University Press, 2005), 142–72. p. 144.
[53] Webber, "A Difference Paradigm for Planning." p. 152.

such as standard tests: a "good" student performs well on tests[54].

- In 2005, Mirowski discussed the importance of rejecting the notion that there is knowledge "self-contained and unsullied by social considerations"[55]: research does not merely reflect an empirical reality but plays a role in constructing it[56].
- In 2020, Touboulic and McCarthy observed the way political processes are present at every stage and organization: "Under virtually all the social circumstances in which planners work, the acceptable way is necessarily the outcome of political processes."[57]

A normative approach that takes into account ethical norms and value judgments is compatible with science. The IPCC and UNESCO recognize the value of integrating scientific and local knowledge:

> *Local knowledge*: The understandings and skills developed by individuals and populations, specific to the places where they live. Local knowledge informs decision-making about fundamental aspects of life, from day-to-day activities to longer-term actions. This knowledge is a key element of the social and cultural systems which influence observations of and responses to climate change; it also informs governance decisions (UNESCO 2018)[58].

It is only when the complexity of our humanness is rigorously addressed, that opportunities to be inclusive, just, and human in the face of pressing grand challenges emerge.

---

[54] Charles Churchman, *The Systems Approach and Its Enemies* (New York: Basic Books, 1979). p. 22.
[55] Mirowski, "How Positivism Made a Pact with the Postwar Social Sciences in the United States." p. 143.
[56] Anne Touboulic and Lucy McCarthy, "Collective Action in SCM: A Call for Activist Research," *The International Journal of Logistics Management* 31, no. 1 (2020): 3–20, https://doi.org/DOI 10.1108/IJLM-08-2019-0222. p. 4.
[57] Webber, "A Difference Paradigm for Planning." p. 157.
[58] Intergovernmental Panel on Climate Change. "Climate Change 2022: Mitigation of Climate Change. Contribution of Working Group III to the Sixth Assessment Report of the Intergovernmental Panel on Climate Change," *Cambridge University Press*, 2022, https://doi.org/10.1017/9781009157926. p. 1807.

II.   *A System-wide Transformation can be Achieved Only when Everyone Takes a Step Forward Together*

The behaviors of complex adaptive systems (CAS) are notoriously difficult to predict due to their *non-linearity*[59]: "when forecasting a break from the norm, a wholly new development, or the course of change over a long timeframe, even the most seasoned analyst regresses to throwing darts"[60]. Although tipping points may be a useful concept in modelling the climate, it struggles to offer guidance on intervening in human systems[61]: (1) it is not possible to identify *where* the tipping point is in grand challenges such as zero hunger, even if it may theoretically exist in a human system, and (2) it is not possible to identify *how* the tipping point will occur. There is no precise course of action or a proverbial "silver bullet". Inclusive research and practice as a result becomes a strategic imperative because it surfaces the broadest range of possibilities and potential actions[62].

III.   *Proactively Solving Problems of Today in a Just and Inclusive way is an Investment in Future Peace and Prosperity*

In 1987, the United Nations Brundtland Commission defined sustainability as "meeting the needs of the present without compromising the ability of future generations to meet their own needs". During this study, I have seen a tendency to frame this as an either-or problem: *either* prioritize the present *or* prioritize the future. Foundational concepts in systems research show that this is unwise: as a result of *path-dependency*[63], system history influences current behavior and future events. The problems of today accumulate into the future. Expecting some form of new invention to solve *all* of our problems is unrealistic. Proactively solving the problems of today in a just and inclusive way is an investment in future peace and prosperity.

---

[59] See *Table 1.1.*
[60] Bobby W., "The Limits of Prediction - or, How I Learned to Stop Worrying About Black Swans and Love Analysis," *Studies in Intelligence* 63, no. 4 (December 2019). p. 7.
[61] Mark Nuttall, "Tipping Points and the Human World: Living with Change and Thinking about the Future," *Ambio* 41, no. 1 (January 2012): 96–105, https://doi.org/10.1007/s13280-011-0228-3. p. 96.
[62] Jonathan Antonio Edelman et al., "Designing as Performance: Bridging the Gap Between Research and Practice in Design Thinking Education," in *Design Thinking Research*, ed. Christoph Meinel and Larry Leifer, Understanding Innovation (Switzerland: Springer Nature, 2021), 75–101. p. 87.
[63] See *Table 1.1.*

IV. *Expect Rapid Change, Re-Evaluation, and Realignment of Guidance*

Technology has significantly increased the speed of *feedback loops*[64]. The rapidly changing global landscape invalidates even recent decisions – it is unproductive to force a rigid model on a fluid reality[65]. Researchers and practitioners who intend to respond to current challenges will have to expect rapid change, re-evaluation, and realignment of guidance.

V. *Use the Properties of Complex Adaptive Systems (CAS) in Table 1.1 and Properties of Wicked Problems in Table 1.2 as Checklists When Solving Grand Challenges (GC)*

Section 1.2.3 examined inconsistencies in approaches toward a system-wide transformation. *Table 1.1 Properties of CAS* and *Table 1.2 Properties of Wicked Problems* can be used as checklists to ensure that proposed solutions to grand challenges have carefully considered foundational concepts in systems research.

---

[64] See *Table 1.1*.

[65] Erich Jantsch, *Design for Evolution: Self Organization and Planning in the Life of Human Systems*, The International Library of Systems Theory and Philosophy (New York: George Braziller, 1975). p. 9.

1.3 Systems Research

> *"Systems research sounds really... messy. Is it*
> *actually helpful?" – At a bar talking to a*
> *bartender / activist*

Systems research began eighty or so years ago, in the 1940s, as a response to the increasing fragmentation and specialization of scientific disciplines[66]. The International Society for the Systems Sciences (ISSS)[67], founded in 1954 at the Stanford Center for Advanced Study in the Behavioral Sciences[68], was one of the first organizations dedicated to interdisciplinary inquiry into the nature of complex systems. In 2021, systems research received a wider range of support: researchers from 53 countries were affiliated with the International Institute for Applied Systems Analysis (IIASA)[69] and the institute received funding from organizations in Africa, the Americas, Asia, and Europe[70].

Despite the increasing awareness of systems change's importance in advancing the 2030 Sustainable Development Goals, systems research has historically faced difficulty gaining traction. In 1981, systems researcher Checkland went as far as to claim that it was "not readily recognized as a legitimate subject"[71] because its concern is not a particular set of theories or phenomena such as chemistry or physics, nor a particular problem area such as business or public administration[72]. Instead, systems research can be considered a meta-discipline that can be applied to almost any other discipline[73]. The

---

[66] OECD Science, Technology and Industry, "Addressing Societal Challenges Using Transdisciplinary Research" (OECD DSTI/STP/GSF(2020)4/FINAL, June 2020).
[67] International Society for the Systems Sciences, "About ISSS," accessed March 3, 2023, https://www.isss.org/about-isss/.
[68] *ibid.*
[69] International Institute for Applied Systems Analysis, "Annual Report 2021" (Vienna: International Institute for Applied Systems Analysis (IIASA), June 2022). p. 30.
[70] *ibid.* p. 34.
[71] Checkland, *Systems Thinking, Systems Practice.* p. 5.
[72] *ibid.*
[73] *ibid.*

perception that systems research is not a legitimate subject has changed in the past forty years: there are now systems research departments at Hull University (Systems Science)[74], Massachusetts Institute of Technology (Systems Dynamics)[75], National University of Singapore (Industrial Systems Engineering & Management)[76], University of Buenos Aires (Complex Systems)[77], and the University of Pretoria (Health Systems and Public Health)[78] to name a few.

It is important to address the (mis)perception that systems research is non-humanistic[79]. To offer a short response, it is vital to remember that our civilization — a society where people live in towns or cities, communicate by writing, and build monumental structures[80], is a system connected by our relationships. The subject of systems cannot be more human.

---

[74] Hull University Business School, "Business and Management Postgraduate Research Degrees | University of Hull," accessed March 1, 2023, https://www.hull.ac.uk/study/postgraduate/research/business-and-management-research-degrees.

[75] MIT Sloan School of Management, "System Dynamics," accessed March 1, 2023, https://mitsloan.mit.edu/phd/program-overview/system-dynamics.

[76] National University of Singapore College of Design and Engineering, "Research Degrees – Industrial Systems Engineering and Management," accessed March 4, 2023, https://cde.nus.edu.sg/isem/graduate/research-degrees/.

[77] University of Buenos Aires, "Research - Instituto de Cálculo, Universidad de Buenos Aires," accessed March 4, 2023, https://www.ic.fcen.uba.ar/en/academic-activity/research/complex-systems.

[78] University of Pretoria, "School of Health Systems and Public Health," accessed March 5, 2023, https://www.up.ac.za/school-of-health-systems-and-public-health.

[79] Laszlo, *The Systems View of the World: The Natural Philosophy of the New Developments in the Sciences*. p. 118.

[80] Sterling J. Kernek and Charles H. O'Brien, *Civiliazation Past and Present*, Studying Civilization (Glenview and London: Scott, Foresman and Company, 1987). ch. 1.

1.3.1 Definition of Systems Research (Sustained and Iterative Process of Applying Systems Thinking) and Common Elements of Systems Thinking

"How do you think about systems?"

– A common question

The exploration of systems research begins with the thinking process, a guide to help problem-solve and navigate the field[81]. This thinking process is known as systems thinking. *Systems thinking* frames a phenomenon as a system (by applying systems theories and concepts) to predict behaviors and support analysis of potential actions for improvement[82]. It has been a rapidly evolving field since its ideation in the 1960s[83]. This is in contrast to *systems research*, which could mean (1) a sustained and iterative process of applying systems thinking, or (2) conducting generalizable research into the nature of complex adaptive systems (CAS) such as their properties[84]. *Iterative* describes a repeated process that demonstrate *reciprocity* i.e. responsiveness to feedback.

---

[81] Churchman, *The Systems Approach*. p. 6.

[82] Raghav Rajagopalan, *Immersive Systemic Knowing: Advancing Systems Thinking Beyond Rational Analysis*, Contemporary Systems Thinking (Switzerland: Springer Nature, 2020). p. 24; Ross D. Arnold and Jon P. Wade, "A Definition of Systems Thinking: A Systems Approach | Elsevier Enhanced Reader," *Procedia Computer Science* 44 (2015): 669–78, https://doi.org/10.1016/j.procs.2015.03.050. p. 675.

[83] Lucia Urbani Ulivi, "Preface," in *The Systemic Turn in Human and Natural Sciences: A Rock in The Pond*, ed. Lucia Urbani Ulivi, Contemporary Systems Thinking (Switzerland: Springer Nature, 2019), V–VIII. p. VI.

[84] Debora Hammond, "Philosophical Foundations of Systems Research," in *A Guide to Systems Research: Philosophy, Processes and Practice*, ed. Mary C. Edson, Pamela Buckle Henning, and Shankar Sankaran, vol. 10, Traditional Systems Sciences (Singapore: Springer Nature, 2017), 1–19. p. 2.

Systems research represents a paradigm break from the scientific method of *reductionism* which seeks to identify and reduce a system to a sum of its parts[85]. CAS resists such an approach and demands *holism* which considers systems to be more than the sum of their parts. Holism focuses on the relationships between the parts and how they give rise to a whole[86]. Some scholars attribute the idea "the whole is greater than the sum of its parts", to Aristotle who lived between 384 and 322 BC[87]. In 1995, Reid described holistic thinking as a particularly important means of change for sustainable development as it seeks to anticipate unintended consequences and identify structural solutions[88]. There is however some uncertainty about the origins of the exact phrase[89]. Over the years, different approaches to think about systems have emerged. Despite the variation in approaches, there are common elements of systems thinking, as shown in *Table 1.4.*

---

[85] Michael C. Jackson, *Systems Thinking: Creative Holism for Managers* (West Sussex: John Wiley & Sons, 2003). p. 3.

[86] *ibid.* p. 4.

[87] Christopher Shields, "Aristotle," in *The Stanford Encyclopedia of Philosophy*, ed. Edward N. Zalta (Metaphysics Research Lab, Stanford University, 2022), https://plato.stanford.edu/archives/spr2022/entries/aristotle/.

[88] David Reid, *Sustainable Development: An Introductory Guide* (London: Earthscan Publications Ltd., 1995). p. 153.

[89] The sentence which contains such an idea can be found in Aristotle's Metaphysics Book 8 Section 1045a, but is translated differently across different versions (for example, see Ross 1924 Edition, Tredennick 1933 Edition, or Lawson-Tancred 1998 Edition); Hesiod in c. 700 BC also expressed the idea "They know not how much more the half is than the whole" (Work and Days 25-41).

Table 1.4 Common elements of contemporary systems thinking (ST)

Note: italicized terms refer to Table 1.1 Properties of CAS

Element	Description
1. Recognizing interconnections	Recognizing interconnections is the foundation of systems thinking. It involves identifying key connections between the deeply interwoven parts and whole within a system. Every link may be considered a missing link within the complexly interwoven web, and systems thinking involves tracing these links step by step. *One cannot simply leave a step out of the process of recognizing interconnections.*
2. Identifying and understanding feedback	Some interconnections come together to form cause-effect *feedback loops.* Systems thinking involves identifying the feedback loops and understanding how they affect system behavior.
3. Understanding system structure	The parts and interconnections within a system form a structure. An understanding of interconnections (Element 1) and feedback loops (Element 2) contribute towards the understanding of system structure.
4. Identifying and understanding non-linear relationships	*Non-linearity* is a key property of CAS. Understanding non-linear relationships contributes towards understanding system behavior. It is vital to be wary of reverse causation where the causes and effects of a phenomenon are mistakenly inverted (see Hill's criteria for causation).
5. Understanding dynamic behavior	Understanding interconnections, *feedback loops*, *emergence*, and *non-linearity* contribute to an understanding of dynamic behavior.
6. Reducing complexity by modelling systems conceptually	This involves using different frameworks to view a system in different ways and at different levels of abstraction.
7. Understanding systems at different scales	In 1994, Barry Richmond described this as keeping one eye on the forest and the other one on the trees: it is important to recognize different scales of systems and *systems of systems*.

8. Understanding goals, priorities, and intentions	CAS are *intentional*; it is therefore important to understand their goals, priorities, and intentions.

Sources: Ross D. Arnold and Jon P. Wade, "A Definition of Systems Thinking: A Systems Approach | Elsevier Enhanced Reader," *Procedia Computer Science* 44 (2015): 669–78, https://doi.org/10.1016/j.procs.2015.03.050. p. 676-677; Barry Richmond, "Systems Thinking/ System Dynamics: Let's Just Get on with It," *System Dynamics Review* 10, no. 2–3 (1994), https://doi.org/10.1002/sdr.4260100204. p. 140; Ton Jörg, *New Thinking in Complexity for the Social Sciences and Humanities: A Generative, Transdiciplinary Approach*, Springer Complexity (Springer, 2011). p. 49; Ervin Laszlo, *The Systems View of the World: The Natural Philosophy of the New Developments in the Sciences* (New York: George Braziller, 1972). p. 105-106; "Bradford Hill Criteria," Oxford Reference, accessed May 15, 2023, https://doi.org/10.1093/oi/authority.20110803095523346.

1.3.2 Review of Contemporary Systems Thinking for Solving Grand Challenges: Hard Systems Thinking (HST), Soft Systems Thinking (SST), and Critical Systems Thinking (CST)

"I used to be a computer systems analysts, are you talking about those kinds of systems?" – In a conversation with an Uber driver

Delineating contemporary systems thinking approaches is challenging because they exist simultaneously and influence each other. Some disciplines have historically been associated with a particular approach. For example, Hard Systems Thinking (HST) with operations research, cybernetics, and systems engineering[90]. However, just because systems researchers do not agree on one approach, does not mean a systems approach does not exist. In 1979, Churchman compared this to inferring that art does not exist because no two artists describe it the same way.

---

[90] Rajagopalan, *Immersive Systemic Knowing: Advancing Systems Thinking Beyond Rational Analysis*. p. 26.

To offer a quick overview, Checkland in 1981 coined the terms Hard Systems Thinking (HST) and Soft Systems Thinking (SST) to distinguish his interpretative approach. It was later built upon by Jackson in 1991 who coined Critical Systems Thinking (CST)[91]. This section presents a summary of the critiques and developments of contemporary systems thinking, and focuses on their ability to solve grand challenges. It offers some context for and outlines the demand for Transdisciplinary Research (*Section 1.4*) and Transdisciplinary Systems Research (*Chapter 2*). It is vital to acknowledge the value of different approaches despite the critiques. Each of the approaches has and continues to contribute towards our understanding of systems, especially on the nature of systems.

I.   Hard Systems Thinking (HST)

Hard Systems Thinking (HST) or the functionalist approach[92], refers to an approach that often takes a positivist position (i.e. empirical observations of a system will reveal law-like determinants of system behavior) or a structuralist view (i.e. underlying structures determine system behavior)[93]. Core disciplines that use the HST approach include operational research, cybernetics, systems analysis, and systems engineering[94]. HST tends to emphasize quantification and optimization through model-building[95].

Critics of HST have raised several concerns over HST's ability to solve social problems. In 1983, Hoos found that HST approaches at times reduce social problems so that they can be tackled through quantitative models[96]. In extreme cases, HST institutionalizes and legitimizes the neglect of vital parts of the social problem[97]. In 1988, Jackson further noted that the reduction of complexity can take place

---

[91] Rajagopalan, *Immersive Systemic Knowing: Advancing Systems Thinking Beyond Rational Analysis*. p. 26.

[92] *ibid*. p. 27.

[93] Michael C. Jackson, *Systems Approaches to Management* (New York: Kluwer/Plenum, 2000). p. 107.

[94] Rajagopalan, *Immersive Systemic Knowing: Advancing Systems Thinking Beyond Rational Analysis*. p. 27.

[95] Michael C. Jackson, *Systems Methodology for the Management Sciences*, Contemporary Systems Thinking (New York and London: Plenum Press, 1991). p. 80.

[96] Ida R. Hoos, *Systems Analysis in Public Policy: A Critique*, Revised (Berkeley: University of California Press, 1983). p. 240-241.

[97] *ibid*.

arbitrarily based on the biases of the modeler[98]. In 1989, Rosenhead raised the concern that HST researchers' opaque mathematical techniques lead to exclusion: both by the analyst when they see themselves as experts in the problem space, and of the analyst because of the process' opacity[99]. Additionally, he argued that this paradigm has a tendency to treat people as "passive objects"[100]. In 1991, Jackson found that HST researchers may define goals according to their own world views, values, and interests, contrary to people who would be impacted by the research findings[101]. He also observed how HST struggled to handle "wicked, messy, and ill-structured problems [...] because of the strict prerequisites that need to be met before those methodologies can be employed"[102]. These critiques point to problems with the use of opaque and reductive quantitative models to capture complex human behavior.

II.   *Soft Systems Thinking (SST)*

As a response to the limitations of HST, Soft Systems Thinking (SST) or the interpretative approach incorporates developments in the social sciences to emphasize the social construction of reality, and uses dialogue as a starting point for explorations towards accommodating competing interests[103]. Analysis in SST involves building up the fullest possible picture of the problem space before applying systems concepts and developing multiple models in parallel to represent different views of the problem[104]. There is also an emphasis on understanding the perceptions of the problem space and how people's activities can create improvements[105]. SST "turns decisively towards the 'people dimension' of complexity"[106].

---

[98] Jackson, "Systems Methodologies as Complementary Tools for Managing Situational Complexity." p. 156.

[99] Jonathan Rosenhead, "Introduction: Old and New Paradigms of Analysis," in *Rational Analysis for a Problematic World: Problem Structuring Methods for Complexity, Uncertainty and Conflict*, ed. Jonathan Rosenhead (Chichester and New York: John Wiley & Sons, 1989). p. 9.

[100] *ibid.* p. 12.

[101] Jackson, "Systems Methodologies as Complementary Tools for Managing Situational Complexity." p. 79.

[102] *ibid.* p. 133.

[103] Rajagopalan, *Immersive Systemic Knowing: Advancing Systems Thinking Beyond Rational Analysis*. p. 29.

[104] Jackson, *Systems Methodology for the Management Sciences*. p. 151.

[105] Rajagopalan, *Immersive Systemic Knowing: Advancing Systems Thinking Beyond Rational Analysis*. p. 31.

[106] Jackson, "Systems Methodologies as Complementary Tools for Managing Situational Complexity." p. 157.

There has been numerous critiques of SST. In 1989, Flood found a tendency for SST research to (a) claim one research philosophy as the legitimate one or self-sufficient (isolationism), (b) subsume knowledge without respecting the disparate methodological logic underpinning it (imperialism), and (c) develop systems research into a purely technology-driven or method-driven discipline as a result of a "pick-and-mix" strategy (unreflective pragmatism)[107]. In 1991, Jackson argued that SST takes free and open discussion among stakeholders for granted without considering the complexity and time it takes to plan such a discussion[108]. Historically underrepresented people and communities are disadvantaged in public forums[109], because power shapes which views are prioritized[110]. Where there are irreconcilable differences among stakeholders, SST methods are "neutral" to the extent that they are unable to provide guidance for action[111]. In 2020, Rajagopalan found the possibility that SST researchers can attain "objective" knowledge across competing worldviews problematic[112]. In short, SST struggles in environments with a high degree of disagreement or uncertainty.

III.   *Critical Systems Thinking (CST)*

Since the 1980s and 1990s, there has been an increasing focus on the potential of applying systems thinking to social problems. Whereas HST and SST aim to improve existing social systems and increase integration, CST was designed to challenge the status quo[113]. CST examines contradictions, conflicts, and power in social systems to support systems change[114], with an emphasis towards the practical outcomes of knowledge processes[115]. In 1991, Flood and Jackson outlined the commitments of CST including sociological awareness,

---

[107] Robert L Flood, "Six Scenarios for the Future of Systems 'Problem Solving,'" *Systems Practice* 2, no. 1 (1989), https://doi.org/10.1007/BF01061618. p. 78-82.
[108] Jackson, "Systems Methodologies as Complementary Tools for Managing Situational Complexity." p. 163.
[109] *ibid.*
[110] *ibid.*
[111] *ibid.* p. 84.
[112] Rajagopalan, *Immersive Systemic Knowing: Advancing Systems Thinking Beyond Rational Analysis.* p. 31.
[113] Jackson, "Systems Methodologies as Complementary Tools for Managing Situational Complexity." p. 158.
[114] *ibid.*
[115] *ibid.* p. 195.

human well-being and emancipation, as well as complementarism[116]. Pluralism suggests the co-existence of disparate perspectives, but complementarism emphasizes the synthesis of disparate perspectives[117]. Methods of CST include creative holism, Total System Intervention, and Systemic Intervention.

Critics of CST argue that it does not sufficiently consider the types of knowledge produced by non-academic stakeholders. In 1996, Midgley expressed concern over the use of "human emancipation" in early (pre-1992) CST as it can give the impression that human well-being is detached from the environment[118]. He also questioned whether CST can be described as meta-paradigmatic as a result of CST's theoretical incommensurability with other systems paradigms[119]. In 2020, Rajagopalan argued that CST is strongly rooted in rationalism and struggles to include non-academic stakeholders in the process of knowledge production[120]. Transdisciplinary research in the next section provides the means to address critiques of CST.

---

[116] Robert L. Flood and Michael C. Jackson, "Total Systems Intervention: A Practical Face to Critical Systems Thinking," *Systems Practice* 4, no. 3 (June 1991): 197–213, https://doi.org/10.1007/BF01059565. p. 198.
[117] Jackson, *Systems Methodology for the Management Sciences*. p. 262-264.
[118] Gerald Midgley, "What Is This Thing Called CST," in *Critical Systems Thinking: Current Research and Practice*, ed. Robert L Flood and Norma R. A. Romm (New York and London: Plenum Press, 1996), 11–24. p. 21.
[119] *ibid.* p. 22.
[120] Rajagopalan, *Immersive Systemic Knowing: Advancing Systems Thinking Beyond Rational Analysis*. p. XIV.

1.4 Transdisciplinary Research (TDR)

"What do you mean by transdisciplinary?" – At a
playground with an environmental scientist from
a government agency

Scholz offers a succinct introduction to transdisciplinary research (TDR): "Transdisciplinarity aspires to make the change *from research for society to research with society*"[121].

TDR first emerged at the OECD International Conference on Interdisciplinary Research and Education in 1970[122]. It is a knowledge-creation and problem solving approach where academic and non-academic stakeholders (such as private and public sector actors as well as local or underrepresented communities) work together across disciplinary boundaries to meet the complex[123] challenges of society[124]. In 1993, Mittelstraß observed how "Disciplines are historical entities and their boundaries are historical boundaries"[125]. In 2001, Sholz and Marks observed: "universities have departments, the real world has problems"[126]. By bridging theory and

---

[121] Roland W. Scholz, "Mutual Learning as a Basic Principle of Transdisciplinarity" (International Transdisciplinarity Conference. Transdisciplinarity: Joint Problem-Solving among Science, Technology and Society, Zürich, 2000), 13–17, https://www.researchgate.net/publication/258820048_Mutual_Learning_as_a_Basic_Principle_of_Transdisciplinarity. p. 13.

[122] OECD Science, Technology and Industry, "Addressing Societal Challenges Using Transdisciplinary Research" (OECD DSTI/STP/GSF(2020)4/FINAL, June 2020). p. 9.

[123] *ibid.*

[124] Rudolf Häberli, Walter Grossenbacher-Mansuy, and Julie Thompson Klein, "Summary and Synthesis," in *Transdisciplinarity: Joint Problem Solving among Science, Technology, and Society - An Effective Way for Managing Complexity*, ed. Julie Thompson Klein et al. (Basel, Boston, and Berlin: Springer Basel AG, 2001), 1–22. p. 7.

[125] Jürgen Mittelstraß, "Unity and Transdisciplinarity," *Interdisciplinary Science Reviews* 18, no. 2 (1993): 153–57, https://doi.org/10.1179/isr.1993.18.2.153.

[126] Roland W. Scholz and David Marks, "Learning about Transdisciplinarity: Where Are We? Where Have We Been? Where Should We Go?," in *Transdisciplinarity: Joint Problem Solving among Science, Technology, and Society - An Effective Way for Managing Complexity*, ed. Julie Thompson Klein et al. (Basel, Boston, and Berlin: Springer Basel AG, 2001). p. 236.

practice, TDR has the capacity to advance both simultaneously and develop system-wide transformations for the good of society[127] in a non-reductionist way[128]. TDR has proved effective in fields of societal concern such as ageing, banking, education, energy, health care, migration, nutrition, pollution, and sustainable development[129]. In 2020, the OECD offered a synopsis of the contexts in which TDR is particularly valuable[130]:

- when problems involve the intersection of academic and non-academic (societal) domains
- when problems are context-dependent (e.g. evaluating an initiative's social impact or devising an implementation strategy for a particular place)
- when problems take place in environments that experience systemic and fast-paced technological, environmental, or social change
- when problems involve ethical norms or value judgments
- when problems have a direct or indirect social impact
- when problem-solving demands stakeholder cooperation

The list effectively describes most if not all social and environmental problems.

The value of a transdisciplinary approach has been recognized by UN Deputy Secretary-General Amina Mohamed in 2020: "the SDGs are comprehensive and interconnected and they demand transdisciplinary approaches" (DSG/SM/1430), and in 2021: "Gearing university programs to contribute to the Sustainable Development Goals, fostering more transdisciplinary approaches and encouraging open science are all imperative if we are to unlock solutions that serve the public good" (DSG/SM/1603).

The value of TDR has also been acknowledged by publications from international organizations, such as:

- *UNESCO in 1997*: "Activities undertaken within EPD [Environment and population education and information for development] must be transdisciplinary and intersectoral"[131]

---

[127] OECD Science, Technology and Industry, "Addressing Societal Challenges Using Transdisciplinary Research." p. 9.

[128] Christian Pohl, "What Is Progress in Transdisciplinary Research," *Futures* 43 (2011): 618–26, https://doi.org/10.1016/j.futures.2011.03.001. p. 1.

[129] Häberli, Grossenbacher-Mansuy, and Klein, "Summary and Synthesis." p. 11.

[130] OECD Science, Technology and Industry, "Addressing Societal Challenges Using Transdisciplinary Research." p. 22-23.

[131] UNESCO, "Evaluation of the Entire Transdisciplinary Project: Environment and Population Education and Information for Development" (UNESCO 151 EX/42, April 1997).

- *UNESCO in 2017*: "SDGs are a fundamental framework for sustainability science and diversity and knowledge are key words. Sustainability science can be disciplinary, interdisciplinary or transdisciplinary, but it is user-driven and user-inspired, building from integrated knowledge and territories-based integrated experiences."[132]
- *IPCC in 2018*: "This chapter is necessarily transdisciplinary in its coverage of the climate system, natural and managed ecosystems, and human systems and responses, owing to the integrated nature of the natural and human experience."[133]
- *The European Commission in 2020*: "Proposals should be transdisciplinary and ensure an integrated One Health approach by linking data from a wide range of relevant sources"[134]
- *OECD in 2020*: "Transdisciplinary research (TDR), which involves the integration of knowledge from different science disciplines and (non-academic) stakeholder communities, is required to help address complex societal challenges."[135]
- *The European Commission in 2021*: "Transdisciplinary R&I [Research and Innovation] with a strong social sciences dimension will improve understanding of the political (regulatory) and socio-economic conditions for change, with an emphasis on inequality and gender aspects and the behaviors and values of producers, consumers and all other actors."[136]

Support for and research on TDR has continued since its genesis. TDR is currently pursued in academic departments around the world, some of which include: ETH Zürich (Transdisciplinarity Lab, Department of

---

[132] UNESCO, "Third Symposium on Sustainability Science: Towards Guidelines on Research and Education" (UNESCO, June 2017).
[133] Ove Hoegh-Guldberg et al., "Impacts of 1.5°C Global Warming on Natural and Human Systems," in *Global Warming of 1.5°C. An IPCC Special Report on the Impacts of Global Warming of 1.5°C above Pre-Industrial Levels and Related Global Greenhouse Gas Emission Pathways, in the Context of Strengthening the Global Response to the Threat of Climate Change, Sustainable Development, and Efforts to Eradicate Poverty* (Cambridge and New York: Cambridge University Press, 2018), 175–312. p. 182.
[134] European Commission, "Horizon 2020 - Work Programme 2018-2020 | 8. Health, Demographic Change and Wellbeing" (Brussels: European Commission Decision C(2020)4029, June 2020). p. 49.
[135] OECD Science, Technology and Industry, "Addressing Societal Challenges Using Transdisciplinary Research." p. 4.
[136] European Commission, "Horizon Europe Strategic Plan 2021-2024" (Brussels: European Commission, February 2021). p. 93.

Environmental Systems Science)[137], KU Leuven (Institute for the Future)[138], Parsons School of Design (Transdisciplinary Design)[139], TU Berlin (Transdisciplinary Strategy)[140], TU Delft (Transdisciplinary Lab for Learning and Research)[141], University of British Columbia (Transdisciplinary Collaborative PhD for Climate Action)[142], University of Florence (UNESCO Transdisciplinary Chair in Human Development and Peace Culture)[143], University of Fort Hare (Transdisciplinary Studies)[144], and the University of Technology Sydney (Transdisciplinary Innovation)[145].

1.4.1 Definition of Transdisciplinary Research

The *International Transdisciplinarity 2000 Conference* in Zürich, Switzerland brought clarity to the concepts of inter-, multi-, cross, and transdisciplinary research. After the conference, there was a more wide-spread acknowledgement of the participatory, problem-solving, and action-oriented aspects of TDR[146]. *Table 1.5* describes the differences between the different types of research.

---

[137] ETH Zürich, "Transdisciplinarity Lab | Department of Environmental Systems Science," accessed March 6, 2023, https://usys.ethz.ch/en/research/TdLab.html.
[138] KU Leuven, "Institute for the Future: Transdisciplinary Research Incubator," accessed March 6, 2023, https://rega.kuleuven.be/if/IF.
[139] Parsons School of Design, "Transdisciplinary Design (MFA)," accessed March 9, 2023, https://www.newschool.edu/parsons/mfa-transdisciplinary-design/.
[140] Technical University of Berlin, "Transdisciplinary Strategy," accessed March 10, 2023, https://www.tu.berlin/en/topics/knowledge-exchange/2020/mai/citizen-science-researching-with-society.
[141] TU Delft, "Technology, Policy and Management," TU Delft, accessed March 4, 2023, https://www.tudelft.nl/en/tpm/research/tpm-labs.
[142] University of British Columbia, "Home | Collaborative PhD for Climate Action," accessed March 4, 2023, https://climateaction.collabphd.ubc.ca/.
[143] University of Florence, "UNESCO Chairs | International Relations | UniFI," www.unifi.it, accessed March 11, 2023, https://www.unifi.it/vp-11257-unesco-chairs.html.
[144] University of Fort Hare, "About Us | Faculty of Social Sciences & Humanities," accessed March 4, 2023, https://www.ufh.ac.za/faculties/social-sciences/centres/cts/about-us.
[145] University of Technology Sydney, "Transdisciplinary Innovation," University of Technology Sydney, July 29, 2016, https://www.uts.edu.au/study/transdisciplinary-innovation.
[146] Paul Burger and Rainer Kamber, "Cognitive Integration in Transdisciplinary Science: Knowledge as a Key Notion," *Issues in Integrative Studies* 21 (2003): 43–73. p. 44.

Table 1.5 Multi-, inter-, and transdisciplinary research

Type	Description
Multidisciplinary	*Multidisciplinary research is when researchers study a topic from the perspective of more than one discipline (UNESCO IBE)* Researchers work in parallel or in sequence from a disciplinary base. An example of such is collaborative research, where researchers from different disciplines work independently and the results are brought together at the end of the process. Findings are published as separate chapters and a synthesis or summary is authored by the principle investigator(s).
Interdisciplinary	*Interdisciplinary research is when researchers combine theories, methodologies, ideas, and perspectives from two or more disciplines (UNESCO IBE)* Researchers work jointly and use theories and methods from their disciplinary base to address a common challenge. Findings are often published as a partial, discipline-by-discipline sequence. Interdisciplinary refers to research between two or more disciplines already in existence. For example, social psychology, biochemistry, and environmental economics.
Transdisciplinary	*Transdisciplinary research is when researchers work jointly with non-academic stakeholders across disciplinary boundaries towards a problem-solving, common-good oriented, mutual-learning, and comprehensive approach to complex sustainable development problems (Pohl 2011 and Scholz 2000)* Researchers are encouraged to bridge conceptual, theoretical, and methodological approaches from a range of disciplines and devise a common conceptual framework. However, while transdisciplinary research is the organizing principle for the research, experience in the approach shows that iterating between disciplinary, multidisciplinary, interdisciplinary, and transdisciplinary approaches is critical to addressing continuously emerging research questions.

Sources: UNESCO International Bureau of Education Glossary of Curriculum Terminology; Patricia L. Rosenfield, "The Potential of Transdisciplinary Research for Sustaining and Extending Linkages Between the Health and Social Sciences," *Social Science & Medicine* 35, no. 11 (1992): 1343–57. p. 1351; Boniface P. Kiteme and Urs Wiesmann, "Sustainable River Basin Management in Kenya: Balancing Needs and Requirements," in *Handbook of Transdisciplinary Research*, ed. Gertrude Hirsch Hadorn et al. (Springer, 2008). p. 75; Christian Pohl, "What Is Progress in Transdisciplinary Research," *Futures* 43 (2011): 618–26. Abstract; Joseph J. Kockelmans, "Why Interdisciplinary," in *Interdisciplinarity and Higher Education* (University Park: Pennsylvania State University Press, 1979). p. 124; Roland W. Scholz, "Mutual Learning as a Basic Principle of Transdisciplinarity" (International Transdisciplinarity Conference. Transdisciplinarity: Joint Problem-Solving among Science, Technology and Society, Zürich, 2000), 13–17. p. 13.

TDR's definition can benefit from further clarification, namely the concepts: (1) problem-solving, (2) common-good oriented, (3) mutual learning, (4) comprehensiveness, and (5) approach to complex sustainable development problems.

I.   Problem-solving

The focus on problem-solving was fundamental to the formulation of interdisciplinarity in the 1920s[147]. In 1982, the OECD Centre for Educational Research and Innovation (CERI) identified two streams of interdisciplinary research and argued that *exogenous interdisciplinarity* (i.e. the production of knowledge across disciplinary boundaries to solve the problems of local communities) complements *endogenous interdisciplinarity* (i.e. the production of knowledge with the goal of unifying disciplines within academia)[148]. There has been a growing awareness on the importance of solving social problems with academic research. In 2008, Hadorn et al. argued that: "Societal knowledge demands for a better understanding of, and solutions to, concrete issues in the life-world"[149].

---

[147] Julie Thompson Klein, "Transdisciplinarity and Sustainability: Patterns of Definition," in *Transdisciplinary Research and Practice for Sustainability Outcomes*, ed. Dena Fam et al., Routledge Studies in Sustainability (London and New York: Routledge, 2017), 7–22. p. 9.
[148] OECD Centre for Educational Research and Innovation (CERI), *The University and the Community: The Problems of Changing Relationships* (Paris: OECD, 1982). p. 130.
[149] Gertrude Hirsch Hadorn et al., "The Emergence of Transdisciplinarity as a Form of Research," in *Handbook of Transdisciplinary Research*, ed. Gertrude Hirsch Hadorn et al. (Springer, 2008), 19–42. p. 28.

II.   *Common-good Oriented*

TDR prioritizes the common good in the way it integrates disciplinary boundaries "in order to address socially (as opposed to academically) relevant issues"[150], though the two can intersect. It recognizes that problem-solving "demands awareness of current trends in society, politics and industry, and it cannot be accomplished by reading exclusively scientific journals"[151]. Under conventional research approaches, experts (a) identify problems and solutions, which are then developed, applied, and evaluated to target populations[152], or (b) adapt a pre-determined goal to a community[153]. Traditional public inquiry process also tends to limit general cross-stakeholder learning[154]. In contrast, well-designed TDR involves stakeholders early to understand their perceptions, expectations as well as priorities, and integrates implementation knowledge into the knowledge-creation process through participatory research [155]. Researchers can employ participatory research methods ranging from low intensity (e.g. consulting stakeholders) to high intensity (e.g. collaborating from problem framing to analysis)[156] to identify and pursue a line of inquiry that benefits the common good. This:

- enables collaboration among diverse stakeholders (including experts across disciplinary boundaries)
- familiarizes stakeholders with anticipated guidance[157]
- ensures the relevance and feasibility of the guidance[158]
- clarifies the necessary factors (e.g. circumstances or processes) for a recommendation's adoption[159]

---

[150] Pohl, "What Is Progress in Transdisciplinary Research." p. 619.

[151] Richard Ernst, "The Responsibility of Science and Scientists," in *Transdisciplinarity: Joint Problem Solving among Science, Technology, and Society - An Effective Way for Managing Complexity*, ed. Julie Thompson Klein et al. (Basel, Boston, and Berlin: Springer Basel AG, 2001), 81–93. p. 83.

[152] OECD Science, Technology and Industry, "Addressing Societal Challenges Using Transdisciplinary Research." p. 16.

[153] Tony Meppem and Roderic Gill, "Planning for Sustainability as a Learning Concept," *Ecological Economics* 26 (1998): 121–37. p. 127.

[154] *ibid.* p. 131.

[155] *ibid.* p. 16.

[156] Pohl, "What Is Progress in Transdisciplinary Research." p. 619-620.

[157] OECD Science, Technology and Industry, "Addressing Societal Challenges Using Transdisciplinary Research." p. 24.

[158] Heidi Diggelmann et al., "Introduction: Goals and Criteria of the Award," in *Transdisciplinarity: Joint Problem Solving among Science, Technology, and Society - An Effective Way for Managing Complexity*, ed. Julie Thompson Klein et al. (Basel, Boston, and Berlin: Springer Basel AG, 2001), 141–46. p. 150.

[159] OECD Science, Technology and Industry, "Addressing Societal Challenges Using Transdisciplinary Research." p. 24.

- encourages stakeholders to be part of a responsible and inclusive solution[160]
- enhances stakeholders' ability to improve practices[161]

The inclusion of non-academic actors (such as private and public sector actors as well as historically underrepresented communities) in knowledge-creation is critical to TDR[162]. Häberli in 2001 found that "Every proposal for a research project, in order to produce reliable and socially robust knowledge, has to answer the question: 'Where is the place of people in our knowledge?'"[163]

III.   Mutual Learning

In 1993, Thompson argued that the traditional linear progression from facts ("hard science") to values ("softer" topics in politics and culture) is incoherent with *policy loops* (i.e. the cycle of problem definition, solution monitoring, evaluation, and redefinition of a problem) in practice[164]: the outcome of value-oriented implementation stages circles back and exerts influence over the problem definition stages[165]. As a result, facts and values are intertwined within a research project[166] even if that may not be obvious in silos. In 1995, Clark called into question the traditional division of labor between "knowledge seeking" and "knowledge use"[167]. He described the challenges of the institutional model of knowledge production, where knowledge filters down from pure research to applications across policy and practice[168]. This model is unable to cope with the demands of a rapidly changing complex world, where knowledge is context dependent[169].

---

[160] Häberli, Grossenbacher-Mansuy, and Klein, "Summary and Synthesis." p. 9.

[161] Diggelmann et al., "Introduction: Goals and Criteria of the Award." p. 150.

[162] Pohl, "What Is Progress in Transdisciplinary Research." p. 619-620.

[163] Häberli, Grossenbacher-Mansuy, and Klein, "Summary and Synthesis." p. 4.

[164] Michael Thompson, "Good Science for Public Policy," *Journal of International Development* 5, no. 6 (1993): 669–79, https://doi.org/10.1002/jid.3380050608. p. 670.

[165] *ibid.*

[166] *ibid.*

[167] Norman Clark, "Interactive Nature of Knowledge Systems: Some Implications for the Third World," *Science and Public Policy* 22, no. 4 (1995): 249–58, https://doi.org/10.1093/spp/22.4.249. p. 250.

[168] *ibid.*

[169] *ibid.* p. 249.

In 1998, Meppem and Gill advocated for the use of TDR to manage sustainable development's complexity by enabling "perpetually evolving learning"[170] and "transdisciplinary participation"[171]. They identified surfacing assumptions through mutual learning as the starting point to sustainable development[172]. Recognizing the nuances of our assumptions help mitigate the challenges of intervening in complex adaptive systems (CAS). Assumptions can be cultural and difficult to know or articulate[173]. For example, societies in the North and South can perceive problems in different ways[174].

In 2000, Scholz described mutual learning between scientists and society as "a basic principle of transdisciplinarity"[175]. The multitude of stakeholders bring diverse skills and expertise to the problem solving process[176]. Mutual learning fosters a healthy atmosphere of open collaboration rather than an oppositional one[177]. It also enhances the knowledge of participants including local, academic, industry, and policy stakeholders[178]. In 2008, Kiteme and Wiesmann addressed the importance of extending mutual learning beyond formal political and local leadership structures, and instead to a broad range of stakeholders[179]. This enables researchers to refine and adapt theories to the context in which they are applied[180].

---

[170] Meppem and Gill, "Planning for Sustainability as a Learning Concept." Abstract.

[171] *ibid.* p. 134.

[172] *ibid.* p. 126.

[173] *ibid.* p. 129.

[174] Heidi Diggelmann et al., "Introduction: Goals and Criteria of the Award," in *Transdisciplinarity: Joint Problem Solving among Science, Technology, and Society - An Effective Way for Managing Complexity*, ed. Julie Thompson Klein et al. (Basel, Boston, and Berlin: Springer Basel AG, 2001). p. 151.

[175] Scholz, "Mutual Learning as a Basic Principle of Transdisciplinarity." p. 13.

[176] Michael Gibbons and Helga Nowotny, "The Potential of Transdisciplinarity," in *Transdisciplinarity: Joint Problem Solving among Science, Technology, and Society - An Effective Way for Managing Complexity*, ed. Julie Thompson Klein et al. (Basel, Boston, and Berlin: Springer Basel AG, 2001), 67–80. p. 69.

[177] Meppem and Gill, "Planning for Sustainability as a Learning Concept." p. 122.

[178] Häberli, Grossenbacher-Mansuy, and Klein, "Summary and Synthesis." p. 6.

[179] Boniface P. Kiteme and Urs Wiesmann, "Sustainable River Basin Management in Kenya: Balancing Needs and Requirements," in *Handbook of Transdisciplinary Research*, ed. Gertrude Hirsch Hadorn et al. (Springer, 2008), 63–78. p. 67.

[180] Patricia L. Rosenfield, "The Potential of Transdisciplinary Research for Sustaining and Extending Linkages Between the Health and Social Sciences," *Social Science & Medicine* 35, no. 11 (1992): 1343–57, https://doi.org/10.1016/0277-9536(92)90038-r. p. 1344.

IV.   Comprehensiveness

Research questions in TDR are formulated with stakeholders to offer a better understanding of context[181]. As a result, a larger number of interests are considered, thereby increasing the research's comprehensiveness[182]. While academic pursuits have historically centered around disciplines, some problems may not always be reducible to disciplinary logic[183]. By transcending and integrating disciplinary paradigms, new lines of inquiry can emerge and further the comprehensiveness of the research[184].

V.   Approach to complex sustainable development problems

The OECD, recalled by Sholz et al., made one of the earliest connections between TDR and environmental sustainability in 1973[185]. In 1995, Reid noted primary obstacles to sustainable development include the "lack of awareness of the issues, the political unacceptability of an 'obvious' step forward, the opposition of entrenched interests, and the inadequacy of institutional mechanism for integrating environment and development"[186]. In 1998, Meppem and Gill supplemented the observation by identifying the diverging interpretations of and recommendations for sustainability challenges among ecologists, economists, industry leaders, and activists as a key barriers to consensus on policy action[187]. TDR researchers took note of several key developments in understanding complex sustainable development problems:

- In 1972, Laszlo observed how disciplinary specialists have difficulty communicating when their interests do not coincide[188]. Researchers acquire detailed but isolated fragments of knowledge instead of a continuous and coherent

---

[181] Gibbons and Nowotny, "The Potential of Transdisciplinarity." p. 69.
[182] *ibid.*
[183] *ibid.*
[184] Hadorn et al., "The Emergence of Transdisciplinarity as a Form of Research." p. 29.
[185] Scholz and Marks, "Learning about Transdisciplinarity: Where Are We? Where Have We Been? Where Should We Go?" p. 237.
[186] Reid, *Sustainable Development: An Introductory Guide.* p. 129.
[187] Meppem and Gill, "Planning for Sustainability as a Learning Concept." p. 122.
[188] Laszlo, *The Systems View of the World: The Natural Philosophy of the New Developments in the Sciences.* p. 3-4.

picture[189]. They then struggle to understand how subjects exposed to many influences simultaneously would behave[190].

- In 1973, Rittel and Webber theorized wicked problems[191].
- In 1983, Mitroff argued that the complexity of human systems is not only derived from the system itself: "The very existence of sharp differences among research perspectives is itself evidence for the complexity of human systems"[192].
- In 1993, TDR researchers Funtowicz and Ravet responded to the complexity of sustainable development through 'post-normal science'[193]. It recognizes researchers' broadened scope of obligation to future generations[194] and the insufficient understanding of research's impact on policy or practice[195]. It was formulated for problems that combine *high decision stakes* (i.e. high costs, benefits, or value commitments[196]) and *high systems uncertainties* (i.e. high dependence on the comprehension or management of a complex reality rather than a particular fact[197]), such as sustainable development problems[198]. They have a plurality of legitimate perspectives[199] with multiple points of view for measurement, analysis, and evaluation[200]. Funtowicz and Ravet advocated for the use *of extended peer communities*[201], including communities whose livelihood may depend on the recommendations and have "general principles [...] realized in their 'back yards'"[202].

---

[189] Laszlo, *The Systems View of the World: The Natural Philosophy of the New Developments in the Sciences*. p. 4.
[190] *ibid.* p. 5.
[191] Rittel and Webber, "Dilemmas in a General Theory of Planning." Abstract; see *Table 1.2 Properties of Wicked Problems*
[192] Ian I. Mitroff, "Archetypal Social Systems Analysis: On the Deeper Structure of Human Systems," *The Academy of Management Review* 8, no. 3 (1983): 387–97, https://doi.org/10.2307/257827. p. 387.
[193] Klein, "Transdisciplinarity and Sustainability: Patterns of Definition." p. 10-11.
[194] Silvio O Funtowicz and Jerome R. Ravetz, "Science for the Post-Normal Age," *Futures* 25, no. 7 (1993): 739–55, https://doi.org/10.1016/0016-3287(93)90022-L. p. 754.
[195] *ibid.* p. 743.
[196] *ibid.* p. 744.
[197] *ibid.* p. 744.
[198] *ibid.* p. 750.
[199] *ibid.* p. 739.
[200] Silvio O Funtowicz and Jerome R. Ravetz, "Post-Normal Science," in *Internet Encyclopaedia of Ecological Economics* (International Society for Ecological Economics, 2003). p. 2.
[201] Funtowicz and Ravetz, "Science for the Post-Normal Age." p. 740-741.
[202] *ibid.* p. 753.

Box 1-2 Global Diplomacy for a Paradigm Shift

Global diplomacy is the set of principles, methods, and actions to achieve the common goals of the global community within the contemporary global governance network[203]. Global diplomacy encompasses a broad range of topics that converge around *interactions* i.e. the process whereby individuals mutually influence each other and, in so doing, create, maintain, change, or terminate a pattern of joint action[204].

The importance of interaction is often overlooked. In 1981, Turner put forward the idea that interactions are critical to our civilization. This is because humans are products of a dual evolution, both biological and cultural[205]. To cooperate or even to come into conflict with others, we have to "recognize, assess and anticipate the responses of other people"[206]. Consequently, interactions play a pivotal role in constructing, maintaining, and altering our society[207]. In 1998, Meppem and Gill described the pursuit of sustainable development as "essentially the facilitation of a social process"[208].

The next section on the types of knowledge in Transdisciplinary Research (TDR) offers an opportunity to reflect on global diplomacy in knowledge production through the concept of paradigm shift proposed by Kuhn in 1962[209]. A paradigm is "a basic set of beliefs that guides action, whether of the everyday garden variety or action taken in connection with a disciplined inquiry"[210]. A paradigm shift involves winning acceptance for ideas that have not been accepted and appear to challenge conventions[211]. It can only be achieved through meticulous

[203] Sergeyev, Yuriy. "Sergeyev's Letter," November 9, 2021. p. 1.

[204] Jonathan Turner, *Sociology: Studying the Human System*, 2nd ed. (Santa Monica, California: Goodyear Publishing Company, 1981). p. 93.

[205] Turner, *Sociology: Studying the Human System*. p. 68.

[206] *ibid*. p. 92.

[207] Meppem and Gill, "Planning for Sustainability as a Learning Concept." p. 92.

[208] *ibid*. p. 131.

[209] Egon Guba, "The Alternative Paradigm Dialog," in *The Paradigm Dialog*, ed. Egon Guba (Newbury Park and London: Sage Publications, 1990), 17–30. p. 17.

[210] *ibid*; there is some ambiguity to the definition of paradigm by Kuhn, who is credited for bringing the concept into our collective awareness in 1962, therefore the definition by Guba in 1990 has been adopted.

[211] Reid, *Sustainable Development: An Introductory Guide*. p. 153.

negotiations within social groups[212]. During these interactions, people see new and different things, even with the same tools, in places they have looked before[213]. The criteria used to determine the legitimacy of problems and proposed solutions also tend to change[214].

Austin's theory on *paradigm accommodation* in 1990 offers some insights on how one can practice global diplomacy in knowledge production processes. She described three possible levels at which accommodation among paradigms can be achieved[215]: (a) *at a philosophical level*: is there a win-win scenario where multiple paradigms can come together philosophically? (b) *at a social-community level*: can we co-exist and learn from each other despite being in different paradigms? (c) *at a personal level*: how can I, as an individual, work with different paradigms? She further highlighted the importance of *"dialogical accommodation"*. Researchers can accommodate different paradigms by (a) recognizing and learning to speak to and through different paradigms[216], (b) respecting what each paradigm can contribute[217], and (c) combining different paradigms to solve problems in policy or practice[218].

---

[212] Reid, *Sustainable Development: An Introductory Guide*. p. 153.

[213] Thomas S. Kuhn, *The Structure of Scientific Revolutions* (Chicago: University of Chicago Press, 1962). p. 110.

[214] *ibid.* p. 108.

[215] Ann Austin, "Discussion on Accommodation," in *The Paradigm Dialog*, ed. Egon Guba (Newbury Park and London: Sage Publications, 1990), 136–38. p. 136.

[216] Austin, "Discussion on Accommodation." p. 137.

[217] *ibid.* p. 137.

[218] *ibid.* p. 138.

1.4.2 Types of Knowledge in Transdisciplinary Research

"How might we apply TDR to our work?" – On a
Zoom call with a consultant for governments

In 2008, Kiteme and Wiesmann noted the importance of iterating between different types of knowledge[219]. There have been some variations in the definitions and explanations of the four types of knowledge in transdisciplinary research (TDR). They are: (1) systems knowledge, (2) target knowledge, (3) transformation knowledge, and (4) implementation knowledge. This has been synthesized in *Table 1.6.*

Systems knowledge, target knowledge, and transformation knowledge have been investigated in academia to different extents. However, implementation knowledge has been historically underappreciated in academic knowledge production processes. Researchers in the early 2000s recognized the multiple barriers to disseminating and implementing effective initiatives[220]. In 2006, Eccles and Mittman defined implementation research for the founding of the academic journal *Implementation Sciences*: "the scientific study of methods to promote the systematic uptake of research findings and other evidence-based practices into routine practice, and hence, to improve the quality and effectiveness of health services and care"[221]. The importance of implementation knowledge has been highlighted by Shea in 2023: "the failure to reach goals including the SDGs is not usually because solutions are not known (unlike treatment of incurable diseases for example). The failure is a failure of implementation, as explained by the increasingly prominent discipline of Implementation Science."[222]

---

[219] Kiteme and Wiesmann, "Sustainable River Basin Management in Kenya: Balancing Needs and Requirements." p. 75.
[220] Ross C. Brownson, Graham A. Colditz, and Enola K. Proctor, eds., *Dissemination and Implementation Research in Health: Translating Science to Practice* (Oxford and New York: Oxford University Press, 2012). p. VIII.
[221] Martin P. Eccles and Brian S. Mittman, "Welcome to Implementation Science," *Implementation Science* 1, no. 1 (2006): 1–3, https://doi.org/10.1186/1748-5908-1-1.. Abstract.
[222] Brent Shea, "Collaborative Peer Review Process, Part I," May 8, 2023.

Table 1.6 Types of knowledge in transdisciplinary research (TDR)

Type	Description
1. Systems knowledge	Knowledge derived from systems research[223]
2. Target knowledge	Knowledge that is goal-oriented and future-oriented[224]
3. Transformation knowledge	Knowledge on the methods to create meaningful and responsible large-scale, longer term change within complex adaptive systems[225]
4. Implementation knowledge	Practical knowledge, operational expertise, and the practice of transdisciplinary research[226]

[223] *Previous interpretations* include (1) ProClim in 1997: Knowledge on current situation (eg. systems knowledge of structures and processes, variabilities, and long-term system observations to assess the causes and the extent of change as well as impact of remedial measures); (2) Kiteme and Wiesmann in 2008: Baseline studies create a better understanding of the problem; (3) Lawrence et al. in 2022: Systems knowledge (empirical and theoretical studies from specific disciplinary understanding of one phenomenon to an integrative interdisciplinary perspective on complex relationships between phenomena)

[224] *Previous interpretations* include (1) ProClim in 1997: Knowledge on target situation (eg. scenarios, risk evaluation and assessment, ethical boundary conditions, and visions); (2) Kiteme and Wiesmann in 2008: People's development needs, constraints, and aspirations; (3) Renn in 2019: Goal-oriented knowledge (to overcome the mismatch between scientific results and specific contexts); and (4) Lawrence et al. in 2022: Orientation knowledge (formulation and justification of the goals and objectives of social change processes)

[225] *Previous interpretations* include (1) ProClim in 1997: Knowledge to transition from current to target situation (eg. how to shape and implement the transition, interest and power structures that may be able to transform political and socioeconomic institutions, and draw up scenarios, options, as well as instruments that may reorient socioeconomic structures); (2) Kiteme and Wiesmann in 2008: How to influence investment designs and priorities; (3) Messerli and Messerli in 2008: Action knowledge; (4) Lawrence et al. in 2022: Transformation knowledge (understanding and or development of practical i.e. technical, legal, social, and cultural, means to achieve the desired goals or objectives

[226] *Previous interpretations* include (1) ProClim in 1997: knowledge is also influenced by perceptions, attitudes, and conditions (eg. basic needs, norms, technology, access to resources, power, institutions, ethics, networks etc.). There is insufficient concern about how and how efficiently knowledge on process and problems are being integrated into problem-solving actions. This also calls for a transdisciplinary, non-reductionist, and participatory approach; (2) Renn in 2019: Process knowledge (eg. how co-creative processes can create systems change with and within institutions); (3) Lawrence et al. in 2022: Process knowledge

Sources: ProClim, "Research on Sustainability and Global Change - Visions in Science Policy by Swiss Researchers" (Bern: ProClim - Forum for Climate and Global Change, 1997). p. 15-23; Boniface P. Kiteme and Urs Wiesmann, "Sustainable River Basin Management in Kenya: Balancing Needs and Requirements," in *Handbook of Transdisciplinary Research*, ed. Gertrude Hirsch Hadorn et al. (Springer, 2008), 63–78. p. 67; Bruno Messerli and Paul Messerli, "From Local Projects in the Alps to Global Change Programmes in the Mountains of the World: Milestones in Transdisciplinary Research," in *Handbook of Transdisciplinary Research*, ed. Gertrude Hirsch Hadorn et al. (Springer, 2008), 43–62. p. 59; Ortwin Renn, "Die Rolle(n) Transdisziplinärer Wissenschaft Bei Konfliktgeladenen Transformationsprozessen," trans. Google Translate (via OnlineDocTranslator.com), *GAIA - Ecological Perspectives for Science and Society* 28, no. 1 (2019): 44–51, https://doi.org/10.14512/gaia.28.1.11. p. 46-49; Mark G. Lawrence et al., "Characteristics, Potentials, and Challenges of Transdisciplinary Research," *One Earth* 5, no. 1 (2022): 44–61, https://doi.org/10.1016/j.oneear.2021.12.010.

(methodologies and procedures to design and carry out TDR projects i.e. (a) knowledge on effectively integrating the activities of academic and non-academic actors, (b) knowledge on designing structures to support continuous, reflective learning and adjustment processes, and (c) knowledge on effectively integrating systems, orientation, as well as transformation knowledge)

1.4.3 Evaluation of Transdisciplinary Research (with Supplements for Transdisciplinary Systems Research)

> *"How do we assess the quality of our work on this*
> *complex project?" – At one of the weekly reflection*
> *meetings at the Center for Global Agenda (CGA) at*
> *Unbuilt Labs*

Research evaluation asks: what concepts ought to apply when we examine transdisciplinary research (TDR), what do we value, and why? This section addresses three questions[227]:

1. What are the major works on evaluation criteria in transdisciplinary research?
2. What contributions do Transdisciplinary Systems Research make to transdisciplinary research evaluation?

I.   What are the major works on evaluation criteria in transdisciplinary research?

In 2011, Pohl identified the challenges of evaluating transdisciplinary research (TDR): "In disciplinary research progress is reached and assessed by referring to the state of research in a specific field. But what is progress in transdisciplinary research, where several disciplines and further societal actors may be involved?"[228] Since then, there has been diverse literature on evaluating TDR. Major works are discussed below:

- The OECD in 1982 suggested progress in TDR can advance *exogenous interdisciplinarity* (i.e. knowledge across disciplines to solve local communities' problems) and or *endogenous interdisciplinarity* (i.e. knowledge with the goal of bringing together concepts from different disciplines)[229].
- Pohl in 2011 described progress as (a) a better approach to manage a real world issue, (b) progress within a "thought-

---

[227] Correction: there was a citation error in an earlier version of this preprint.
[228] Christian Pohl, "What Is Progress in Transdisciplinary Research," *Futures* 43 (2011): 618–26, https://doi.org/10.1016/j.futures.2011.03.001. p. 618.
[229] *OECD Centre for Educational Research and Innovation (CERI), The University and the Community: The Problems of Changing Relationships (Paris: OECD, 1982).* p. 130.

style" which is similar to a paradigm in the Kuhnian sense but each individual is a member of multiple thought-styles, (c) the opportunity to experience alternate thought-styles, and (d) the advancement of TDR methods and processes[230].

- Belcher et al. in 2016 presented the most extensive study on the topic as part of a systematic review. The article features a table that clearly identifies assessment rubrics, definitions, and criteria. The authors describe four principles of TDR quality assessment based on Cash et al. in 2003, including (a) relevance, (b) credibility, (c) legitimacy, and (d) effectiveness[231]. The framework has been updated recently[232].
- Willetts and Mitchell in 2017 acknowledged the role different worldviews play in ideas of quality, and propose five quality criteria: (a) original contribution to knowledge and broader societal outcomes, (b) reflexivity and responsiveness, (c) research integrity based on credibility, legitimacy, and alignment, (d) sufficient engagement with both research context and literature, and (e) coherent argument across diverse approaches and perspectives[233].

Evaluation criteria in transdisciplinary research typically builds on established research evaluation in the social sciences, with additional criteria that emphasize the integration of knowledge, engagement with stakeholders, and solving community problems — many of the hallmarks of transdisciplinarity.

---

[230] Pohl, "What Is Progress in Transdisciplinary Research." p. 625.
[231] Brian M. Belcher et al., "Defining and Assessing Research Quality in a Transdisciplinary Context," *Research Evaluation* 25 (2016): 1–17, https://doi.org/10.1093/reseval/rvv025. p. 8-12.
[232] See https://researcheffectiveness.ca/.
[233] Juliet Willetts and Cynthia Mitchell, "Assessing Transdisciplinary Doctoral Research," in *Transdisciplinary Research and Practice for Sustainability Outcomes*, ed. Dena Fam et al., Routledge Studies in Sustainability (London and New York: Routledge, 2017), 122–36. p. 123, 126.

II.   What contributions do Transdisciplinary Systems
*   Research make to transdisciplinary research evaluation?*

This section brings together ideas on research evaluation based on the
Transdisciplinary Systems Research (TSR) approach developed in the
next chapters. To solve complex sustainable development problems,
TSR adds the following evaluation criteria:

1.   *Pathways-to-impact and actionable recommendations*: The
     research takes into account implementation knowledge and
     identifies how the guidance will contribute to shared goals
     within a target timeframe. See *Sections 1.2.3* and *6.2*.
2.   *Properties of complex adaptive systems (CAS) and grand
     challenges*: The research does not contradict the known
     properties of CAS and grand challenges (including the
     properties of wicked problems). See *Sections 1.2.1 and 1.2.2*.
3.   *Legal and legitimate*: The research and outputs are ethical and
     in accordance with international law, including international
     human rights law. Extra care is taken when working with
     vulnerable populations or in volatile environments. The
     research followed a principled process and meet the standard
     of proof necessary based on shared goals. See *Section 2.2.2*.
4.   *Non-academic outcomes*: Rarely are stakeholders focused
     solely on academic outcomes. TSR explicitly highlights the
     importance of non-academic outcomes such as changes in
     policy, practices, perspectives, and financing. See *Sections 5.1*
     and *5.2*.

[Blank page]

1.5 Key Concepts from Systems, Systems Research, and Transdisciplinary Research

This chapter examined many theoretical concepts with which to understand a system-wide transformation for sustainable development. *Table 1.7* summarizes key concepts in *Chapter 1*. It also describes their relationship to Transdisciplinary Systems Research (TSR), which will be introduced in the next chapter.

Table 1.7 Key concepts from systems, systems research, and transdisciplinary research, in Transdisciplinary Systems Research (TSR)

Section	Concepts	TSR
1.2.1	*System*: a collection of parts that interact to form a whole, whose characteristics depend both on the characteristics of the parts and their interconnections.	Applies to TSR.
	Complex adaptive systems (CAS): a collection of deeply interwoven parts and wholes that (1) cannot be understood in isolation, and (2) responds unpredictably to input.	
	Properties of complex adaptive systems (CAS): see *Table 1.1*.	
	System-wide transformation: large scale, longer term changes to close the compliance gap and advance the 2030 Sustainable Development Goals.	
1.2.2	*Grand challenges*: challenges that are characterized by their (1) global scope, (2) high significance, (3) potential to be solvable, and (4) wickedness.	Applies to TSR.
	Wicked problems: problems associated with intervening in complex adaptive systems (CAS).	

	Properties of wicked problems: see *Table 1.2.*	
1.3.1	*Systems thinking*: an approach that frames a phenomenon as a system (by applying systems theories and concepts) to predict behaviors and support analysis of potential actions for improvement. *Systems research*: this includes (1) a sustained and iterative process of applying systems thinking, or (2) conducting generalizable research into the nature of complex adaptive systems (CAS) such as their properties. *Common elements of contemporary systems thinking*: see *Table 1.4.*	Applies to TSR.
1.3.2	*Hard Systems Thinking (HST), Soft Systems Thinking (SST)*, and *Critical Systems Thinking (CST)*	TSR responds to critiques of HST, SST, and CST.
1.4.1	*Transdisciplinary research (TDR)*: when researchers work jointly with non-academic stakeholders across disciplinary boundaries towards a problem-solving, common-good oriented, mutual-learning, and comprehensive approach to complex sustainable development problems.	Applies to TSR.
1.4.2	*Systems knowledge*: knowledge derived from systems research. *Target knowledge*: goal-oriented and future-oriented knowledge (such as the 2030 Sustainable Development Goals). *Transformation knowledge:* knowledge on the methods to create meaningful and responsible large-scale, longer term change within complex adaptive systems. *Implementation knowledge*: practical knowledge, operational expertise, and the practice of (transdisciplinary) research.	Applies to TSR.

1.4.3	*Evaluation criteria for transdisciplinary research.*	Applies to TSR

1.6 References

Agazzi, Evandro. "Systemic Thinking: An Introduction." In *The Systemic Turn in Human and Natural Sciences: A Rock in The Pond*, edited by Lucia Urbani Ulivi, IX–XVII. Contemporary Systems Thinking. Switzerland: Springer Nature, 2019.

Aristotle. *Metaphysics, Book 8, Section 1045a (Tredennick 1933 Edition)*. Translated by Hugh Tredennick. Boston: Harvard University Press, 1933. https://www.perseus.tufts.edu/hopper/text?doc=Perseus%3Atext%3A19 99.01.0052%3Abook%3D8%3Asection%3D1045a.

———. "Metaphysics: Book Theta." In *The Metaphysics*, translated by Hugh Lawson-Tancred, 253–82. Penguin Classics, 1999.

Arnold, Ross D., and Jon P. Wade. "A Definition of Systems Thinking: A Systems Approach | Elsevier Enhanced Reader." *Procedia Computer Science* 44 (2015): 669–78. https://doi.org/10.1016/j.procs.2015.03.050.

Austin, Ann. "Discussion on Accommodation." In *The Paradigm Dialog*, edited by Egon Guba, 136–38. Newbury Park and London: Sage Publications, 1990.

Bammer, Gabriele. "Tools for Transdisciplinary Research." In *Transdisciplinary Research and Practice for Sustainability Outcomes*, edited by Dena Fam, Jane Palmer, Chris Riedy, and Cynthia Mitchell, 39–54. Routledge Studies in Sustainability. London and New York: Routledge, 2017.

Belcher, Brian M., Katherine E. Rasmussen, Matthew R. Kemshaw, and Deborah A. Zornes. "Defining and Assessing Research Quality in a Transdisciplinary Context." *Research Evaluation* 25 (2016): 1–17. https://doi.org/10.1093/reseval/rvv025.

Bobby W. "The Limits of Prediction - or, How I Learned to Stop Worrying About Black Swans and Love Analysis." *Studies in Intelligence* 63, no. 4 (December 2019).

Boulding, Kenneth, Elise Boulding, and Guy Burgess. *The Social System of the Planet Earth*. Massachusetts: Addison-Wesley Publishing Company, 1980.

Brownson, Ross C., Graham A. Colditz, and Enola K. Proctor, eds. *Dissemination and Implementation Research in Health: Translating Science to Practice*. Oxford and New York: Oxford University Press, 2012.

Burger, Paul, and Rainer Kamber. "Cognitive Integration in Transdisciplinary Science: Knowledge as a Key Notion." *Issues in Integrative Studies* 21 (2003): 43–73.

Checkland, Peter. *Systems Thinking, Systems Practice*. Chichester and New York: John Wiley & Sons, 1981.

Churchman, Charles. *The Systems Approach*. New York: A Delta Book, 1968.

————. *The Systems Approach and Its Enemies*. New York: Basic Books, 1979.

Clark, Norman. "Interactive Nature of Knowledge Systems: Some Implications for the Third World." *Science and Public Policy* 22, no. 4 (1995): 249–58. https://doi.org/10.1093/spp/22.4.249.

Cohen, S. Marc. "Aristotle's Metaphysics." In *The Stanford Encyclopedia of Philosophy*. Metaphysics Research Lab, Stanford University, November 21, 2020. https://plato.stanford.edu/entries/aristotle-metaphysics/.

Czakon, Wojciech. "Grand Challenges: A Way Out of the Ivory Tower for Management Academic Discipline." *Management Issues* 17, no. 4 (October 17, 2019). https://doi.org/10.7172/1644-9584.84.1.

Diggelmann, Heidi, Gertrude Hirsch Hadorn, Ruth Kaufmann-Hayoz, Johannes R Randegger, and Christian Smoliner. "Introduction: Goals and Criteria of the Award." In *Transdisciplinarity: Joint Problem Solving among Science, Technology, and Society - An Effective Way for Managing Complexity*, edited by Julie Thompson Klein, Walter Grossenbacher-Mansuy, Rudolf Häberli, Alain Bill, Roland W. Scholz, and Myrtha Welti, 141–46. Basel, Boston, and Berlin: Springer Basel AG, 2001.

Eccles, Martin P., and Brian S. Mittman. "Welcome to Implementation Science." *Implementation Science* 1, no. 1 (2006): 1–3. https://doi.org/10.1186/1748-5908-1-1.

Edelman, Jonathan Antonio, Babajide Owoyele, Joaquin Santuber, and Anne Victoria Talbot. "Designing as Performance: Bridging the Gap Between Research and Practice in Design Thinking Education." In *Design Thinking Research*, edited by Christoph Meinel and Larry Leifer, 75–101. Understanding Innovation. Switzerland: Springer Nature, 2021.

Ernst, Richard. "The Responsibility of Science and Scientists." In *Transdisciplinarity: Joint Problem Solving among Science, Technology, and Society - An Effective Way for Managing Complexity*, edited by Julie Thompson Klein, Walter Grossenbacher-Mansuy, Rudolf Häberli, Alain Bill, Roland W. Scholz, and Myrtha Welti, 81–93. Basel, Boston, and Berlin: Springer Basel AG, 2001.

ETH Zürich. "Transdisciplinarity Lab | Department of Environmental Systems Science." Accessed March 6, 2023. https://usys.ethz.ch/en/research/TdLab.html.

European Commission. "Horizon 2020 - Work Programme 2018-2020 | 8. Health, Demographic Change and Wellbeing." Brussels: European Commission Decision C(2020)4029, June 2020.

————. "Horizon Europe Strategic Plan 2021-2024." Brussels: European Commission, February 2021.

Evelyn-White, Hugh G., trans. "Hesiod: Works And Days," 1914.

Flood, Robert L. "Six Scenarios for the Future of Systems 'Problem Solving.'" *Systems Practice* 2, no. 1 (1989). https://doi.org/10.1007/BF01061618.

Flood, Robert L., and Michael C. Jackson. "Total Systems Intervention: A Practical Face to Critical Systems Thinking." *Systems Practice* 4, no. 3 (June 1991): 197–213. https://doi.org/10.1007/BF01059565.

Funtowicz, Silvio O, and Jerome R. Ravetz. "Post-Normal Science." In
    Internet Encyclopaedia of Ecological Economics. International Society
    for Ecological Economics, 2003.
———. "Science for the Post-Normal Age." *Futures* 25, no. 7 (1993): 739–
    55. https://doi.org/10.1016/0016-3287(93)90022-L.
Gear, Claire, Elizabeth Eppel, and Jane Koziol-Mclain. "Advancing
    Complexity Theory as a Qualitative Research Methodology."
    International Journal of Qualitative Methods 17, no. 1 (December 1,
    2018): 1609406918782557. https://doi.org/10.1177/1609406918782557.
Gibbons, Michael, and Helga Nowotny. "The Potential of
    Transdisciplinarity." In *Transdisciplinarity: Joint Problem Solving
    among Science, Technology, and Society - An Effective Way for
    Managing Complexity*, edited by Julie Thompson Klein, Walter
    Grossenbacher-Mansuy, Rudolf Häberli, Alain Bill, Roland W. Scholz,
    and Myrtha Welti, 67–80. Basel, Boston, and Berlin: Springer Basel
    AG, 2001.
Gomersall, Tim. "Complex Adaptive Systems: A New Approach for
    Understanding Health Practices." *Health Psychology Review* 12, no. 4
    (December 2018): 405–18.
    https://doi.org/10.1080/17437199.2018.1488603.
Guba, Egon. "The Alternative Paradigm Dialog." In *The Paradigm Dialog*,
    edited by Egon Guba, 17–30. Newbury Park and London: Sage
    Publications, 1990.
Häberli, Rudolf, Walter Grossenbacher-Mansuy, and Julie Thompson Klein.
    "Summary and Synthesis." In *Transdisciplinarity: Joint Problem
    Solving among Science, Technology, and Society - An Effective Way for
    Managing Complexity*, edited by Julie Thompson Klein, Walter
    Grossenbacher-Mansuy, Rudolf Häberli, Alain Bill, Roland W. Scholz,
    and Myrtha Welti, 1–22. Basel, Boston, and Berlin: Springer Basel AG,
    2001.
Hadorn, Gertrude Hirsch, Susette Biber-Klemm, Walter Grossenbacher-
    Mansuy, Holger Hoffmann-Riem, Dominique Joye, Christian Pohl, Urs
    Wiesmann, and Elisabeth Zemp. "The Emergence of Transdisciplinarity
    as a Form of Research." In *Handbook of Transdisciplinary Research*,
    edited by Gertrude Hirsch Hadorn, Holger Hoffmann-Riem, Susette
    Biber-Klemm, Walter Grossenbacher-Mansuy, Dominique Joye,
    Christian Pohl, Urs Wiesmann, and Elisabeth Zemp, 19–42. Springer,
    2008.
Hammond, Debora. "Philosophical Foundations of Systems Research." In *A
    Guide to Systems Research: Philosophy, Processes and Practice*, edited
    by Mary C. Edson, Pamela Buckle Henning, and Shankar Sankaran,
    10:1–19. Traditional Systems Sciences. Singapore: Springer Nature,
    2017.
Head, Brian W. *Wicked Problems in Public Policy: Understanding and
    Responding to Complex Challenges*. Switzerland: Palgrave Macmillan,
    2022.
Henning, Pamela Buckle. "Competencies Necessary for Systems Research."
    In *A Guide to Systems Research: Philosophy, Processes and Practice*,
    edited by Mary C. Edson, Pamela Buckle Henning, and Shankar

Sankaran, 10:177–98. Traditional Systems Sciences. Singapore: Springer Nature, 2017.

Hoegh-Guldberg, Ove, Daniela Jacob, Michael Taylor, Marco Bindi, Sally Brown, Ines Camilloni, Arona Diedhiou, et al. "Impacts of 1.5°C Global Warming on Natural and Human Systems." In *Global Warming of 1.5°C. An IPCC Special Report on the Impacts of Global Warming of 1.5°C above Pre-Industrial Levels and Related Global Greenhouse Gas Emission Pathways, in the Context of Strengthening the Global Response to the Threat of Climate Change, Sustainable Development, and Efforts to Eradicate Poverty*, 175–312. Cambridge and New York: Cambridge University Press, 2018.

Hoos, Ida R. *Systems Analysis in Public Policy: A Critique*. Revised. Berkeley: University of California Press, 1983.

Hull University Business School. "Business and Management Postgraduate Research Degrees | University of Hull." Accessed March 1, 2023. https://www.hull.ac.uk/study/postgraduate/research/business-and-management-research-degrees.

Independent Group of Scientists appointed by the Secretary-General. "Global Sustainable Development Report (GSDR) 2019: The Future Is Now - Science for Achieving Sustainable Development." New York: United Nations, 2019.

Intergovernmental Panel on Climate Change. "Climate Change 2022: Mitigation of Climate Change. Contribution of Working Group III to the Sixth Assessment Report of the Intergovernmental Panel on Climate Change." *Cambridge University Press*, 2022. https://doi.org/10.1017/9781009157926.

International Institute for Applied Systems Analysis. "Annual Report 2021." Vienna: International Institute for Applied Systems Analysis (IIASA), June 2022.

International Society for the Systems Sciences. "About ISSS." Accessed March 3, 2023. https://www.isss.org/about-isss/.

Jackson, Michael C. "Creative Holism: A Critical Systems Approach to Complex Problem Situations." *Systems Research and Behavioural Science* 23 (2006): 647–57. https://doi.org/10.1002/sres.799.

———. *Systems Approaches to Management*. New York: Kluwer/Plenum, 2000.

———. "Systems Methodologies as Complementary Tools for Managing Situational Complexity." *Transactions of the Institute of Measurement and Control* 10, no. 3 (1988): 155–60. https://doi.org/10.1177/014233128801000307.

———. *Systems Methodology for the Management Sciences*. Contemporary Systems Thinking. New York and London: Plenum Press, 1991.

———. *Systems Thinking: Creative Holism for Managers*. West Sussex: John Wiley & Sons, 2003.

Jantsch, Erich. *Design for Evolution: Self Organization and Planning in the Life of Human Systems*. The International Library of Systems Theory and Philosophy. New York: George Braziller, 1975.

Jörg, Ton. *New Thinking in Complexity for the Social Sciences and Humanities: A Generative, Transdiciplinary Approach*. Springer Complexity. Springer, 2011.

Kernek, Sterling J., and Charles H. O'Brien. *Civiliazation Past and Present*. Studying Civilization. Glenview and London: Scott, Foresman and Company, 1987.

Khan, Sobia, Ashley Vandermorris, John Shepherd, James W. Begun, Holly Jordan Lanham, Mary Uhl-Bien, and Berta Whitney. "Embracing Uncertainty, Managing Complexity: Applying Complexity Thinking Principles to Transformation Efforts in Healthcare Systems." *BMC Health Services Research*, March 21, 2018. https://doi.org/10.1186/s12913-018-2994-0.

Kiteme, Boniface P., and Urs Wiesmann. "Sustainable River Basin Management in Kenya: Balancing Needs and Requirements." In *Handbook of Transdisciplinary Research*, edited by Gertrude Hirsch Hadorn, Holger Hoffmann-Riem, Susette Biber-Klemm, Walter Grossenbacher-Mansuy, Dominique Joye, Christian Pohl, Urs Wiesmann, and Elisabeth Zemp, 63–78. Springer, 2008.

Klein, Julie Thompson. "Transdisciplinarity and Sustainability: Patterns of Definition." In *Transdisciplinary Research and Practice for Sustainability Outcomes*, edited by Dena Fam, Jane Palmer, Chris Riedy, and Cynthia Mitchell, 7–22. Routledge Studies in Sustainability. London and New York: Routledge, 2017.

Kockelmans, Joseph J. "Why Interdisciplinary." In *Interdisciplinarity and Higher Education*. University Park: Pennsylvania State University Press, 1979.

KU Leuven. "Institute for the Future: Transdisciplinary Research Incubator." Accessed March 6, 2023. https://rega.kuleuven.be/if/IF.

Kuhn, Thomas S. *The Structure of Scientific Revolutions*. Chicago: University of Chicago Press, 1962.

Lamperti, Francesco, Irene Monasterolo, and Andrea Roventini. "Climate Risks, Economics and Finance: Insights from Complex Systems." In *The Systemic Turn in Human and Natural Sciences: A Rock in The Pond*, edited by Lucia Urbani Ulivi, 97–119. Contemporary Systems Thinking. Switzerland: Springer Nature, 2019.

Laszlo, Ervin. *The Systems View of the World: The Natural Philosophy of the New Developments in the Sciences*. New York: George Braziller, 1972.

Lawrence, Mark G., Stephen Williams, Patrizia Nanz, and Ortwin Renn. "Characteristics, Potentials, and Challenges of Transdisciplinary Research." *One Earth* 5, no. 1 (2022): 44–61. https://doi.org/10.1016/j.oneear.2021.12.010.

Lönngren, Johanna, and Katrien Van Poeck. "Wicked Problems: A Mapping Review of the Literature." *International Journal of Sustainable Development & World Ecology* 28, no. 6 (August 18, 2021): 481–502. https://doi.org/10.1080/13504509.2020.1859415.

Meppem, Tony, and Roderic Gill. "Planning for Sustainability as a Learning Concept." *Ecological Economics* 26 (1998): 121–37.

Messerli, Bruno, and Paul Messerli. "From Local Projects in the Alps to Global Change Programmes in the Mountains of the World: Milestones in Transdisciplinary Research." In *Handbook of Transdisciplinary Research*, edited by Gertrude Hirsch Hadorn, Holger Hoffmann-Riem, Susette Biber-Klemm, Walter Grossenbacher-Mansuy, Dominique Joye, Christian Pohl, Urs Wiesmann, and Elisabeth Zemp, 43–62. Springer, 2008.

Midgley, Gerald. *Systemic Intervention: Philosophy, Methodology, and Practice*. Contemporary Systems Thinking. New York: Springer Science+Business Media, 2000.

———. "What Is This Thing Called CST." In *Critical Systems Thinking: Current Research and Practice*, edited by Robert L Flood and Norma R. A. Romm, 11–24. New York and London: Plenum Press, 1996.

Mirowski, Philip. "How Positivism Made a Pact with the Postwar Social Sciences in the United States." In *The Politics of Method in the Human Sciences: Positivism and Its Epistemological Others*, edited by George Steinmetz, 142–72. Durham, London: Duke University Press, 2005.

MIT Sloan School of Management. "System Dynamics." Accessed March 1, 2023. https://mitsloan.mit.edu/phd/program-overview/system-dynamics.

Mitroff, Ian I. "Archetypal Social Systems Analysis: On the Deeper Structure of Human Systems." *The Academy of Management Review* 8, no. 3 (1983): 387–97. https://doi.org/10.2307/257827.

Mittelstraß, Jürgen. "Unity and Transdisciplinarity." *Interdisciplinary Science Reviews* 18, no. 2 (1993): 153–57. https://doi.org/10.1179/isr.1993.18.2.153.

National University of Singapore College of Design and Engineering. "Research Degrees – Industrial Systems Engineering and Management." Accessed March 4, 2023. https://cde.nus.edu.sg/isem/graduate/research-degrees/.

Nuttall, Mark. "Tipping Points and the Human World: Living with Change and Thinking about the Future." *Ambio* 41, no. 1 (January 2012): 96–105. https://doi.org/10.1007/s13280-011-0228-3.

OECD Centre for Educational Research and Innovation (CERI). *The University and the Community: The Problems of Changing Relationships*. Paris: OECD, 1982.

OECD Science, Technology and Industry. "Addressing Societal Challenges Using Transdisciplinary Research." OECD DSTI/STP/GSF(2020)4/FINAL, June 2020.

Oxford Reference. "Bradford Hill Criteria." Oxford Reference. Accessed May 15, 2023. https://doi.org/10.1093/oi/authority.20110803095523346.

Palmer, Jane, Chris Riedy, Dena Fam, and Cynthia Mitchell. "Transdisciplinary Research and Practice for Sustainable Outcomes: An Introduction." In *Transdisciplinary Research and Practice for Sustainability Outcomes*, edited by Dena Fam, Jane Palmer, Chris Riedy, and Cynthia Mitchell, 1–6. Routledge Studies in Sustainability. London and New York: Routledge, 2017.

Parsons School of Design. "Transdisciplinary Design (MFA)." Accessed March 9, 2023. https://www.newschool.edu/parsons/mfa-transdisciplinary-design/.

Peters, B Guy. "What Is so Wicked about Wicked Problems? A Conceptual Analysis and a Research Program." *Policy and Society* 36, no. 3 (July 3, 2017): 385–96. https://doi.org/10.1080/14494035.2017.1361633.

Plsek, Paul E, and Trisha Greenhalgh. "Complexity Science: The Challenge of Complexity in Health Care." *BMJ* 323 (September 15, 2001).

Pohl, Christian. "What Is Progress in Transdisciplinary Research." *Futures* 43 (2011): 618–26. https://doi.org/10.1016/j.futures.2011.03.001.

ProClim. "Research on Sustainability and Global Change - Visions in Science Policy by Swiss Researchers." Bern: ProClim - Forum for Climate and Global Change, 1997.

Rajagopalan, Raghav. *Immersive Systemic Knowing: Advancing Systems Thinking Beyond Rational Analysis*. Contemporary Systems Thinking. Switzerland: Springer Nature, 2020.

Reid, David. *Sustainable Development: An Introductory Guide*. London: Earthscan Publications Ltd., 1995.

Renn, Ortwin. "Die Rolle(n) Transdisziplinärer Wissenschaft Bei Konfliktgeladenen Transformationsprozessen." Translated by Google Translate (via OnlineDocTranslator.com). *GAIA - Ecological Perspectives for Science and Society* 28, no. 1 (2019): 44–51. https://doi.org/10.14512/gaia.28.1.11.

Richmond, Barry. "Systems Thinking/ System Dynamics: Let's Just Get on with It." *System Dynamics Review* 10, no. 2–3 (1994). https://doi.org/10.1002/sdr.4260100204.

Rittel, Horst W. J., and Melvin M. Webber. "Dilemmas in a General Theory of Planning." *Policy Sciences, Springer* 4, no. 2 (June 1973). https://doi.org/10.1007/BF01405730.

Rosenfield, Patricia L. "The Potential of Transdisciplinary Research for Sustaining and Extending Linkages Between the Health and Social Sciences." *Social Science & Medicine* 35, no. 11 (1992): 1343–57. https://doi.org/10.1016/0277-9536(92)90038-r.

Rosenhead, Jonathan. "Introduction: Old and New Paradigms of Analysis." In *Rational Analysis for a Problematic World: Problem Structuring Methods for Complexity, Uncertainty and Conflict*, edited by Jonathan Rosenhead. Chichester and New York: John Wiley & Sons, 1989.

Sachs, Jeffrey D., Guido Schmidt-Traub, Mariana Mazzucato, Dirk Messner, Nebojsa Nakicenovic, and Johan Rockström. "Six Transformations to Achieve the Sustainable Development Goals." *Nature Sustainability* 2, no. 9 (September 2019): 805–14. https://doi.org/10.1038/s41893-019-0352-9.

Samad, Tariq, and Anuradha Annaswamy. "The Impact of Control Technology." Institute of Electrical and Electronics Engineers Control Systems Society, 2011.

Scholz, Roland W. "Mutual Learning as a Basic Principle of Transdisciplinarity," 13–17. Zürich, 2000. https://www.researchgate.net/publication/258820048_Mutual_Learning_as_a_Basic_Principle_of_Transdisciplinarity.

Scholz, Roland W., and David Marks. "Learning about Transdisciplinarity: Where Are We? Where Have We Been? Where Should We Go?" In *Transdisciplinarity: Joint Problem Solving among Science, Technology, and Society - An Effective Way for Managing Complexity*, edited by Julie Thompson Klein, Walter Grossenbacher-Mansuy, Rudolf Häberli, Alain Bill, Roland W. Scholz, and Myrtha Welti. Basel, Boston, and Berlin: Springer Basel AG, 2001.

Sergeyev, Yuriy. "Sergeyev's Letter," November 24, 2021.

Shea, Brent. "Collaborative Peer Review Process, Part I," May 8, 2023.

Shields, Christopher. "Aristotle." In *The Stanford Encyclopedia of Philosophy*, edited by Edward N. Zalta. Metaphysics Research Lab, Stanford University, 2022. https://plato.stanford.edu/archives/spr2022/entries/aristotle/.

Singer, Marcus George. *The Ideal of a Rational Morality: Philosophical Compositions*. Oxford: Oxford University Press, 2003.

Solmsen, Friedrich. "Hesiod | Greek Poet | Britannica." Accessed March 3, 2023. https://www.britannica.com/biography/Hesiod.

Srivastava, Leena, Luis Gomez Echeverri, and Flavia Schlegel. "Transformations within Reach: Pathways to a Sustainable and Resilient World, Synthesis Report." Laxenburg, Paris: International Institute for Applied Systems Analysis (IIASA), International Science Council (ISC), January 2021.

Sterman, John D. *Business Dynamics: Systems Thinking and Modeling for a Complex World*. McGraw-Hill Higher Education, 2000.

Technical University of Berlin. "Transdisciplinary Strategy." Accessed March 10, 2023. https://www.tu.berlin/en/topics/knowledge-exchange/2020/mai/citizen-science-researching-with-society.

Thompson, Michael. "Good Science for Public Policy." *Journal of International Development* 5, no. 6 (1993): 669–79. https://doi.org/10.1002/jid.3380050608.

Touboulic, Anne, and Lucy McCarthy. "Collective Action in SCM: A Call for Activist Research." *The International Journal of Logistics Management* 31, no. 1 (2020): 3–20. https://doi.org/DOI 10.1108/IJLM-08-2019-0222.

TU Delft. "Technology, Policy and Management." TU Delft. Accessed March 4, 2023. https://www.tudelft.nl/en/tpm/research/tpm-labs.

Turner, Jonathan. *Sociology: Studying the Human System*. 2nd ed. Santa Monica, California: Goodyear Publishing Company, 1981.

Ulivi, Lucia Urbani. "Preface." In *The Systemic Turn in Human and Natural Sciences: A Rock in The Pond*, edited by Lucia Urbani Ulivi, V–VIII. Contemporary Systems Thinking. Switzerland: Springer Nature, 2019.

UNESCO. "Evaluation of the Entire Transdisciplinary Project: Environment and Population Education and Information for Development." UNESCO 151 EX/42, April 1997.

———. "The Scientific Advisory Board of the United Nations Secretary-General." UNESCO, October 31, 2013. https://en.unesco.org/themes/science-sustainable-future/scientific-advisory-board-united-nations-secretary-general.

———. "Third Symposium on Sustainability Science: Towards Guidelines on Research and Education." UNESCO, June 2017.

UNESCO International Bureau of Education. "Transdisciplinary Approach." Text, May 23, 2016. https://www.ibe.unesco.org/en/glossary-curriculum-terminology/t/transdisciplinary-approach.

University of British Columbia. "Home | Collaborative PhD for Climate Action." Accessed March 4, 2023. https://climateaction.collabphd.ubc.ca/.

University of Buenos Aires. "Research - Instituto de Cálculo, Universidad de Buenos Aires." Accessed March 4, 2023. https://www.ic.fcen.uba.ar/en/academic-activity/research/complex-systems.

University of Florence. "UNESCO Chairs | International Relations | UniFI." www.unifi.it. Accessed March 11, 2023. https://www.unifi.it/vp-11257-unesco-chairs.html.

University of Fort Hare. "About Us | Faculty of Social Sciences & Humanities." Accessed March 4, 2023. https://www.ufh.ac.za/faculties/social-sciences/centres/cts/about-us.

University of Pretoria. "School of Health Systems and Public Health." Accessed March 5, 2023. https://www.up.ac.za/school-of-health-systems-and-public-health.

University of Technology Sydney. "Transdisciplinary Innovation." University of Technology Sydney, July 29, 2016. https://www.uts.edu.au/study/transdisciplinary-innovation.

Urlings, L. "Set a System to Change a System: Seven Systems Transformations for Benchmarking Companies on the SDGs." Amsterdam: World Benchmarking Alliance, 2021.

Waddock, Sandra. "Thinking Transformational System Change." *Journal of Change Management*, March 5, 2020. https://doi.org/10.1080/14697017.2020.1737179.

Webber, Melvin M. "A Difference Paradigm for Planning." In *Planning Theory in the 1980's: A Search for Future Directions*, edited by Robert W. Burchell and George Sternlieb, 151–62. New Brunswick, N.J.: Center for Urban Policy Research, Rutgers University, 1978.

Willetts, Juliet, and Cynthia Mitchell. "Assessing Transdisciplinary Doctoral Research." In *Transdisciplinary Research and Practice for Sustainability Outcomes*, edited by Dena Fam, Jane Palmer, Chris Riedy, and Cynthia Mitchell, 122–36. Routledge Studies in Sustainability. London and New York: Routledge, 2017.

Williams, Bob, and Richard Hummelbrunner. *Systems Concepts in Action: A Practitioner's Toolkit*. California: Stanford Business Books, 2011.

World Business Council for Sustainable Development (WBCSD). "Unlocking Systems Transformation: Vision 2050 Issue Brief." Geneva, June 2020.

2

Research Philosophy: Transdisciplinary Systems Research (TSR)

2.0 Outline

This chapter builds on the idea in *Chapter 1* that transdisciplinary research has the potential to address critiques of past systems thinking approaches. It develops a novel approach known as Transdisciplinary Systems Research (TSR), as well as corresponding concepts Transdisciplinary Systems Thinking (TST) and Transdisciplinary Systems Guidance (TSG). TSR was formulated to solve grand challenges by combining transdisciplinary research and systems thinking, with a dedicated research philosophy that includes a theory on boundaries (ontology), procedures for examining evidence (epistemology), and valuation lenses (axiology). A key feature of TSR is it sets as boundaries the properties of complex adaptive systems (CAS) and the properties of grand challenges including those of wicked problems. In more practical terms, this chapter identifies a series of filters through which evidence is funneled through to arrive at the final synthesis. While research philosophy may seem esoteric, practitioners would also derive value from topics such as assumptions, evidence-based decision-making, and frameworks that have been used to guide judgment.

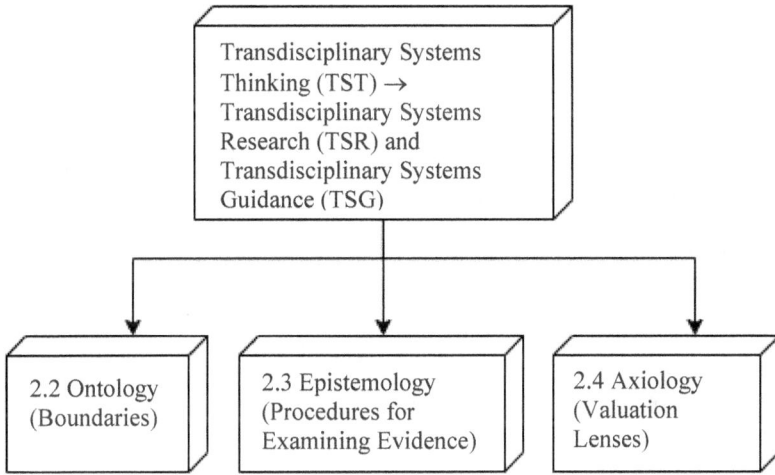

Figure 2.1 Outline for *Chapter 2*

2.1 Understanding the Construction of Transdisciplinary Systems Research for Future Revisions and Updates

Recognizing the *dynamic* property of complex adaptive systems (CAS), the theory on Transdisciplinary Systems Research (TSR) has been structured so that it can be easily adapted and updated, as shown in *Figure 2.2*. For example, researchers and practitioners can update the properties of CAS, include additional boundaries, or modify TSR in the future e.g. "The project uses Transdisciplinary Systems Research with [*x, y, and z*] modifications."

Box 2-1: Definitions of Transdisciplinary Systems Thinking (TST), Transdisciplinary Systems Research (TSR), and Transdisciplinary Systems Guidance (TSG)

Transdisciplinary Systems Thinking (TST) is formulated to solve grand challenges by combining transdisciplinary research and systems thinking, with a dedicated research philosophy that includes a theory on boundaries (ontology), procedures for examining evidence (epistemology), and valuation lenses (axiology).

Transdisciplinary Systems Research (TSR) describes a sustained and iterative process of applying TST.

Transdisciplinary Systems Guidance (TSG) is the outcome of a TSR research process. It refers to advice that is grounded in implementation knowledge and formulated to help stakeholders achieve shared goals e.g. policy recommendations, investment recommendations, and other recommended actions.

Transdisciplinary Systems Thinking (TST)
→ Transdisciplinary Systems Research
(TSR) and Transdisciplinary Systems
Guidance (TSG)

Ontology (Boundaries)	Epistemology (Procedures for Examining Evidence)	Axiology (Valuation lenses)
Boundary 1: A complex reality	*Procedure 1*: Treatment on uncertainty	*Valuation lens 1*: 2030 Sustainable Development Goals shared principles and commitments
Boundary 2: International law	*Procedure 2*: Concepts in modern law of evidence	
Definitions of systems thinking, systems research, complex adaptive systems, system-wide transformation, grand challenges, wicked problems	*Procedure 3*: Futures studies	*Valuation lens 2*: Four principles of biomedical ethics
	Definitions of transdisciplinary research, systems knowledge, target knowledge, transformation knowledge, implementation knowledge	*Valuation lens 3*: Crisis management and risk management
		Valuation lens 4: Operational expertise and stress-testing
Properties of complex adaptive systems, grand challenges, wicked problems		*Valuation lens 5*: Just transition
		Evaluation criteria for transdisciplinary research (with supplements)

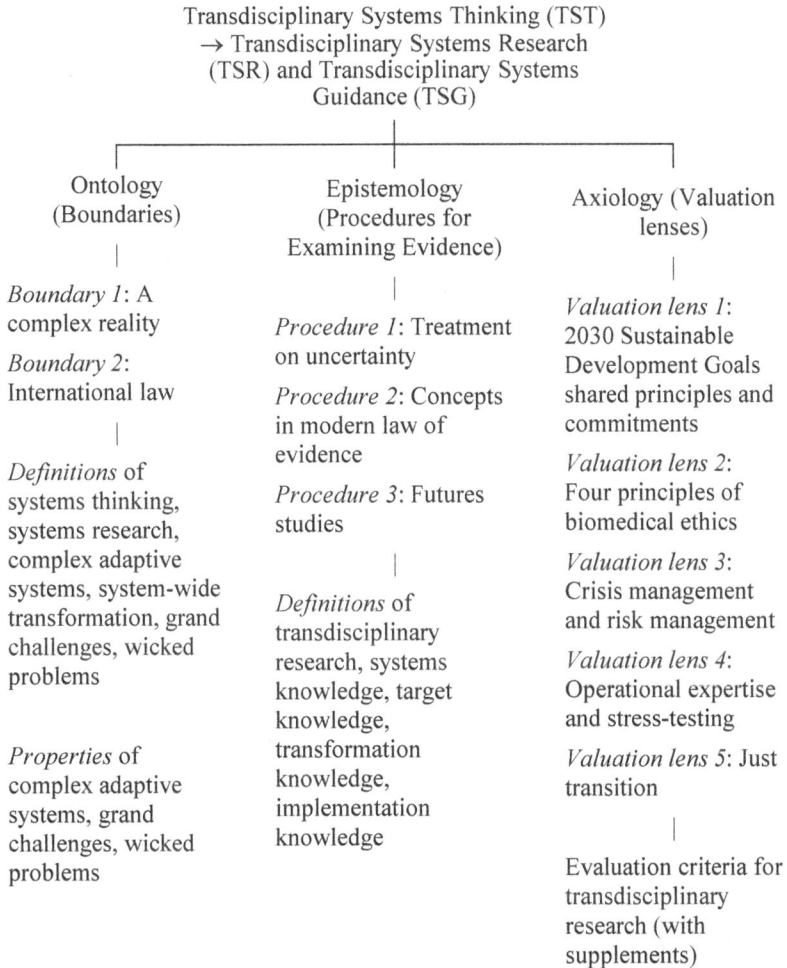

Figure 2.2 Construction of Transdisciplinary Systems Research (TSR) for future revisions and updates

2.2 *Ontology*: Boundaries in Transdisciplinary Systems Research

The theory on Transdisciplinary Systems Research (TSR) begins with a consideration of its *ontology* (i.e. the study of being, existence, identity, property, relation, fact, and world)[234]. This addresses TSR's fundamental assumptions. The ontology of TSR largely follows the philosophy articulated by Jörg in 2011. *A complex reality* is used to describe the transdisciplinary, nonlinear, self-organizing, dynamically interdependent, fluid-like, ever-evolving nature of reality[235], "as a potential outcome of complex processes and generative mechanisms"[236]. To clarify[237]:

- *A transdisciplinary reality* describes a reality that transcends artificial disciplinary boundaries[238].
- *A fluid reality* describes a shift from "being" to "becoming", where reality no longer unfolds in stages, but is in transition and in the process of transformation[239].
- *Generative mechanisms* describe the creation of ideas[240]. This is in contrast to the generic use of the term: "to produce (something) or cause (something) to be produced"[241]. Generative in this context posits that actors within complex adaptive systems are capable of composing original thought and actions, which can be seen as emergent behavior in a non-linear process[242]. Subsequently, actors have (some) agency

---

[234] Peter Simons, "Ontology | Metaphysics | Britannica," accessed March 20, 2023, https://www.britannica.com/topic/ontology-metaphysics.

[235] Ton Jörg, *New Thinking in Complexity for the Social Sciences and Humanities: A Generative, Transdiciplinary Approach*, Springer Complexity (Springer, 2011). p. 70, 90, 96.

[236] *ibid.* p. 67.

[237] For *complexity*, see *Section 1.2.1*. For *nonlinear, self-organizing, dynamically interdependent, ever-evolving*, see *Table 1.1*.

[238] Jörg, *New Thinking in Complexity for the Social Sciences and Humanities: A Generative, Transdiciplinary Approach*. p. 90.

[239] *ibid.* p. 39.

[240] Claire Tatro and Jack Fleming, "Generative Design Research: Using Metaphor to Capture Complexity," in *Proceedings of the 2017 International Symposium on Human Factors and Ergonomics in Health Care*, 2017, 59–65. p. 59.

[241] Britannica Dictionary, "Generate Definition & Meaning," accessed March 17, 2023, https://www.britannica.com/dictionary/generate.

[242] Tatro and Fleming, "Generative Design Research: Using Metaphor to Capture Complexity." p. 164.

and power to act in a way that is not prescribed by the overarching system. This view humanizes the social sciences[243], allows the possibility of innovation[244], and shifts towards an understanding of the world of *"unrealized potential"*[245]. Jörg argued that the focus on the "unknown realms of possibilities"[246], the world of the possible by Kauffman in 1993 and an enlarged space of the possible by Osberg in 2009 *"is* the world of real-world complexity"[247].

A second series of concepts crucial to the ontology of TSR is complementarism introduced by Flood and Jackson in 1991. *Complementarism* posits that, unlike pluralism (i.e. the presence or co-existence of different ways of being), a synthesis of different ways of being is possible[248]. It moves from a binary view e.g. reductionism *or* holism, towards a transdisciplinary view of reductionism *and* holism. Recall the expression, "it is both a science *and* an art". Complementarism is a response to *unreflective pragmatism*, where a "tool-kit" of techniques is assembled without regard for theory[249]. Unreflective pragmatism is not a requirement to solve problems. For example, by understanding transdisciplinary research as an iterative process between disciplinary and cross-disciplinary approaches[250], TSR researchers can engage with methods in a way that appreciates their philosophical underpinnings. More generally, in scenarios where theories are incompatible, I find it helpful to focus on the entities (e.g. people or organizations) who see the world through these seemingly incompatible lenses: how, why, and at what venues do these "incompatible" theories interact?

The third series of concepts critical to the ontology of Transdisciplinary Systems Research is the idea of boundary from Critical Systems Thinking (CST) by Churchman in 1970[251].

---

[243] Jörg, *New Thinking in Complexity for the Social Sciences and Humanities: A Generative, Transdiciplinary Approach.* p. 67.
[244] *ibid.* p. 63.
[245] *ibid.* p. 244.
[246] *ibid.* p. 2.
[247] *ibid.* p. 2.
[248] Robert L. Flood and Michael C. Jackson, *Creative Problem Solving: Total Systems Intervention* (New York: John Wiley & Sons, 1991). p. 47.
[249] *ibid.* p. 47.
[250] Boniface P. Kiteme and Urs Wiesmann, "Sustainable River Basin Management in Kenya: Balancing Needs and Requirements," in *Handbook of Transdisciplinary Research*, ed. Gertrude Hirsch Hadorn et al. (Springer, 2008), 63–78. p. 75.
[251] Shankar Sankaran, "Taking Action Using Systems Research," in *A Guide to Systems Research: Philosophy, Processes and Practice*, ed. Mary C. Edson,

Boundaries define the subject of study i.e. what is considered relevant[252]. Boundaries are significant because they determine what issues exist, how issues are seen, and what actions will be taken[253]. An improvement within a narrow boundary may not be perceived as one within a broader boundary[254]. Where there are multiple subjects, an overarching boundary or framework emerges[255].

Boundary judgments describe judgment on where boundaries are constructed and the values that guide their construction[256]. In 2000, Midgley pointed to their importance because it is impossible for any analysis to be fully "comprehensive" as a result of *a complex reality*. Boundaries can be constructed by looking outwards into the world or within theory[257], through (a) *critique* (boundary critique): reflection on and choices between boundaries with consideration to project goals[258], (b) *judgment*: decisions relating to the appropriateness of theory and methods[259], and (c) *action*: implementation and foreseeable recommendations as a result of pursuing a line of inquiry[260]. These three activities are inseparable and influence each other[261]: boundary choices determine the theories applicable to the research, and the theoretical limitations in turn affect the project's boundaries. Another way to approach boundary critique is known as Critical Systems Heuristics (CSH), created by Ulrich in 1983[262] and built upon by Reynolds and Midgley[263]. This is shown in *Table 2.1*.

Pamela Buckle Henning, and Shankar Sankaran, vol. 10, Translational Systems Sciences (Springer, 2017), 111–42. p. 119.

[252] Gerald Midgley, *Systemic Intervention: Philosophy, Methodology, and Practice*, Contemporary Systems Thinking (New York: Springer Science+Business Media, 2000). p. 79.

[253] *ibid.* p. 36.

[254] Gerald Midgley, Isaac Munlo, and Mandy Brown, "The Theory and Practice of Boundary Critique: Developing Housing Services for Older People," *Journal of the Operational Research Society* 49 (1998): 467–78, https://doi.org/10.2307/3009885. p. 467.

[255] Midgley, *Systemic Intervention: Philosophy, Methodology, and Practice*. p. 79; see also *Table 1.2*.

[256] *ibid.* p. 36.

[257] *ibid.* p. 80; see parallel concepts *exogenous* and *endogenous interdisciplinarity* in *Section 1.4.1*

[258] *ibid.* p. 82.

[259] *ibid.* p. 132.

[260] *ibid.*

[261] *ibid.* p. 131-132.

[262] Werner Ulrich, "A Brief Introduction to Critical Systems Heuristics (CSH)" (ECOSENSUS, The Open University, 2005), https://www.wulrich.com/downloads/ulrich_2005f.pdf.

[263] Bob Williams and Richard Hummelbrunner, *Systems Concepts in Action: A Practitioner's Toolkit* (California: Stanford Business Books, 2011). p. 303.

Table 2.1 Components of Critical Systems Heuristics

Component	Questions with reference to systems knowledge ("what is") and target knowledge ("what ought to be")
1. Purpose	What is / ought to be the purpose of the system?
2. Targets	What is / ought to be the targets of the system?
3. Indicators	What is / ought to be the metrics for the system's targets?
4. Resources	What is / ought to be the resources (such as financial, time, natural, or expertise) available to achieve the system's purpose?
5. Decision-maker	Who is / ought to be in control of the resources to enable the system to achieve its purpose?
6. Decision environment	What factors are / ought to be in place to ensure accountability?
7. Knowledge	What knowledge is / ought to be considered?
8. System designer	Who is / ought to be the designer of the system?
9. Inclusion	What mechanisms are / ought to be in place for inclusive participation?
10. Improvement	When inefficiencies arise, what is / ought to be the process for stakeholders to enact change?
11. Representation	Who is / ought to be representing the interests of historically underrepresented people and communities?
12. Conflict resolution	What is / ought to be the process for reconciling differences?

Sources: Bob Williams and Richard Hummelbrunner, *Systems Concepts in Action: A Practitioner's Toolkit* (California: Stanford Business Books, 2011). p. 305-306

TSR recognizes its fundamental assumptions through the concept of boundaries, as shown in the next subsections.

2.2.1 *Boundary 1*: A Complex Reality

The first boundary is *a complex reality*. Transdisciplinary Systems Research (TSR) assumes reality is as defined earlier in this section, and the subject of study exists as described by the definitions and properties of complex adaptive systems (CAS), grand challenges (GC), and systems thinking in *Chapter 1*. These definitions and properties can be updated according to new consensuses. It is uncertain how suspending or contradicting one or some of the properties would affect the project outcome. It is as such generally inadvisable.

2.2.2 *Boundary 2*: International Law

Transdisciplinary Systems Research (TSR), Transdisciplinary Systems Thinking (TST), and Transdisciplinary Systems Guidance (TSG) operate in accordance with international law, including international human rights law. This boundary addresses the practicalities of operating within a dynamic environment and considers international law as an imperfect but practical reflection of global values, norms, and sentiments. Providing guidance on international law is outside the scope of this book. I recommend consulting international law experts when uncertainty arises[264].

---

[264] For readers interested in the topic, UCLouvain offers an online MicroMasters Program in International Law on edX, which at the time of writing, can be audited for free and accessed any time.

Box 2-2: Closing the Compliance Gap

Decisions by consensus, such as the Glasglow Climate Pact at COP26 and the 2030 Sustainable Development Goals, were made unanimously[265]. While any signed international document is a manifestation of the *political will* of the signatory states except in cases such as political or economic despair[266], *decisions by consensus,* "understood as the absence of objection rather than a particular majority"[267] command a stronger moral imperative to act and in turn demonstrate a stronger political commitment[268]. When "deeds lag behind words, or compliance falls short of commitment"[269], a *compliance gap* appears.

One of the compliance gaps that has been well studied is in international human rights law. Literature on the transition from *commitment* to *compliance* is contested in the realm of human rights[270]. Scholars have disagreed on whether the compliance gap has increased in the thirty years between the early 1980s and late 2000s[271]. In 2015, Harrison and Sekalala questioned the relationship between commitment on paper and action[272]. Some scholars have even argued that a commitment may be a smokescreen to hide worse abuses[273]. There are, however, two areas that scholars have agreed on since. First, commitment to human rights norms does not by itself lead to compliance[274]. Second, the engagement of intermediaries, such as international

[265] Yuriy Sergeyev, "Sergeyev's Letter," November 24, 2021.

[266] *ibid.*

[267] United Nations Dag Hammarskjöld Library, "What Does It Mean When a Decision Is Taken 'by Consensus'? - Ask DAG!," accessed November 26, 2021, https://ask.un.org/faq/260981.

[268] Sergeyev, "Sergeyev's Letter," November 24, 2021.

[269] Xinyuan Dai, "The 'Compliance Gap' and the Efficacy of International Human Rights Institutions," in *The Persistent Power of Human Rights: From Commitment to Compliance*, ed. Thomas Risse, Stephen C. Ropp, and Kathryn Sikkink (Cambridge: Cambridge University Press, 2013), 85–102. p. 85.

[270] James Harrison and Sharifah Sekalala, "Addressing the Compliance Gap? UN Initiatives to Benchmark the Human Rights Performance of States and Corporations," *Review of International Studies* 41, no. 5 (December 2015): 925–45, https://doi.org/10.1017/S026021051500039X. p. 926.

[271] Dai, "The 'Compliance Gap' and the Efficacy of International Human Rights Institutions." p. 85.

[272] Harrison and Sekalala, "Addressing the Compliance Gap?". p. 926.

[273] *ibid.*

[274] *ibid.*

organizations and domestic civil society organizations, is necessary to increase compliance[275].

"Today, we have a surplus of multilateral challenges and a deficit of multilateral solutions", says United Nations Secretary-General António Guterres at the General Assembly meeting marking the organization's seventy-fifth anniversary, as he introduces the networked multilateralism agenda (SG/SM/20264). Scholarship on networked governance has increased, advocating for the mobilization and engagement of citizens as well as organizations across the contemporary global governance network[276]. The rise of networked governance can be attributed to two main reasons. First, issues now confronting the world, such as climate change, cannot be solved without global participation. There is a higher degree of interdependency between state and non-state actors[277]. Second, technological advancements have provided a wider array of non-state actors to disseminate information and organize[278]. Some non-state actors have become such important actors that their influence has been recognized to be on par with that of state diplomats since they now perform similar functions[279]. This includes aggregating interests, public speaking, negotiations, and providing policy recommendations[280].

---

[275] Harrison and Sekalala, "Addressing the Compliance Gap?". p. 926.
[276] John Lim, "Networked Governance: Why It Is Different and How It Can Work," *Civil Service College Singapore, ETHOS,* 2011. p. 19.
[277] David Held, "The Diffusion of Authority," in *International Organizations and Global Governance*, ed. Thomas G. Weiss and Rorden Wilkinson (London and New York: Routledge, 2014). p. 64.
[278] Lim, "Networked Governance: Why It Is Different and How It Can Work." p. 20.
[279] Held, "The Diffusion of Authority." p. 64.
[280] *ibid.*

2.3 *Epistemology*: Procedures for Examining Evidence in Transdisciplinary Systems Research

The *epistemology* (i.e. the study of knowledge) [281] of Transdisciplinary Systems Research (TSR) asks: What constitutes knowledge within a complex reality and what knowledge informs recommendations? Given the ontological underpinnings of TSR as discussed in the previous section, it is vital to acknowledge the uncertainty of knowledge[282]. This changes conventional epistemology into an "epistemology of the possible"[283] with greater awareness of the role of the future[284]. For example: how relevant will a research question be by the time it is answered, how will knowledge (not) created today affect the future, and how future-resilient are our guidance?

TSR largely follows the epistemology of transdisciplinary research (TDR) and this section will identify supplementary concepts. Recall TDR's definition: TDR is when researchers work jointly with non-academic stakeholders across disciplinary boundaries towards a problem-solving, common-good oriented, mutual-learning, and comprehensive approach to complex sustainable development problems[285]. TDR responds to challenges in problem-solving. In 1979, Lindblom and Cohen noted the general dissatisfaction with social research in solving social problems: practitioners are frustrated with the research they are offered, and researchers wish to be listened to more[286]. In 1985, Argyris, Putnam, and Smith argued that social scientists at times respond to disappointments by conducting research that seems increasingly esoteric and disconnected with reality[287].

---

[281] Johan R. Edelheim, *Ontological, Epistemological and Axiological Issues* (Routledge Handbooks Online, 2014), https://doi.org/10.4324/9780203763308.ch3. ch3.

[282] Jörg, *New Thinking in Complexity for the Social Sciences and Humanities: A Generative, Transdiciplinary Approach.* p. 5.

[283] *ibid.* p. 257.

[284] See also *target knowledge* in *Table 1.6 Types of Knowledge in TDR.*

[285] See *Section 1.4.1 Definition of Transdisciplinary Research.*

[286] Charles E. Lindblom and David K. Cohen, *Usable Knowledge: Social Science and Social Problem Solving* (New Haven and London: Yale University Press, 1979). p. VII.

[287] Chris Argyris, Robert Putnam, and Diana McLain Smith, *Action Science* (San Francisco: Jossey-Bass Publishers, 1985). p. IX-X.

In 2021, Renn identified some of the important epistemological questions for TDR[288]. I address these with supplements for TSR in this section:

1. How do we evaluate research design and measure the quality and applicability of outputs?
2. How do we integrate distinct research methods into a coherent approach?
3. How do we understand research credibility?
4. How do we reconcile the academic (such as positivist or normative) and non-academic ways of knowing?

I.   How do we evaluate research design and measure the quality and applicability of outputs?

This has already been addressed in *Section 1.4.3 Evaluation Criteria for Transdisciplinary Research*. There is no additional information in this section.

II.   How do we integrate distinct research methods into a coherent approach?

Scholars in transdisciplinary research have identified strategies to integrate distinct research methods. For example, Schwaninger, Edenhofer, and Kaufmann-Hayoz in 2008 argued that frameworks can help manage the relevant body of knowledge. Frameworks integrate diverse disciplinary perspectives, structure an issue in a transdisciplinary way, and prompt a systematic process of learning[289]. TSR supplements TDR by leveraging the concepts of *boundary*, *boundary judgment*, and *boundary critique* from Critical Systems Thinking (CST) to help increase coherence in research.

---

[288] Ortwin Renn, "Transdisciplinarity: Synthesis towards a Modular Approach," *Futures* 130 (June 1, 2021), https://doi.org/10.1016/j.futures.2021.102744. p. 6.
[289] Markus Schwaninger, Silvia Edenhofer, and Ruth Kaufmann-Hayoz, "Policy Analysis and Design in Local Public Management: A System Dynamics Approach," in *Handbook of Transdisciplinary Research*, ed. Gertrude Hirsch Hadorn et al. (Springer, 2008), 205–22. p. 218.

III.   How do we understand research credibility?

The summary of the *International Transdisciplinarity 2000 Conference* recognized that "Transdisciplinary research is a form of action research"[290]. The term *action research* was coined by Lewin in 1946[291]. It is a form of research practice that involves evidence gathering, reflection on actions, and making evidence-based claims to knowledge[292]. Greenwood and Levin in 1998 argued that action research distinguishes between *internal credibility* (i.e. knowledge that is convincing to the stakeholder group generating it) and *external credibility* (i.e. knowledge that is convincing to people who are outside of the stakeholder group generating it)[293]. External credibility is critical to research credibility in TSR. Communities are unlikely to find the "'objective' theories of outsiders"[294] credible if they cannot see a connection to the local context. In 2020, Keahey citing Bryndon-Miller et al. in 2003 clarified this idea: "action research does not rely upon value neutrality to demonstrate research validity, but rather engages a validity-in-action approach that emphasizes stakeholder relevance and outcomes"[295]. TSR highlights the value of knowledge on and knowledge tested in practice.

IV.   How do we reconcile the academic (such as positivist or normative) and non-academic ways of knowing?

Research in *action science* can offer some insights. Argyris, Putnam, and Smith in 1985 developed the theory of action science based on Lewin's theory of action research[296]. They identified several key features of action science: (a) empirically falsifiable propositions

---

[290] Rudolf Häberli, Walter Grossenbacher-Mansuy, and Julie Thompson Klein, "Summary and Synthesis," in *Transdisciplinarity: Joint Problem Solving among Science, Technology, and Society - An Effective Way for Managing Complexity*, ed. Julie Thompson Klein et al. (Basel, Boston, and Berlin: Springer Basel AG, 2001), 1–22..

[291] Greenwood and Levin, *Introduction to Action Research: Social Research for Social Change*. p. 17; scholars generally agree that Lewin coined the term "action research".

[292] Jean McNiff and Jack Whitehead, *Action Research: Principles and Practice*, 2nd ed. (London and New York: Routledge Palmer, 2002). p. 16.

[293] Greenwood and Levin, *Introduction to Action Research: Social Research for Social Change*. p. 81.

[294] *ibid.*

[295] Jennifer Keahey, "Sustainable Development and Participatory Action Research: A Systematic Review," *Systematic Practice and Action Research* 39 (2020): 291–306, https://doi.org/10.1007/s11213-020-09535-8. p. 293.

[296] Argyris, Putnam, and Smith, *Action Science*. p. 6.

organized into a theory, (b) knowledge that can impact policy or practice, and (c) alternatives to the status quo[297]. They argued that researchers who do not explore ways of changing the *status quo* (i.e. the interdependence among norms, rules, skills, and values that create a pervasive pattern[298]) risk perpetuating it[299].

One of the methods action science employs to bridge academic and non-academic ways of knowing is "communities of inquiry in communities of social practice"[300]. Through mutual learning, communities of inquiry offer a space for stakeholders to make, challenge, and justify claims to knowledge[301]. Other methods to bridge academic and non-academic ways of knowing are also available. Burns in 2014 identified a few examples and an explanation of their purposes. For example: (a) *reflective practice* (individuals reflect on their own practice), (b) *action learning, action science, and action inquiry* (group process to support individual reflection), (c) *co-operative inquiry* (group reflection on group endeavor), (d) *participatory action research* (community-based knowledge generation for community action), and (e) *systemic action research* (system-wide learning)[302]. These methods inform the methodology of this study, which is discussed in *Chapter 3*.

Although the aforementioned methods provide space for reflection, they offer little guidance on how researchers and practitioners can reconcile academic and non-academic ways of knowing *when evidence is in conflict*. Recognizing the wide range of methods available and diverse ways of knowing[303], TSR offers three procedures for examining evidence. TSR supplements the science-based treatment on uncertainty with concepts from the modern law of evidence and futures studies to offer guidance on reconciling conflicting evidence from diverse ways of knowing. Well articulated procedures for examining evidence are pivotal to problem-solving, especially since grand challenges are characterized by *conflicting theories* and *real world consequences*[304].

---

[297] Argyris, Putnam, and Smith, *Action Science*. p. 4.

[298] *ibid*. p. XI.

[299] *ibid*. p. XII; see parallel concepts *systems change* in *Section 1.2.1* and *paradigm shift* in *Box 1-2*.

[300] Argyris, Putnam, and Smith, *Action Science*. p. 6. p. 34.

[301] *ibid*.

[302] Danny Burns, "Systemic Action Research: Changing System Dynamics to Support Sustainable Change," *Action Research* 12, no. 1 (2014): 3–18, https://doi.org/0.1177/1476750313513910. p. 4.

[303] See *Table 1.2*.

[304] *ibid*.

Before addressing the subject in greater detail, it is important to recognize the issue of *epistemic hegemony*, a term that is typically used to describe the lack of receptivity to non-Western scholars and epistemologies[305]. Epistemic hegemony extends to the sharp divide between generalizable and local knowledge, academics and practitioners, theoretical and applied subjects etc. Consider: (a) what constitutes "valid knowledge", (b) what knowledge is "valued", (c) what methods can produce knowledge, (d) what level of rigor is necessary, and (e) who is considered legitimate producers of knowledge within this broader knowledge industry[306]. This is compounded by *the fear of epistemic trespassing* in academia as observed by Shea in 2023: "a trained aversion for those who go beyond the knowledge base of their academic disciplines"[307].

There is a lot of value in mutual learning if researchers in academia seek to influence practice or policy. The private sector expects a high degree of internal credibility (i.e. are you willing to bet thousands or millions of dollars on the recommendations?), and the public sector expects a high degree of external credibility (i.e. will the recommendations stand up to the scrutiny of hundreds of cross-disciplinary experts and move forward to impact policy?). These challenges are not common to academia.

2.3.1 *Procedure 1*: Treatment on Uncertainty

The first procedure for examining evidence is well established within academia. It is the science-based treatment on uncertainty. The IPCC issued a "Guidance Note for Lead Authors of the IPCC Fifth Assessment Report (AR5) on Consistent Treatment of Uncertainties" in 2010[308]. This subsection provides an overview of the key concepts.

---

[305] Orion Noda, "Epistemic Hegemony: The Western Straitjacket and Post-Colonial Scars in Academic Publishing," *Revista Brasileira de Política Internacional* 63, no. 1 (2020): e007, https://doi.org/10.1590/0034-7329202000107. Abstract.

[306] Rajesh Tandon, "Social Transformation and Participatory Research," *Convergence: An International Journal of Adult Education* 21, no. 2–3 (1988): 5–18. p. 8.

[307] Brent Shea, "Collaborative Peer Review Process, Part I," May 8, 2023.

[308] Michael D. Mastrandea et al., "Guidance Note for Lead Authors of the IPCC Fifth Assessment Report on Consistent Treatment of Uncertainties" (Intergovernmental Panel on Climate Change (IPCC), 2010), https://www.ipcc.ch/site/assets/uploads/2018/05/uncertainty-guidance-note.pdf.

First, the AR5 relies on two metrics for communicating the degree of certainty in key findings, taking into account evidence such as mechanistic understanding, theory, data, models, and expert judgment:

1. Confidence in qualitative terms
    - The validity of a finding, based on the type, amount, quality, and consistency of the evidence is described by "limited", "medium", or "robust" (when multiple consistent independent lines of high-quality evidence are available).
    - The degree of agreement is described by "low", "medium", or "high"[309].
2. Quantified measures of uncertainty in a finding
    - Expressed probabilistically based on statistical analysis of observations or model results, or expert judgment[310].

Second, expert judgment includes an evaluation of the type, amount, quality, and consistency of evidence and the degree of agreement[311]. It may also include standards of evidence applied, approaches to combining or reconciling multiple lines of evidence, conditional assumptions, and explanation of critical factors[312]. The guidance note further acknowledges that experts tend to underestimate uncertainty from an incomplete understanding of or competing frameworks for systems and processes[313].

Third, the guidance note recognizes that sound decision-making depends on information about the full range of possible consequences and associated possibilities, including low-probability high-impact outcomes, often from a risk management perspective[314]. The table below describes the common language used to describe the likelihood of an outcome.

---

[309] Mastrandea et al., "Guidance Note for Lead Authors of the IPCC Fifth Assessment Report on Consistent Treatment of Uncertainties." p. 2.
[310] *ibid.* p. 1.
[311] Mastrandea et al., "Guidance Note for Lead Authors of the IPCC Fifth Assessment Report on Consistent Treatment of Uncertainties." p. 2.
[312] *ibid.*
[313] *ibid.*
[314] *ibid.* p. 1.

Table 2.2 Terminology to describe the likelihood of an outcome

Terminology	Likelihood of the Outcome
Virtually certain	99-100% probability
Very likely	90-100% probability
Likely	66-100% probability
About as likely as not	33-66% probability
Unlikely	0-33% probability
Very unlikely	0-10% probability
Exceptionally unlikely	0-1% probability

Source: Michael D. Mastrandea et al., "Guidance Note for Lead Authors of the IPCC Fifth Assessment Report on Consistent Treatment of Uncertainties" (Intergovernmental Panel on Climate Change (IPCC), 2010), https://www.ipcc.ch/site/assets/uploads/2018/05/uncertainty-guidance-note.pdf. p. 3.

2.3.2 *Procedure 2*: Concepts from the Modern Law of Evidence

As an extension of *Boundary 2: International Law*, Transdisciplinary Systems Research (TSR) introduces concepts from the modern law of evidence[315] to help researchers reconcile conflicting evidence and identify a persuasive course of action. It broadens the range of evidence considered and offers a series of concepts to guide judgment. I have made some modifications to adapt the concepts for use in research. For example, researchers are unlikely to encounter the concept of admissibility or admissible evidence in everyday practice.

---

[315] This subsection cites *The Modern Law of Evidence* (11th edition) by Keane and McKeown in 2016, which is at the time of writing the latest edition available to borrow on the Internet Archive for readers interested in the topic, and the Cornell Law School Legal Information Institute WEX legal encyclopaedia, which is also available online. The 2nd edition of *The Modern Law of Evidence* has been cited at the International Criminal Tribunal for the former Yugoslavia (ICTY).

Evidence is "an item or information proffered to make the existence of a fact more or less probable"[316]. *The law of evidence* is the "body of law and discretion regulating the means by which facts may be proved in both courts of law and tribunals and arbitrations in which the struct rules of evidence apply"[317]. While in an ideal world, all evidence relevant to the dispute is taken into account[318], in the real world a variety of factors restrict the evidence considered including practical constraints such as time, resources, and the need for finality[319]. The modern law of evidence operates in an environment where aspirations to ascertain the truth have to be balanced with the need for a decision even if the evidence is inadequate or inconclusive[320]. This is a more accurate portrayal of the context in which researchers work within *a complex reality*[321], and takes into account the properties of grand challenges[322].

Facts that are open to proof or disproof are:
1. *Facts in issue*: facts that have to be proved in order to succeed in making a claim[323]
2. *Relevant facts*: facts from which the existence or non-existence of a fact in issue may be inferred, when direct evidence is unavailable[324]
3. *Collateral facts*: sometimes referred to as 'subordinate facts', which can include facts affecting the competence of a witness and facts affecting the credibility of a witness[325]

Together, they offer a more complete understanding of the uncertainty within complex adaptive systems (CAS).

---

[316] Cornell Law School, "Evidence," LII / Legal Information Institute, accessed March 23, 2023, https://www.law.cornell.edu/wex/evidence.
[317] Adrian Keane and Paul McKeown, *The Modern Law of Evidence*, 11th ed. (Oxford: Oxford University Press, 2016). p. 2.
[318] *ibid*; understood as "all evidence that logically goes to prove or disprove the existence of those facts, and would thereby get to the truth of the matter"
[319] Keane and McKeown, *The Modern Law of Evidence*. p. 2.
[320] *ibid*.
[321] See *Section 2.2.1*
[322] See *Table 1.2*. Also see *Section 2.2*: in 2000, Midgley pointed out that it is impossible for any analysis to be fully "comprehensive" as a result of *a complex reality*.
[323] Keane and McKeown, *The Modern Law of Evidence*. p. 9.
[324] *ibid*. p. 10.
[325] *ibid*.

Evidence takes three forms: oral evidence, documentary evidence, and things[326]. They can be grouped by labels such as:

- *Direct testimony*: an oral statement by a witness who has perceived a fact in issue with one of five senses, and has or claims to have personal or first-hand knowledge[327]
- *Documentary evidence*: a document has no single definition and can include not only documents in writing, but also maps, plans, graphs, drawings, photographs, videotapes, films, and negatives[328]
- *Real evidence*: a material object to allow an inference based on its existence, condition, or value; however, no weight is attached to such evidence without accompanying testimony identifying the object in question and explaining its significance in relation to the facts in issue or relevant to the issue[329]
- *Hearsay*: any statement other than one made by a witness[330]
- *Circumstantial evidence*: evidence of *relevant facts* is described as circumstantial evidence[331], and is particularly powerful when it proves multiple facts all of which point to the same direction[332]
- *Conclusive evidence*: evidence that, regardless of its weight, concludes the fact in issue[333]

Transdisciplinary Systems Research (TSR) takes into account a wide range of evidence. However, conclusive evidence is by definition more desirable, and documentary evidence is preferred as they can be examined by third-parties to enhance the credibility of the research. Within this broadened scope, TSR researchers can cite global agreements and statements from indigenous people or local communities as a valid source of knowledge. It is helpful to make a remark in-text about the sources of knowledge when they deviate from academic conventions, both for clarity and for giving proper credit.

---

[326] Keane and McKeown, *The Modern Law of Evidence*. p. 11.

[327] *ibid*. p. 11-12.

[328] *ibid*. p. 12-13.

[329] *ibid*. p. 13.

[330] *ibid*. p. 12.

[331] *ibid*. p. 10.

[332] *ibid*. p. 14.

[333] *ibid*. p. 33.

There are four principles that may be used to justify the exclusion of evidence obtained illegally or unfairly[334]:

1. *Reliability principle*: evidence is excluded if its reliability or the ability to test reliability has been impaired because of how it was obtained
2. *Integrity principle*: evidence is excluded to disassociate from how it was obtained or to maintain the process' integrity
3. *Disciplinary principle*: evidence is excluded to "discipline" and discourage obtaining evidence in such a way
4. *Rights-based or protective principle*: evidence is excluded when there is a breach of rights

There is a particular application that TSR researchers are likely to encounter: under the *integrity principle*, researchers are not obligated to reproduce advertisements for products or services, or self-promotion materials that have been submitted.

The *burden of proof* or the obligation to prove[335] consists of the *burden of production* (i.e. the obligation to present sufficient evidence to support a particular proposition of fact[336]) and the *burden of persuasion* (i.e. the obligation to convince a particular proposition of fact is true[337]). The burden of persuasion is an important idea that emphasizes the importance of effective and persuasive communication in research. Different *standards of proof* are necessary for a fact to gain *credibility[338]* depending on the goals and context of the project:

- *Preponderance of the evidence*: the burden of proof is met when there is a greater than 50% chance that the claim is true
- *Clear and convincing evidence*: evidence is highly and substantially more likely to be true than untrue
- *Beyond a reasonable doubt*: there is no other reasonable explanation that can come from the evidence presented

In most cases, TSR researchers will aim for clear and convincing evidence, or beyond a reasonable doubt. However, preponderance of the evidence may suffice if researchers are looking to launch a pilot study. The necessary standard of proof is highly context-dependent. These concepts from the modern law of evidence offer guidance for evidence-gathering in collaboration with non-academic stakeholders.

---

[334] *ibid.* p. 59-60.
[335] Keane and McKeown, *The Modern Law of Evidence*. p. 87.
[336] Cornell Law School, "Burden of Production," LII / Legal Information Institute, accessed March 23, 2023,
https://www.law.cornell.edu/wex/burden_of_production.
[337] Cornell Law School, "Burden of Persuasion," LII / Legal Information Institute, accessed March 23, 2023,
https://www.law.cornell.edu/wex/burden_of_persuasion.
[338] See *Section 2.3.*

2.3.3 *Procedure 3*: Futures Studies

The UN Global Pulse (UNGP) Foresight Glossary provides a
description of futures studies:
> *Futures studies*: the academic discipline, research methods,
> and tools used to develop knowledge about the future. It
> includes foresight, forecasting and strategic planning.
> Following recent developments shifting the focus form futures
> studies to anticipation, futures studies now capture Indigenous
> futurity and non-dominant conceptions of time[339].

Futures studies is compatible with academic ways of knowing.
Considerations of the future is present in almost every academic
discipline. Demographers project population changes, economists
provide macroeconomic outlooks, meteorologists offer weather
forecasts[340]. In 1989, Bell and Olick further observed some of the
topics that can be studied through established methods of science and
social science, such as (a) people's present images of the possible
future; (b) people's expectations of the future; (c) people's preferences
among perceived alternative futures; (d) people's present intention to
act in particular ways such as how they intend to invest; (e) people's
obligations and commitment to others; (f) people's past decisions in
particular situations; and (g) trend analysis of time series data[341].

From the perspective of Transdisciplinary Systems Research (TSR),
futures studies address several challenges. First, it acknowledges the
fundamental challenge of influencing complex adaptive
systems (CAS): our inability to fully anticipate initiatives' effects[342].
Second, it directly addresses target knowledge in Transdisciplinary
Systems Research (TSR)[343]. Third, it expands the ways of knowing to
include ones historically underrepresented in academia. For example,
one can ask: how might we draw from implementation knowledge to
help understand the future of a CAS, or how will local knowledge help
understand the future impact of an intervention?

---

[339] UN Global Pulse, "HOW - Glossary," UNGP - Foresight Project, accessed
April 30, 2023, https://foresight.unglobalpulse.net/how-glossary/.
[340] Wendell Bell and Jeffrey K. Olick, "An Epistemology for the Futures Field:
Problems and Possibilities of Prediction," *Futures* 21, no. 2 (1989): 115–35,
https://doi.org/10.1016/0016-3287(89)90001-3. p. 118.
[341] *ibid*. p. 122.
[342] See *Box 1-1*.
[343] See *Table 1.6* and *Section 2.3*.

More generally, a sound understanding of the future is fundamental to policy and planning. As Jantsch observed in 1972 and 1975[344]: "Action is bound to a belief in the future"[345]. Vickers noted a macro-level observation in 1983: "Human systems both design and predict their own future history – they are sometimes blind, often obdurate, often misguided, but seldom negligible as agents"[346]. Bell and Olick noted a micro-level observation in 1989: people in their everyday lives act by iterating mental images of the future, including consequences of their own behavior, other actors' behaviors, and forces beyond their control[347]. Our understanding of the future implicitly shapes the guidance offered. An exhaustive list of future scenarios is not within the scope of this publication, but *Section 5.2* on featured statements offers some of the crucial foresight that has been taken into account.

To offer some definitions, *prediction* is "a statement about the expected occurrence of some future event, outcome, state or process", in contrast to a *forecast* per the UNGP Glossary: "Predicting or estimating the likelihood of a future event or trend based on quantitative analysis and modelling"[348]. In 1989, Bell and Olick observed a fundamental paradox of futures studies: researchers make claims to knowledge but the future "cannot be known"[349]. Some scholars minimize the goal of prediction, others argue that futures studies ought to reveal alternative possibilities[350] because "there are no future facts"[351]. Some predictions can be plausible when they are made, but may portray such an undesirable future that it influences behavior and creates a self-negating or self-fulfilling prophecy[352]. It is therefore vital to differentiate between *presumptively true* (i.e. a plausible prediction congruent with relevant evidence) and *terminally true* (i.e. a prediction that accurately describes the eventual outcome)[353].

---

[344] Erich Jantsch, *Technological Planning and Social Futures* (New York: John Wiley & Sons, 1972). p. 11.

[345] Erich Jantsch, *Design for Evolution: Self Organization and Planning in the Life of Human Systems*, The International Library of Systems Theory and Philosophy (New York: George Braziller, 1975). p. 33.

[346] Geoffrey Vickers, *Human Systems Are Different* (London: Harper & Row, Publishers, 1983). p. XV.

[347] Bell and Olick, "An Epistemology for the Futures Field: Problems and Possibilities of Prediction." p. 117.

[348] UN Global Pulse, "HOW - Glossary."

[349] Bell and Olick, "An Epistemology for the Futures Field: Problems and Possibilities of Prediction." p. 115.

[350] *ibid.* p. 119.

[351] *ibid.* p. 121.

[352] *ibid.* p. 129.

[353] *ibid.*

In 2003, Aligica identified mismatches between theoretical truth (explanation) and predictive success (prediction)[354]: predictions are evidential rather than demonstrative i.e. it is not possible to deduce or prove a theory about the future through formal logic alone[355]. Claims to knowledge are made by synthesizing evidence to argue for a predictive thesis, and therefore the epistemology of futures studies depends not only on formal logic but also on a "larger theory of argumentation"[356]. The evidential nature of predictive argumentation reinforces the concepts from the modern law of evidence[357] and broadens the types of evidence for knowledge, including "non-formal and tacit knowledge"[358]. *Table 2.3* highlights a few futures studies concepts from the UNGP Glossary[359].

---

[354] Paul Dragos Aligica, "Prediction, Explanation and the Epistemology of Future Studies," *Futures* 35, no. 10 (December 2003): 1027–40, https://doi.org/10.1016/S0016-3287(03)00067-3. p. 1035.

[355] *ibid.*

[356] *ibid.*

[357] See *Section 2.3.2*.

[358] Aligica, "Prediction, Explanation and the Epistemology of Future Studies." p. 1035.

[359] For the complete list, consult the UNGP website.

Table 2.3 Highlights of futures studies concepts

Concept	Definition
Anticipatory governance	A strategy and policy-making process with due consideration to strategic foresight.
Driver of change	Ideas or emerging patterns of actions that may shape the future. These may have a direct or indirect effect.
Futures cone	A tool designed by futurist Joseph Voros that helps to visualize and explore a range of different futures including *projected future* (the default "business as usual" future), *probable futures* (likely based on current trends), *plausible futures* (credible based on current knowledge), *possible futures* (potentially possible), *preferred futures* (desired), and *preposterous futures* (unlikely or improbable).
Participatory futures	Potential futures derived from knowledge co-creation with stakeholders.
Risk management	An iterative process to identify, assess, evaluate, and plan for undesirable futures.
Weak signals	Early indicators of potential futures that may contribute to planning and risk management.

Source: UN Global Pulse, "HOW - Glossary," UNGP - Foresight Project, accessed April 30, 2023, https://foresight.unglobalpulse.net/how-glossary/.

2.4 *Axiology*: Valuating Transdisciplinary Systems Research

In 1971, Churchman offered an important insight about valuating systems research: "when one is considering systems it's always wise to raise questions about the most obvious and simple assumptions"[360]. This section on *axiology* (i.e. the study of values)[361] considers the values and valuation lenses associated with Transdisciplinary Systems Research (TSR).

2.4.1 *Valuation Lens 1*: 2030 Sustainable Development Goals Shared Principles and Commitments

This subsection highlights some of the 2030 Sustainable Development Goals Shared Principles and Commitments[362]:
  - Guided by the purposes and principles of the Charter of the United Nations, including full respect for international law
  - Grounded in the Universal Declaration of Human Rights, international human rights treaties, the Millennium Declaration and the 2005 World Summit Outcome
  - Recognizing that eradicating poverty in all its forms and dimensions, combating inequality within and among countries, preserving the planet, creating sustained, inclusive and sustainable economic growth and fostering social inclusion are linked to each other and are interdependent

These shared principles and commitments show some of the crucial principles that underlie the Goals and targets.

---

[360] Charles Churchman, *The Design of Inquiring Systems: Basic Concepts of Systems and Organization* (New York: Basic Books, 1971). p. IX,
[361] Mark Schroeder, "Value Theory," in *The Stanford Encyclopedia of Philosophy*, ed. Edward N. Zalta, Fall 2021 (Metaphysics Research Lab, Stanford University, 2021), https://plato.stanford.edu/archives/fall2021/entries/value-theory/.
[362] For the complete list, see A/Res/70/1 ¶ 10, 11, 12, and 13.

2.4.2 *Valuation Lens 2*: Four Principles of Biomedical Ethics

Beauchamp and Childress' four principles of biomedical ethics offer guidance for conducting research that involves human interventions[363].

1. *Respect for Autonomy[364]*: to respect an autonomous actor is to acknowledge that actor's right to hold views and make choices – in practice, this typically refers to informed consent and the right to refuse an intervention
2. *Nonmaleficence[365]*: to do no harm according to our best ability and judgment, including mitigating unintentional consequences
3. *Beneficence[366]*: to actively help others, and to do more good than harm to our best ability and judgment
4. *Justice[367]*: to distribute the benefits and burdens of an intervention equitably

The principles offer some clarity towards the notion of emancipation in Critical Systems Thinking (CST) which is embedded within Transdisciplinary Systems Research (TSR).

2.4.3 *Valuation Lens 3*: Crisis Management and Risk Management

I.   Crisis Management

A *crisis* is when a low-probability, high-impact event threatens the integrity and or survival of an individual or group and has no clear means of resolution[368]. It has social, environmental, political, or

---

[363] This subsection cites *Principles of Biomedical Ethics* (5th edition) by Beauchamp and Childress in 2001, which is at the time of writing the latest edition available for free to borrow on the Internet Archive for readers interested in the topic. Guidance for when the principles are in conflict is outside of the scope of this publication, but readers can consult Beauchamp and Childress' work for more information.

[364] Tom L. Beauchamp and James F. Childress, *Principles of Biomedical Ethics*, 5th ed. (Oxford and New York: Oxford University Press, 2001). p. 57-63.

[365] *ibid.* p. 113.

[366] *ibid.* p. 165.

[367] *ibid.* p. 234.

[368] Christine M. Pearson and Judith A. Clair, "Reframing Crisis Management," *The Academy of Management Review* 23, no. 1 (1998): 59–76. p. 60.

economic repercussions, which can in turn become crises as well[369]. An event that has a minor impact and is easy to solve does not constitute a crisis. The *severity* of a crisis is the amount of damage generated by the crisis[370], which can affect specific populations disproportionately depending on each individual crisis. Populations that struggle to anticipate, cope with, resist, and recover from a crisis are more *vulnerable* than others[371].

A basic 3-stage crisis intervention model involves a *pre-crisis stage*, *crisis stage*, and a *post-crisis stage*[372]:

1. the *pre-crisis stage* involves early detection, prevention, and preparation
2. the *crisis* stage involves the recognition and response to the immediate crisis
3. the *post-crisis* stage involves investigation and reflection[373]

While this model serves as a good starting point towards understanding the structure of a crisis and is particularly helpful when dealing with abrupt natural hazards e.g. hurricanes and wildfires, a more detailed model is helpful to understand human-made crises.

The 5-phase conflict model by Samarasinghe et. al. from 2001 better represents the escalating tensions within a local human-made crisis[374]:

1. the *pre-conflict phase* is defined by informal protests and the emergence of political tension
2. the *conflict emergence phase* is defined by sporadic and random cases of violence, the degree of which is determined by local conditions
3. the *conflict and crisis phase* marks the point when violence leads to the collapse of certain parts of the country

---

[369] Kevin MacKay, "The Ecological Crisis Is a Political Crisis," *MAHB.Stanford.Edu* (blog), September 25, 2018, https://mahb.stanford.edu/blog/ecological-crisis-political-crisis/.

[370] W Timothy Coombs, "Protecting Organization Reputations During a Crisis: The Development and Application of Situational Crisis Communication Theory," *Corporate Reputation Review* 10, no. 3 (September 1, 2007): 163–76, https://doi.org/10.1057/palgrave.crr.1550049. p. 169.

[371] William Donner and Havidán Rodríguez, "Disaster Risk and Vulnerability: The Role and Impact of Population and Society | PRB," Population Reference Bureau, 2011, https://www.prb.org/resources/disaster-risk/.

[372] Sanjeev M A, Neerja Pande, and Santhosh Kumar P K, "Role of Effective Crisis Communication by the Government in Managing the First Wave Covid-19 Pandemic - A Study of Kerala Government's Success," *Journal of Public Affairs* 21, no. 4 (November 2021): e2721, https://doi.org/10.1002/pa.2721.

[373] *ibid.*

[374] Stanley Samarasinghe, Brian Donaldson, and Colleen McGinn, "Conflict Vulnerability Analysis: Issues, Tools & Responses" (USAID, 2001). p. 8.

4. the *conflict settlement phase* is when efforts to find a lasting resolution begin
5. the *post conflict transition phase* signifies the end of violence, when rehabilitation, reconstruction, and sustainable development can happen

Preventive diplomacy, which aims to "prevent disputes from arising between parties, to prevent existing disputes from escalating into conflicts and to limit the spread of the latter when they occur" (A/47/277 ¶ 20) is an important concept when considering recommendations. The loss of life and property after a conflict breaks out dramatically, increases grievances on all sides, hardens the position of all sides, and escalates the conflict further[375]. As such, intervening early, when the chances of success are greater, is preferable.

II.   *Risk Management*

There is a wide range of risk management models. I have included one of such frameworks adapted from JPMorgan Chase & Co's 2015 Code of Conduct[376]. When uncertainty arises in decision-making, it can be helpful to use the following decision tree for guidance:

1. Is it legal and legitimate?
2. Does it comply with globally accepted norms and practices, and the principles of ethical behavior they reflect?
3. Are you certain it would not cause loss or harm to others?
4. Would it be okay if everyone did it?
5. Would you feel comfortable if the activity is on the front page of the newspaper?

For any of the questions, if the answer is:

- "Not sure": seek advice before proceeding
- "No": stop and seek assistance as the action could have serious consequences.

If the answer is "Yes" for all of the questions, the activity appears to be acceptable. Risk management is an important consideration when researchers offer guidance to shape complex adaptive systems (CAS).

---

[375] Connie Peck, "An Interest-Based, Problem-Solving Approach to United Nations Mediation," in *Strengthening the Practice of Peacemaking and Preventive Diplomacy in the United Nations : The UNITAR Approach*, ed. Connie Peck and Eleanor Wrtheim (Geneva: The United Nations Institute for Training and Research (UNITAR), 2014). p. 58.

[376] JPMorgan Chase & Co., "Code of Conduct," 2015, https://www.jpmorgan.com/content/dam/jpm/global/disclosures/CO/code-of-conduct.pdf.

2.4.4 *Valuation Lens 4*: Operational Expertise and Stress-Testing

Operational expertise and stress-testing are important valuation lens. Operational expertise can include the practice of transdisciplinary research, and other know-how associated with the implementation of potential guidance. One example of how to conduct stress-tests has been explored by Schwaninger, Edenhofer, and Kaufmann-Hayoz in 2008 through experiments with "What If" questions[377]: What if an initiative is successful or not successful? What if some (unknown) parameters or variables not within our control were to change dramatically? This can lead to a closer examination of previous initiatives or future activities[378]. Sensitivity analysis can also be helpful to understand the uncertainty in a system[379].

2.4.5 *Valuation Lens 5*: Just Transition

In 2015, the International Labour Organization (ILO)[380] published the "Guidelines for a just transition towards environmentally sustainable economies and societies for all" based on the Outcome of the Tripartite Meeting of Experts on Sustainable Development, Decent Work and Green Jobs in 2015 (GB.325/POL/3). Highlights of the Guidelines are included below:
- The four pillars of the Decent Work Agenda: (1) social dialogue, (2) social protection, (3) rights at work, and (4) employment – are indispensable building blocks of sustainable development
- "Managed well, transitions to environmentally and socially sustainable economies can become a strong driver of job creation, job upgrading, social justice, and poverty eradication"

---

[377] Schwaninger, Edenhofer, and Kaufmann-Hayoz, "Policy Analysis and Design in Local Public Management: A System Dynamics Approach." p. 214-215.
[378] *ibid.*
[379] *ibid.*
[380] The ILO is the tripartite UN agency that brings together governments, employers, and workers representatives of 187 member states to set labor standards, develop policies, and devise programmes promoting decent work for all women and men.

- "Strong social consensus on the goal and pathways to sustainability is fundamental; social dialogue has to be an integral part of the institutional framework for policy-making and implementation at all levels"
- "Several institutional labor standards, including those covering freedom of association and the right to collective bargaining, prohibition of forced labor, child labor and non-discrimination, social dialogue, tripartite consultation, minimum wage, labor administration and inspection, employment policy, human resource development, occupational safety and health, as well as social security, are important in this regard"

Just transition is a strategic imperative in a system-wide transformation for two reasons. First, *a system-wide transformation can be achieved only when everyone takes a step forward together, like a puzzle that will be solved only when we turn all the keys at the same time*[381]. Second, there is a tendency to attribute the resistance to change to actors with more power as they attempt to maintain the status quo[382]. However, actors with less power can also resist change if they perceive that such changes are likely to worsen their situation[383]. Consequently, a just transition is pivotal to reducing resistance towards sustainable development.

---

[381] See *Section 1.2.4*.
[382] Ariel Macaspac Hernández, *Taming the Big Green Elephant: Setting the Motion for Transformation towards Sustainability*, Globale Gesellschaft Und Internationale Beziehungen (Wiesbaden: Springer VS. Springer Fachmedien Wiesbaden GmbH, 2021). p. 2.
[383] *ibid.*

2.5 References

Aligica, Paul Dragos. "Prediction, Explanation and the Epistemology of Future Studies." *Futures* 35, no. 10 (December 2003): 1027–40. https://doi.org/10.1016/S0016-3287(03)00067-3.

Argyris, Chris, Robert Putnam, and Diana McLain Smith. *Action Science*. San Francisco: Jossey-Bass Publishers, 1985.

Beauchamp, Tom L., and James F. Childress. *Principles of Biomedical Ethics*. 5th ed. Oxford and New York: Oxford University Press, 2001.

Bell, Wendell, and Jeffrey K. Olick. "An Epistemology for the Futures Field: Problems and Possibilities of Prediction." *Futures* 21, no. 2 (1989): 115–35. https://doi.org/10.1016/0016-3287(89)90001-3.

Britannica Dictionary. "Generate Definition & Meaning." Accessed March 17, 2023. https://www.britannica.com/dictionary/generate.

Burns, Danny. "Systemic Action Research: Changing System Dynamics to Support Sustainable Change." *Action Research* 12, no. 1 (2014): 3–18. https://doi.org/0.1177/1476750313513910.

Churchman, Charles. "Operations Research as a Profession." *Management Science*, 1970. http://dx.doi.org/10.1287/mnsc.17.2.B37.

———. *The Design of Inquiring Systems: Basic Concepts of Systems and Organization*. New York: Basic Books, 1971.

Coombs, W Timothy. "Protecting Organization Reputations During a Crisis: The Development and Application of Situational Crisis Communication Theory." *Corporate Reputation Review* 10, no. 3 (September 1, 2007): 163–76. https://doi.org/10.1057/palgrave.crr.1550049.

Cornell Law School. "Burden of Persuasion." LII / Legal Information Institute. Accessed March 23, 2023. https://www.law.cornell.edu/wex/burden_of_persuasion.

———. "Burden of Production." LII / Legal Information Institute. Accessed March 23, 2023. https://www.law.cornell.edu/wex/burden_of_production.

———. "Evidence." LII / Legal Information Institute. Accessed March 23, 2023. https://www.law.cornell.edu/wex/evidence.

Dai, Xinyuan. "The 'Compliance Gap' and the Efficacy of International Human Rights Institutions." In *The Persistent Power of Human Rights: From Commitment to Compliance*, edited by Thomas Risse, Stephen C. Ropp, and Kathryn Sikkink, 85–102. Cambridge: Cambridge University Press, 2013.

Donner, William, and Havidán Rodríguez. "Disaster Risk and Vulnerability: The Role and Impact of Population and Society | PRB." Population Reference Bureau, 2011. https://www.prb.org/resources/disaster-risk/.

Edelheim, Johan R. *Ontological, Epistemological and Axiological Issues*. Routledge Handbooks Online, 2014. https://doi.org/10.4324/9780203763308.ch3.

Fam, Dena, Jane Palmer, Chris Riedy, and Cynthia Mitchell, eds.
    Transdisciplinary Research and Practice for Sustainability Outcomes.
    Routledge Studies in Sustainability. London and New York: Routledge,
    2017.
Flood, Robert L., and Michael C. Jackson. *Creative Problem Solving: Total
    Systems Intervention*. New York: John Wiley & Sons, 1991.
Greenwood, Davydd J., and Morten Levin. *Introduction to Action Research:
    Social Research for Social Change*. Thousand Oaks and London: Sage
    Publications, 1998.
Häberli, Rudolf, Walter Grossenbacher-Mansuy, and Julie Thompson Klein.
    "Summary and Synthesis." In *Transdisciplinarity: Joint Problem
    Solving among Science, Technology, and Society - An Effective Way for
    Managing Complexity*, edited by Julie Thompson Klein, Walter
    Grossenbacher-Mansuy, Rudolf Häberli, Alain Bill, Roland W. Scholz,
    and Myrtha Welti, 1–22. Basel, Boston, and Berlin: Springer Basel AG,
    2001.
Harrison, James, and Sharifah Sekalala. "Addressing the Compliance Gap?
    UN Initiatives to Benchmark the Human Rights Performance of States
    and Corporations." *Review of International Studies* 41, no. 5 (December
    2015): 925–45. https://doi.org/10.1017/S026021051500039X.
Held, David. "The Diffusion of Authority." In *International Organizations
    and Global Governance*, edited by Thomas G. Weiss and Rorden
    Wilkinson. London and New York: Routledge, 2014.
Hernández, Ariel Macaspac. *Taming the Big Green Elephant: Setting the
    Motion for Transformation towards Sustainability*. Globale Gesellschaft
    Und Internationale Beziehungen. Wiesbaden: Springer VS. Springer
    Fachmedien Wiesbaden GmbH, 2021.
Jantsch, Erich. *Design for Evolution: Self Organization and Planning in the
    Life of Human Systems*. The International Library of Systems Theory
    and Philosophy. New York: George Braziller, 1975.
———. *Technological Planning and Social Futures*. New York: John Wiley
    & Sons, 1972.
Jörg, Ton. *New Thinking in Complexity for the Social Sciences and
    Humanities: A Generative, Transdiciplinary Approach*. Springer
    Complexity. Springer, 2011.
JPMorgan Chase & Co. "Code of Conduct," 2015.
    https://www.jpmorgan.com/content/dam/jpm/global/disclosures/CO/cod
    e-of-conduct.pdf.
Keahey, Jennifer. "Sustainable Development and Participatory Action
    Research: A Systematic Review." *Systematic Practice and Action
    Research* 39 (2020): 291–306. https://doi.org/10.1007/s11213-020-
    09535-8.
Keane, Adrian, and Paul McKeown. *The Modern Law of Evidence*. 11th ed.
    Oxford: Oxford University Press, 2016.
Kiteme, Boniface P., and Urs Wiesmann. "Sustainable River Basin
    Management in Kenya: Balancing Needs and Requirements." In
    Handbook of Transdisciplinary Research, edited by Gertrude Hirsch
    Hadorn, Holger Hoffmann-Riem, Susette Biber-Klemm, Walter

Grossenbacher-Mansuy, Dominique Joye, Christian Pohl, Urs Wiesmann, and Elisabeth Zemp, 63–78. Springer, 2008.

Lim, John. "Networked Governance: Why It Is Different and How It Can Work." *Civil Service College Singapore, ETHOS*, 2011.

Lindblom, Charles E., and David K. Cohen. *Usable Knowledge: Social Science and Social Problem Solving*. New Haven and London: Yale University Press, 1979.

M A, Sanjeev, Neerja Pande, and Santhosh Kumar P K. "Role of Effective Crisis Communication by the Government in Managing the First Wave Covid-19 Pandemic - A Study of Kerala Government's Success." *Journal of Public Affairs* 21, no. 4 (November 2021): e2721. https://doi.org/10.1002/pa.2721.

MacKay, Kevin. "The Ecological Crisis Is a Political Crisis." *MAHB.Stanford.Edu* (blog), September 25, 2018. https://mahb.stanford.edu/blog/ecological-crisis-political-crisis/.

Mastrandea, Michael D., Christopher B. Field, Thomas F. Stocker, Ottmar Edenhofer, Kristie L. Ebi, David J. Frame, Hermann Held, et al. "Guidance Note for Lead Authors of the IPCC Fifth Assessment Report on Consistent Treatment of Uncertainties." Intergovernmental Panel on Climate Change (IPCC), 2010. https://www.ipcc.ch/site/assets/uploads/2018/05/uncertainty-guidance-note.pdf.

McNiff, Jean, and Jack Whitehead. *Action Research: Principles and Practice*. 2nd ed. London and New York: Routledge Palmer, 2002.

Midgley, Gerald. *Systemic Intervention: Philosophy, Methodology, and Practice*. Contemporary Systems Thinking. New York: Springer Science+Business Media, 2000.

Midgley, Gerald, Isaac Munlo, and Mandy Brown. "The Theory and Practice of Boundary Critique: Developing Housing Services for Older People." *Journal of the Operational Research Society* 49 (1998): 467–78. https://doi.org/10.2307/3009885.

Noda, Orion. "Epistemic Hegemony: The Western Straitjacket and Post-Colonial Scars in Academic Publishing." *Revista Brasileira de Política Internacional* 63, no. 1 (2020): e007. https://doi.org/10.1590/0034-7329202000107.

Pearson, Christine M., and Judith A. Clair. "Reframing Crisis Management." *The Academy of Management Review* 23, no. 1 (1998): 59–76.

Peck, Connie. "An Interest-Based, Problem-Solving Approach to United Nations Mediation." In *Strengthening the Practice of Peacemaking and Preventive Diplomacy in the United Nations : The UNITAR Approach*, edited by Connie Peck and Eleanor Wrtheim. Geneva: The United Nations Institute for Training and Research (UNITAR), 2014.

Renn, Ortwin. "Transdisciplinarity: Synthesis towards a Modular Approach." *Futures* 130 (June 1, 2021). https://doi.org/10.1016/j.futures.2021.102744.

Samarasinghe, Stanley, Brian Donaldson, and Colleen McGinn. "Conflict Vulnerability Analysis: Issues, Tools & Responses." USAID, 2001.

Sankaran, Shankar. "Taking Action Using Systems Research." In *A Guide to Systems Research: Philosophy, Processes and Practice*, edited by Mary

C. Edson, Pamela Buckle Henning, and Shankar Sankaran, 10:111–42. Translational Systems Sciences. Springer, 2017.

Schroeder, Mark. "Value Theory." In *The Stanford Encyclopedia of Philosophy*, edited by Edward N. Zalta, Fall 2021. Metaphysics Research Lab, Stanford University, 2021. https://plato.stanford.edu/archives/fall2021/entries/value-theory/.

Schwaninger, Markus, Silvia Edenhofer, and Ruth Kaufmann-Hayoz. "Policy Analysis and Design in Local Public Management: A System Dynamics Approach." In *Handbook of Transdisciplinary Research*, edited by Gertrude Hirsch Hadorn, Holger Hoffmann-Riem, Susette Biber-Klemm, Walter Grossenbacher-Mansuy, Dominique Joye, Christian Pohl, Urs Wiesmann, and Elisabeth Zemp, 205–22. Springer, 2008.

Sergeyev, Yuriy. "Sergeyev's Letter," November 24, 2021.

Shea, Brent. "Collaborative Peer Review Process, Part I," May 8, 2023.

Simons, Peter. "Ontology | Metaphysics | Britannica." Accessed March 20, 2023. https://www.britannica.com/topic/ontology-metaphysics.

Tandon, Rajesh. "Social Transformation and Participatory Research." *Convergence: An International Journal of Adult Education* 21, no. 2–3 (1988): 5–18.

Tatro, Claire, and Jack Fleming. "Generative Design Research: Using Metaphor to Capture Complexity." In *Proceedings of the 2017 International Symposium on Human Factors and Ergonomics in Health Care*, 59–65, 2017.

UCLouvain. "International Law MicroMasters® Program." edX. Accessed March 19, 2023. https://www.edx.org/micromasters/louvainx-international-law.

Ulrich, Werner. "A Brief Introduction to Critical Systems Heuristics (CSH)." ECOSENSUS, The Open University, 2005. https://www.wulrich.com/downloads/ulrich_2005f.pdf.

UN Global Pulse. "HOW - Glossary." UNGP - Foresight Project. Accessed April 30, 2023. https://foresight.unglobalpulse.net/how-glossary/.

United Nations Dag Hammarskjöld Library. "What Does It Mean When a Decision Is Taken 'by Consensus'? - Ask DAG!" Accessed November 26, 2021. https://ask.un.org/faq/260981.

Vickers, Geoffrey. *Human Systems Are Different*. London: Harper & Row, Publishers, 1983.

Williams, Bob, and Richard Hummelbrunner. *Systems Concepts in Action: A Practitioner's Toolkit*. California: Stanford Business Books, 2011.

3

Research Design: Timeline, Methodologies, and Implementation

3.0 Outline

After clarifying foundational concepts in *Chapter 1*, and research philosophy in *Chapter 2*, this chapter discusses the research design and methodologies of this study to produce four types of knowledge identified by Transdisciplinary Systems Research (TSR)[384]:

1. *Systems knowledge*: *Chapter 1* frames a system-wide transformation as a grand challenge
2. *Transformation knowledge*: *Chapter 4* constructs a model of global change processes within the contemporary global governance network through global governance theory, neo-institutionalist theory, and intentional systems theory with reference to the compliance gap in *Chapter 2*
3. *Target knowledge*: *Chapter 5* examines emerging perspectives on the 2030 Sustainable Development Goals through sustainable development and participatory action research (SDPAR)
4. *Implementation knowledge*: *Chapter 6* formulates guidance through the theory and practice of global diplomacy

---

[384] See *Table 1.7.*

The overarching framework in this book is presented in *Section 3.2.3* on the co-evolution of the problem and solution space. The *problem space* describes the collection of research questions within the mutable boundaries and project goals, and the *solution space* describes the collection of viable alternative solution conjectures. Transdisciplinary Systems Research (TSR) in *Chapters 1 to 5* clarifies the problem space and narrows down the solution-space to produce Transdisciplinary Systems Guidance (TSG) in *Chapter 6*.

For clarity, this chapter first explains the research design in a linear, phase-based way (*Sections 3.1* and *3.2*). It then discusses the non-linear, iterative implementation of TSR (*Section 3.3*). It introduces crucial topics such as intentional systems theory, sustainable development and participatory action research (SDPAR), methods to manage complexity in TSR, and the collaborative peer review process (CPRP).

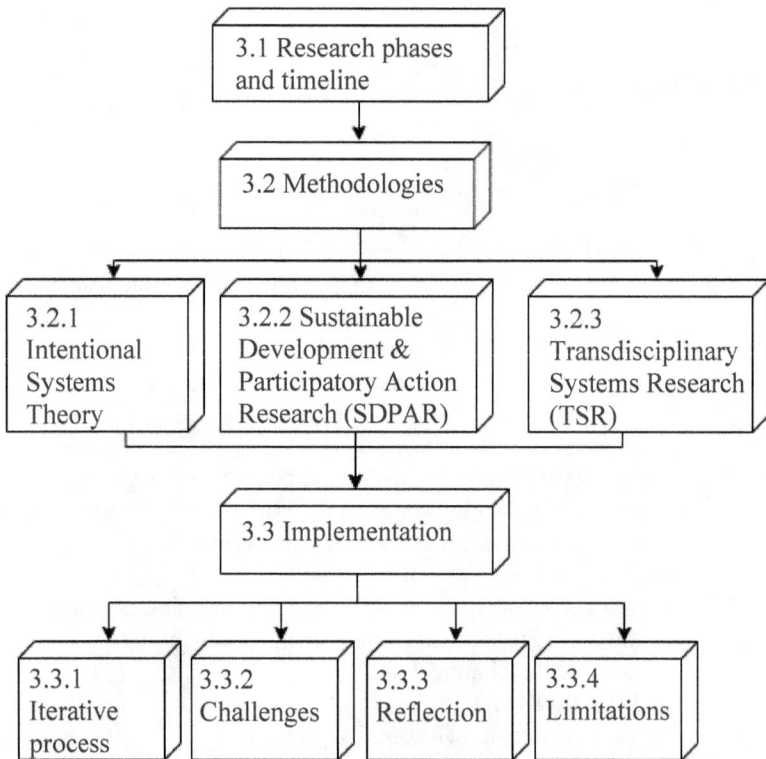

Figure 3.1 Outline for Chapter 3

3.1 Research Phases and Timeline

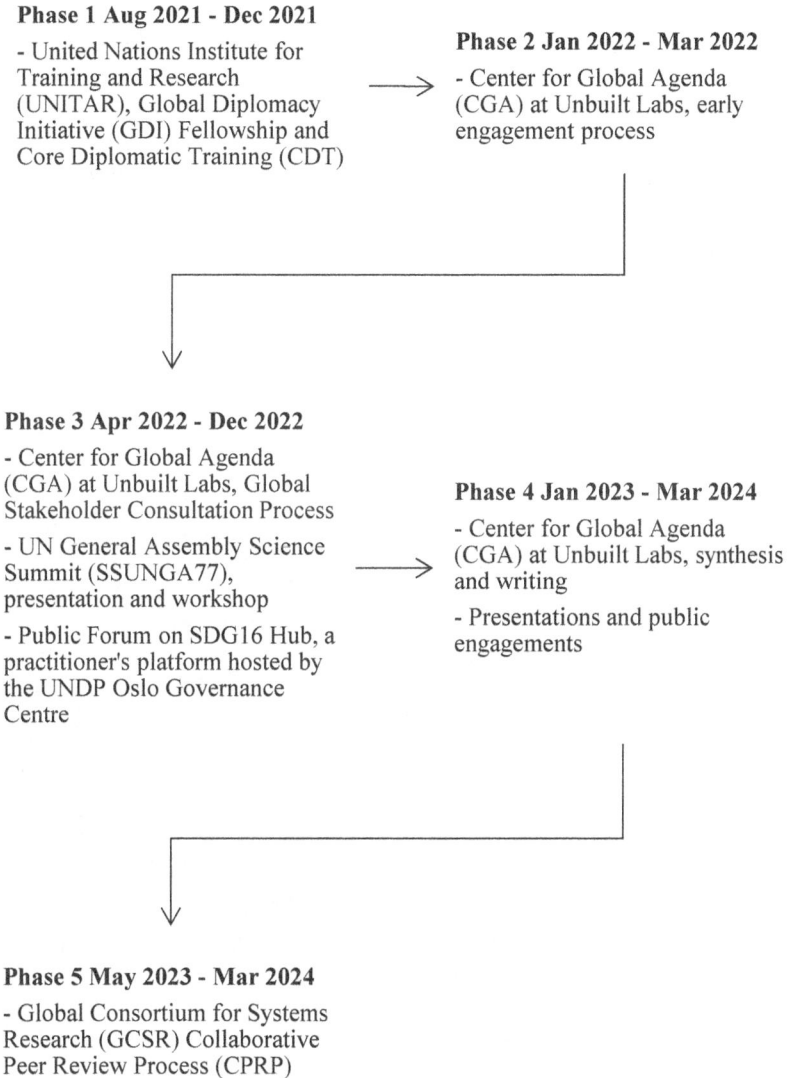

Phase 1 Aug 2021 - Dec 2021

- United Nations Institute for Training and Research (UNITAR), Global Diplomacy Initiative (GDI) Fellowship and Core Diplomatic Training (CDT)

Phase 2 Jan 2022 - Mar 2022

- Center for Global Agenda (CGA) at Unbuilt Labs, early engagement process

Phase 3 Apr 2022 - Dec 2022

- Center for Global Agenda (CGA) at Unbuilt Labs, Global Stakeholder Consultation Process

- UN General Assembly Science Summit (SSUNGA77), presentation and workshop

- Public Forum on SDG16 Hub, a practitioner's platform hosted by the UNDP Oslo Governance Centre

Phase 4 Jan 2023 - Mar 2024

- Center for Global Agenda (CGA) at Unbuilt Labs, synthesis and writing

- Presentations and public engagements

Phase 5 May 2023 - Mar 2024

- Global Consortium for Systems Research (GCSR) Collaborative Peer Review Process (CPRP)

Figure 3.2 Research phases and timeline

Phase 1: United Nations Institute for Training and Research (UNITAR), Global Diplomacy Initiative (GDI) Fellowship and Core Diplomatic Training (CDT) (Aug 2021 – Dec 2021)

This project began with UNITAR's Global Diplomacy Initiative's (GDI) weekly seminars and Core Diplomatic Training (CDT) program. The research process formally began with a Letter of Interest on the 5th of October 2021 to H.E. Ambassador Dr. Yuriy Sergeyev, who was formerly a Lecturer at Yale University, elected member of the Security Council and Human Rights Council, and Chair of the Sixth Committee on Legal Affairs. Dr. Sergeyev later became my advisor at the United Nations Institute for Training and Research (UNITAR). We exchanged many pages of Word Document letters honing in on a literature gap that would have a meaningful impact on current practices. His feedback helped identify frontier topics in the theory and practice of global diplomacy. I am pleased to have gotten to know him through the exchanges and learn how a former member of the Security Council sees the global governance network and the world at large.

On the 1st of November 2021, I sent a formal research proposal to Dr. Sergeyev and UNITAR. One of the interesting observations I made then was the frequent use of the catchall phrase "lack of political will". It became the starting point for a much larger exploration that developed into the theory on closing the compliance gap, system-wide transformation methods, and Transdisciplinary Systems Research (TSR). I submitted a draft chapter to UNITAR on the 2nd of December 2021, which is when I began working with my reader at UNITAR, Ms. Larisa Schelkin. I am grateful for her expertise and for later presenting the opportunity to engage the global community at the UN General Assembly Science Summit (SSUNGA77). I submitted a quarterly project update to my advisor, reader, and UNITAR following the draft chapter.

Phase 2: Center for Global Agenda (CGA) at Unbuilt Labs, early engagement process (Jan 2022 – Mar 2022)

On the 1st of January 2022, I began the early engagement process for the publication through the Center for Global Agenda (CGA) at Unbuilt Labs with the support of my co-director, Dr. Marguerite Van Cook. It involved 50+ confidential in-person and virtual unstructured interviews around the project focused on implementation challenges. Interviewees included students, early-career professionals, startup founders, senior executives, private and public board of directors, advisors to trillion dollar asset management companies, policymakers, activists, and others. After numerous interviews, it became apparent that while the private sector Environmental, Social, Governance (ESG) framework helped increase transparency and guide change, a coherent and comprehensive framework to facilitate a system-wide transformation is necessary in order to achieve the 2030 Sustainable Development Goals.

Phase 3: Center for Global Agenda (CGA) at Unbuilt Labs, Global Stakeholder Consultation Process (Mar 2022 – Dec 2022)

On the 28th of March 2022, the Center for Global Agenda (CGA) at Unbuilt Labs announced the Global Stakeholder Consultation Process through Cision PRWeb as the "Recommended UN Action Plan to Close the Compliance Gap (CCG)" with the draft framework (see revised framework in *Section 6.1*). Anyone could submit a statement to be included in our public archives or propose ways to collaborate. The public access *Future of Global Governance Series* Workshops and Proceedings in *Section 5.1* was developed from this open call. Featured Statements have also been included in full in *Section 5.2*.

The outreach effort to ensure an inclusive knowledge-production process was supported by the SDG16 Hub, a practitioner's platform hosted by the UNDP Oslo Governance Centre, the Swiss Academies of Arts and Sciences Network for Transdisciplinary Research of the (Td-Net), and the Academic Council on the United Nations System (ACUNS). It has also been enabled by the platforms provided by the Planetary Health Alliance (PHA) at Johns Hopkins University, the Global Mental Health Action Network (GMHAN), and JISCMail. I have made personal appeals by inviting historically underrepresented people and communities to participate through email and Linkedin messages. Whenever possible, I worked closely with people who had expressed an interest to facilitate their participation, and tried my very best to support existing initiatives.

On the 26th of April 2022, CGA began hosting a Public Forum on SDG16 Hub, and registered the series of initiatives on Act4SDGs.org, a platform powered by the UN SDG Action Campaign. On the 15th of September 2022, I conducted a mid-project presentation at the UN General Assembly Science Summit (SSUNGA77) as a featured speaker and co-convened a session on the 29th of September 2022 as part of the Future of Global Governance Series. The Global

Stakeholder Consultation Process closed on the 20th of December 2022. With the support of CGA, I directly engaged hundreds of people across many stakeholder groups including historically underrepresented people and communities.

Phase 4: Center for Global Agenda (CGA) at Unbuilt Labs, synthesis and writing process; presentations and public engagements (Jan 2023 – March 2024)

From January 2023 to March 2024, I synthesized the evidence gathered and different written outputs throughout the research process while paying close attention to the changing global landscape. The theoretical foundations of this study established in *Chapters 1* and *2* have been presented and released as abridged conference papers: "What can systems research teach us about conducting impactful research for the 2030 Sustainable Development Goals"[385] and "A Theory of Transdisciplinary Systems Research (TSR)"[386] in November 2023. Key recommendations in *Chapter 6* have also been released to the public in stages as part of the Center for Global Agenda (CGA) High-level Recommendations and Global Strategy[387].

Phase 5: Global Consortium for Systems Research (GCSR), Collaborative Peer Review Process (CPRP) *(May 2023 – March 2024)*

From May 2023 to March 2024, *Parts I (Chapters 1, 2, and 3)*, *II (Chapters 4, and 5)*, and *III (Chapter 6)* each underwent multiple rounds of collaborative peer review with 20+ reviewers. Reviewers received a confidential manuscript and offered suggestions on logic, structure, style, and clarity. I am very grateful for their time, expertise, and patience. I revised the manuscript accordingly.

---

[385] Marvin Cheung, "Keynote: What Can Systems Research Teach Us about Conducting Impactful Research for the 2030 Sustainable Development Goals" (Annual Innovation Conference, PatSnap, November 16, 2023), https://unbuiltlabs.com/conducting-impactful-research-for-the-2030-sdgs.
[386] Marvin Cheung, "A Theory on Transdisciplinary Systems Research (TSR)" (Future of Global Governance Series, Center for Global Agenda (CGA) at Unbuilt Labs, November 11, 2023), https://unbuiltlabs.com/a-theory-on-tsr.
[387] Center for Global Agenda (CGA) at Unbuilt Labs, "High Level Recommendations and Global Strategy," Unbuilt Labs, The Global Think Tank Ecosystem, accessed February 13, 2024, https://unbuiltlabs.com/cga/high-level-recommendations-and-global-strategy.

3.2 Methodologies

Transdisciplinary Systems Research (TSR) methodologies do not aim to directly implicate a solution (many solutions are possible). Rather, it aims to provide the necessary context to understand, evaluate, and argue for or against possible solutions. In so doing, it narrows down the solution space to indicate directions for future actions.

3.2.1 *Intentional Systems Theory*: Physical Stance, Design Stance and Intentional Stance

Dennett coined the term *Intentional Systems Theory* in 1971[388]. According to Intentional Systems Theory, anything that is usefully predictable by the *intentional stance* is by definition an intentional system. The intentional stance is "the strategy of interpreting the behavior of an entity (person, animal, artifact, whatever) by treating it *as if* it were a rational agent who governed its 'choice' of 'action' by a 'consideration' of its 'beliefs' and 'desires'"[389]. *Beliefs* describe the "ideas or conceptions that people hold about what should exist or what *actually does exist* in a *particular* social situation or context"[390]. *Desires* encompass a range of possibilities such as survival, procreation, food, security, and health. In 1989, Dennett argued for belief and desire attribution through the *intentional strategy*: one starts with "rational" beliefs and desires, and revises based on exceptions observed[391]. In other words, we begin with the beliefs[392] a system *ought to have* given its perceptual capabilities, epistemology, and system history; and the desires a system *ought to have* as well as the most practical means of satisfying them. We then revise our

---

[388] Daniel Dennett, "Intentional Systems," *Journal of Philosophy* 68, no. 4 (1971): 87–106, https://doi.org/10.2307/2025382. p. 87.
[389] Daniel Dennett, "Intentional Systems Theory," in *Oxford Handbook of the Philosophy of Mind*, ed. Brian P. McLaughlin, Ansgar Beckermann, and Sven Walter (Oxford and New York: Oxford Handbooks Online, 2009), https://doi.org/10.1093/oxfordhb/9780199262618.003.0020. p. 2.
[390] Jonathan Turner, *Sociology: Studying the Human System*, 2nd ed. (Santa Monica, California: Goodyear Publishing Company, 1981). p. 90.
[391] Dennett, "Intentional Systems Theory." p. 21.
[392] *ibid.* p. 49.

understanding of the complex adaptive system (CAS) based on the evidence gathered. The intentional stance can be contrasted with two other basic stances or strategies of prediction: *the physical stance* (i.e. explains a system's behavior through its physical constitution[393]), and *the design stance* (i.e. explains a system's behavior by how it is designed[394]). These are discussed in greater detail in *Chapter 4* with reference to the model of global change processes. Given the ontological assumptions of Transdisciplinary Systems Research (TSR) including *a complex reality* and the *intentionality* of complex adaptive systems (CAS)[395], Intentional Systems Theory can be adopted directly.

3.2.2 *Sustainable Development and Participatory Action Research (SDPAR)*: Unstructured Interviews, Research Reflection Meetings, Research Forums, and Workshops

In 2001, Parkes and Panelli published a paper that looked to "move beyond the question of *why* it is important to integrate across traditional boundaries and between different stakeholders to focus on *how* this integration may be achieved"[396]. This subsection focuses on the question of "how", and expands on the procedures for examining evidence for Transdisciplinary Systems Research (TSR)[397]. It discusses the methodologies to produce knowledge with stakeholders, including participatory action research (PAR) with reference to system-wide transformation, as well as sustainable development and participatory action research (SDPAR) methods identified by Keahey in 2020.

---

[393] Daniel Dennett, *The Intentional Stance* (Cambridge, Massachusetts: MIT Press, 1989). p. 16.

[394] *ibid.* p. 16-17.

[395] See *Section 2.2.1*: the subject of study is assumed to exist as described by the definitions and properties of complex adaptive systems (CAS), and *Table 1.1* CAS adapt towards some ends depending on what the system prioritizes or values; survival is an example of such.

[396] Margot Parkes and Ruth Panelli, "Integrating Catchment Ecosystems and Community Health: The Value of Participatory Action Research," *Ecosystem Health* 7, no. 2 (2001): 85–106, https://doi.org/10.1046/j.1526-0992.2001.007002085.x. p. 86.

[397] See *Section 2.3*.

PAR refers to a spectrum of approaches that combine research and action to define, address, and reconsider mutually conceived problems[398]. It recognizes the power dynamics within knowledge production processes[399], and seeks to "empower participants to take control of the political and economic forces that shape their lives"[400] through: (a) an interest in action or achieving a wider social goal, which may involve researchers in the risks or politics of the research context[401], and (b) participatory processes that enable the researched populations to be involved in varying degrees in the research program[402].

Numerous scholars have identified a connection between PAR and system-wide transformation. One of the earliest connections was made by Tandon in 1988 through his article "Social Transformation and Participatory Research"[403]. Chaudhary observed that inclusive knowledge production "substantially contributed" to transformation efforts in 1997[404]. Pain, Kindon, and Kesby argued that PAR can "open up possibilities for social change and political transformation"[405] in 2007 by influencing policymakers if the participants demand it or work collaboratively with institutions, policymakers, or not-for-profits[406].

---

[398] Parkes and Panelli, "Integrating Catchment Ecosystems and Community Health: The Value of Participatory Action Research." p. 87.

[399] Jennifer Keahey, "Sustainable Development and Participatory Action Research: A Systematic Review," *Systematic Practice and Action Research* 39 (2020): 291–306, https://doi.org/10.1007/s11213-020-09535-8. p. 292.

[400] Karen Healy, "Participatory Action Research and Social Work: A Critical Appraisal," *International Social Work* 44, no. 1 (January 2001): 93–105, https://doi.org/10.1177/002087280104400108. p. 95.

[401] Keahey, "Sustainable Development and Participatory Action Research: A Systematic Review." p. 292.

[402] *ibid.*

[403] Rajesh Tandon, "Social Transformation and Participatory Research," *Convergence: An International Journal of Adult Education* 21, no. 2–3 (1988): 5–18. p. 5.

[404] Anil Chaudhary, "Toward an Epistemology of Participatory Research," in *Participatory Action Research: International Contexts and Consequences*, ed. Robin McTaggart (Albany: State University of New York Press, 1997). p. 121.

[405] Rachel Pain, Sara Kindon, and Mike Kesby, "Participatory Action Research: Making a Difference to Theory, Practice and Action," in *Participatory Action Research Approaches and Method: Connecting People, Participation and Place*, ed. Sara Kindon, Rachel Pain, and Mike Kesby (New York: Routledge, 2007), 26–32. p. 26.

[406] *ibid.* p. 32.

Table 3.1 Types of participatory research

Mode	Involvement of Local / Researched People	Relationship of Research to People
Co-option	Representatives are selected, but there is little input or power sharing	On
Compliance	Outsiders determine the agenda and direct the actions	For
Consultation	Outsiders examine local knowledge and determine actions	For / With
Cooperation	Local people work alongside outsiders to determine priorities in a process led by outsiders	With
Co-learning	Local people and outsiders share their knowledge to create new understandings and form action plans together	With / By
Collective Action	Local people create their own agenda and mobilize to implement it with or without outside facilitators	By

Source: Margot Parkes and Ruth Panelli, "Integrating Catchment Ecosystems and Community Health: The Value of Participatory Action Research," *Ecosystem Health* 7, no. 2 (2001): 85–106, https://doi.org/10.1046/j.1526-0992.2001.007002085.x. p. 88.

In 2020, Keahey's systematic review identified the concept of Sustainable Development and Participatory Action Research (SDPAR). It is characterized by (1) an effort to shift control to grassroots co-investigators, (2) integrating diverse ways of knowing, and (3) supporting social transformation towards sustainable development[407]. *Table 3.2* describes SDPAR methods supplemented with Cohen et al.'s work published in the same year on research forums as a knowledge co-production method[408]. A *research forum* is a collective space for co-producing research questions, methods, and outputs with historically underrepresented people and communities[409]. *Table 3.3* describes the research methods employed, corresponding to the phases of research.

[407] Keahey, "Sustainable Development and Participatory Action Research: A Systematic Review." p. 292.

[408] Sue Cohen et al., "Co-Production as Experimentation: The Research Forum as Method," in *Imagining Regulation Differently: Co-Creating for Engagement*, ed. Morag McDermont et al. (Bristol: Policy Press, 2020). p. 25.

[409] *ibid.*

Table 3.2 Sustainable Development and Participatory Action Research (SDPAR) methods

Type	Methods
Qualitative Methods	Participant observation, focus group discussions, informal/ semi-structured interviews, field diaries, narrative journals, photographic documentation, documentary analysis, peer exchanges, and shared story telling
Quantitative Methods	Questionnaires, surveys, statistical analysis, crop and field tests, field measurements, remote sensing data, meteorological data, hydrological data, resource clustering, spatial analysis, and logical framework analysis
Participatory Research Methods	Photovoice, participatory video, participatory lesson development, transect walks, participatory rural appraisal, participatory mapping, participatory indicator development, small group assessment, and participatory data analysis
Participatory Action Methods	Research reflection meetings, community meetings, committee meetings, consensus building activities, leadership training, SWOT analysis, knowledge-exchange workshops, participatory planning, participatory networking, and research forum

Sources: Jennifer Keahey, "Sustainable Development and Participatory Action Research: A Systematic Review," *Systematic Practice and Action Research* 39 (2020): 291–306, https://doi.org/10.1007/s11213-020-09535-8. p. 299; Sue Cohen et al., "Co-Production as Experimentation: The Research Forum as Method," in *Imagining Regulation Differently: Co-Creating for Engagement*, ed. Morag McDermont et al. (Bristol: Policy Press, 2020). p. 23.

Table 3.3 Research methods

Phase	Methods	Description
On-going	Reflective practice	*Reflective practice* is the act of working transparently and iteratively based on feedback. Mortari in 2015 described this as "a practice that a researcher should carry out to make the politics of research transparent [... and] the ethical task of making transparent the ways of reasoning that are carried out through the research act"[410]. See, for example: *Sections 2.2, 2.3, and 2.4*
Phases 2 – 4	Research reflection meetings	Weekly group review of the research process and findings at the Center for Global Agenda (CGA) at Unbuilt Labs. See, for example: *Box 3-1 Transdisciplinary Systems Research (TSR) Q&A*
Phase 2. Early engagement process	Unstructured interviews	50+ confidential unstructured interviews focused on (a) how to secure buy-in, (b) who may be interested in the project, and (c) the extent of change necessary to advance the 2030 Sustainable Development Goals. To support a broad exploratory inquiry, the unstructured interview process is characterized by open-ended questions and more spontaneous follow-up questions[411]. Norton et al. in 2018 have used unstructured interviews as part of a broader set of Participatory Action Research (PAR) program, similar to this study[412]. They have

[410] Luigina Mortari, "Reflectivity in Research Practice: An Overview of Different Perspectives," *International Journal of Qualitative Methods* 14, no. 5 (December 9, 2015): 160940691561804, https://doi.org/10.1177/1609406915618045.

[411] Rahul S. Chauhan, "Unstructured Interviews: Are They Really All That Bad?," *Human Resource Development International* 25, no. 4 (August 8, 2022): 474–87, https://doi.org/10.1080/13678868.2019.1603019. p. 476.

[412] Richard K. Norton et al., "Overlooking the Coast: Limited Local Planning for Coastal Area Management along Michigan's Great Lakes," *Land Use Policy* 71

		opted for confidential unstructured interviews as well due to similar concerns that formally recorded or transcribed meetings would discourage participation and honest feedback[413]. These interviews have shaped the direction and structure of the book. See, for example: questions at the beginning of each section in *Chapter 1*
Phase 3. Global Stakeholder Consultation Process	Public access knowledge-exchange workshops	I co-led the public-access Future of Global Governance Series at the Center for Global Agenda (CGA) at Unbuilt Labs with CGA Co-director Dr. Marguerite Van Cook. We invited a wide range of stakeholders to present their perspectives, participate in panel discussions, and co-led exploratory sessions. I directly engaged hundreds of people across many stakeholder groups including historically underrepresented people and communities through this process. See: *Chapter 5*
	Public access research forums	After the draft framework in *Section 6.2* was announced, anyone could initiate and participate in discussions on the project's Public Forum on SDG16 Hub, a practitioner's platform hosted by the UNDP Oslo Governance Centre. Anyone could also submit a statement to the CGA public archive. Unique to this consultation process, featured statements have been printed in full to present diverse voices for reader's consideration as part of a broader effort to empower diverse voices. See: *Section 5.2: Featured Statements*

(February 2018): 183–203, https://doi.org/10.1016/j.landusepol.2017.11.049. Abstract.

[413] Norton et al., "Overlooking the Coast." p. 191.

3.2.3 *Transdisciplinary Systems Research (TSR):* Managing Complexity, Collaborative Peer Review Process

This section discusses the methodologies in this project that is not typically employed in transdisciplinary research or systems research.

I.   *Managing Complexity*

Transdisciplinary Systems Research (TSR) involves working iteratively between theory and practice to question all assumptions. Deleuze in 1968 described the role of reframing problems in effective research, and Maniglier in 2021 discussed its applications in transdisciplinary research[414]. Working iteratively to question all assumptions is a tremendous undertaking: Faced with a vast amount of information in a multi-year research project, how might we structure the line of inquiries? Current systems research methods can produce highly complex diagrams with concerning legibility and seemingly no beginning or end, see example in *Figure 3.3*. The figure shows eight nodes, each representing a piece of information. Imagine what it would look like with hundreds of new pieces of information a day — all the while the unit of analysis or boundaries of investigation may change, and every new piece of information involves a reassessment: Will this improve, contradict, or overhaul previous thinking?

---

[414] Heather J Miles, "Practising Difference across Geography: A Transdisciplinary and Deleuzian Approach to Intradisciplinary Thinking," *Environment and Planning F* 2, no. 4 (December 2023): 495–514, https://doi.org/10.1177/26349825231200607. p. 498.

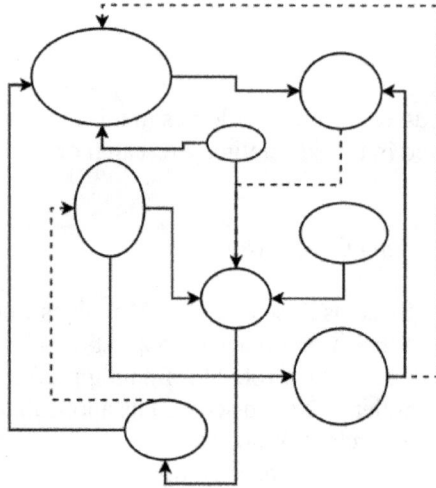

Figure 3.3 Example of a systems research diagram with concerning legibility

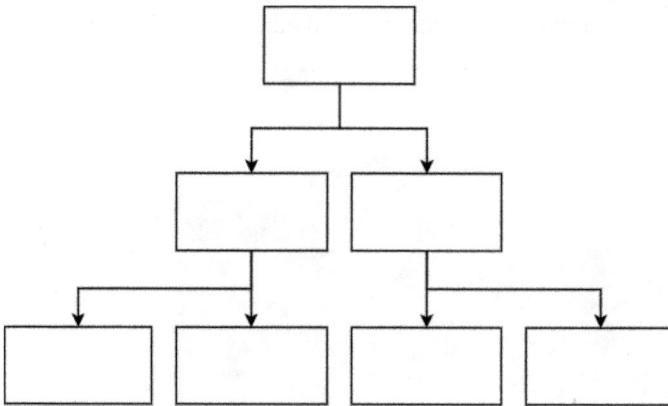

Figure 3.4 Basic tree diagram

Design thinking, "the cognitive processes that are manifested in design action"[415], offers a solution. Design has had a prominent role in systems research and transdisciplinary research[416]. In 1992, following a workshop at TU Delft[417], Cross observed how design problems are a category of "ill-defined problems"[418] (i.e. wicked problems): it is not clear at the start of a design project what the problem is, even if it may have been loosely defined by the client; many constraints (boundaries) and criteria (goals) will benefit from clarification or will be re-defined during the project[419]. Cross further observed how designers' attention oscillates (works iteratively) between "the problem" and "the solution"[420] with the support of "alternative solution conjectures"[421] i.e. potential solutions that serve as hypotheses to support problem exploration. While it may seem that the creative process is like a pendulum swinging between two distinct ends with no apparent start or end, we know this to be untrue. As Cross noted, a design solution is not an arbitrary construct: it usually bears some relationship to the given problem[422]. The design process can be framed as a starting condition followed by a series of problem-solution pairs. This can be structured as a tree diagram with reference to Minto's pyramid principle[423]. *Figure 3.4* shows a basic tree diagram.

---

[415] Nigel Cross, Kees Dorst, and Norbert Roozenburg, "Preface," in *Research in Design Thinking*, ed. Nigel Cross, Kees Dorst, and Norbert Roozenburg (Netherlands: Delft University Press, 1992). p. 1.

[416] For example, see *Section 1.2.2:* wickedness or wicked problems were defined by design theorists and urban design professors Rittel and Webber in 1973

[417] Cross, Dorst, and Roozenburg, "Preface.".

[418] Nigel Cross, "Research in Design Thinking," in *Research in Design Thinking*, ed. Nigel Cross, Kees Dorst, and Norbert Roozenburg (Netherlands: Delft University Press, 1992). p. 4.

[419] *ibid*; also see *Table 1.2* No definitive formulation: There are many theories for the cause and urgency of a wicked problem and the framing determines the preferred intervention.

[420] *ibid*. p. 5.

[421] *ibid*.

[422] *ibid*. p. 6.

[423] For interested readers, *The Minto Pyramid Principle: Logic in writing, thinking, and problem solving* is available for free to borrow on the Internet Archive.

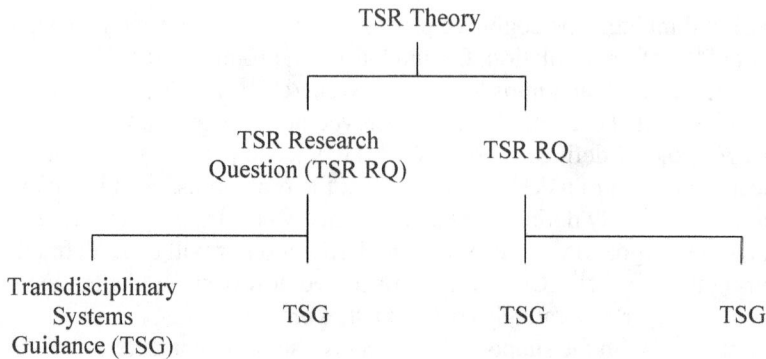

Figure 3.5 Transdisciplinary Systems Research (TSR) line of inquiry tree diagram

Figure 3.5 describes how a line of inquiry can be structured when conducting Transdisciplinary Systems Research (TSR). It connects TSR research questions ("the problem") with Transdisciplinary Systems Guidance (TSG) ("alternative solution conjectures"). To offer an example of how this structure can be applied, below is a case study built around Klein's *This Changes Everything: Capitalism vs the Climate* from 2014:

1. *TSR Theory* broadly describes a perspective, which can be from academia, industry, or other relevant sources: Klein observed that "For decades, regular people have been asked to turn off their lights, put on sweaters, and pay premium prices [...] and then watched as the biggest polluters have been allowed to expand their emissions without penalty."[424] – To what extent has unfairness slowed progress?

2. *TSR Research Question (TSR RQ)* examines the applicability of a perspective to a specific context: Klein referenced a quote, "When local people own the wind farms, and share in the benefits, they will support them. It won't be NIMBY (Not In My Back Yard), it will be POOL (Please On Our Land)."[425] – Is this claim true?

3. *Transdisciplinary Systems Guidance (TSG)* is the outcome of a TSR research process. It refers to advice that is grounded in implementation knowledge and formulated to help stakeholders achieve shared goals: What new or existing initiatives can increase fairness?

---

[424] Naomi Klein, *This Changes Everything: Capitalism vs the Climate* (New York and London: Simon & Schuster Paperbacks, 2014). p. 116.
[425] *ibid.* p. 132.

Depending on the findings at each level, researchers can open new lines of inquiries, reject hypotheses, or build on previous findings. Critical to TSR is flexibility in the selection of TSR theories, and flexibility in exploring different layers of abstraction i.e. one can move in a multi-directional pattern within the tree from theory to guidance or from guidance to theory. *Figure 3.6* shows the mental model of complexity in TSR. Multiple TSR lines of inquiry can be combined to map a complex landscape. This opens up the research process for teams and (external) collaborators to work together: individuals can independently pursue TSR Theories, TSR RQs, and TSG from the same line of inquiry, and discuss findings at regular intervals.

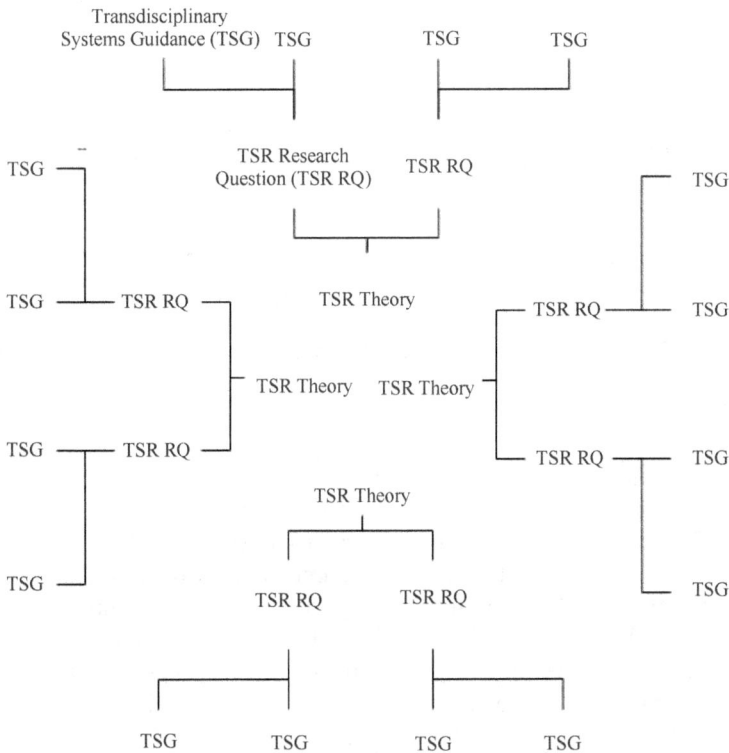

Figure 3.6 Mental model of complexity in Transdisciplinary Systems Research (TSR)

Transdisciplinary Systems Research (TSR) clarifies the problem space and establishes a solution-space for Transdisciplinary Systems Guidance (TSG). The *problem space* consists of the collection of research questions within the mutable boundaries of the project, and the *solution space* consists of the collection of viable alternative solution conjectures. At a project level, guidance can be synthesized through Maher and Poon's model of the co-evolution of the problem and solution space. This is shown in *Figure 3.7*.

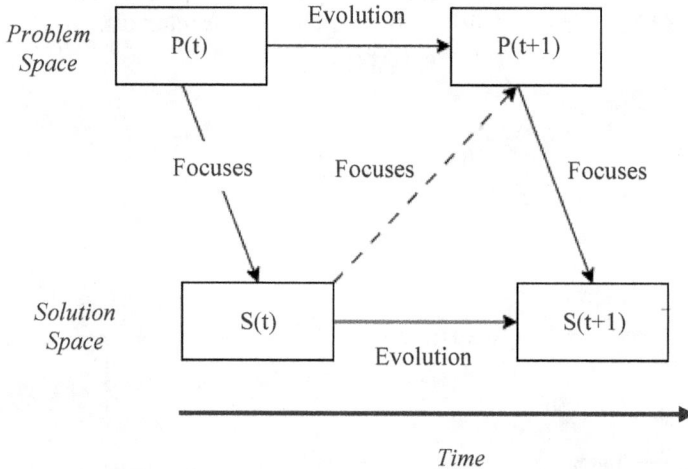

Figure 3.7 Model of the co-evolution of problem space and solution space by Maher and Poon in 1996

In Maher and Poon's model, the problem space and solution space evolve in parallel[426]. The problem space evolves from P(t) to P(t+1), P(t+2), etc. The solution space evolves from S(t) to S(t+1), S(t+2), etc. The problem space and solution space interact in two main ways: (1) the research question focuses the range of solution conjectures (downward arrow), and (2) the refined list of solution conjectures informs future research questions (upward arrow). These interactions occur for the duration of the project. For readability, this publication presents one set of these interactions, though many of these have occurred throughout the project. *Chapters 1* to *5* clarifies the problem space, and *Chapter 6* focuses on the solution space.

---

[426] Mary Lou Maher and Josiah Poon, "Modelling Design Exploration as Co-Evolution," *The Special Issues of Microcomputers in Civil Engineering on Evolutionary Systems in Design*, 1996. p. 4.

II.   *Collaborative Peer Review Process (CPRP)*

A Collaborative Peer Review Process (CPRP) has been employed in *Phase 5* of this study. There are many approaches for teams of people to work together to undertake a review, one of which is where one or more reviewers collaborate with the author to improve the publication[427]. In 2017, Kwon et al. observed how CPRP was able to create new opportunities for interprofessional learning and negotiating feedback[428], in line with the ethos of mutual learning in transdisciplinary research[429]. In 2013, Elsevier launched a series of pilots with academic journals Molecular Cell, Neuron, and Cell, and found that: "Enthusiasm for collaborative review appears to be generally high among researchers"[430]. Despite variations in each pilot, reviewers remained anonymous to one another in all cases[431]. It has also been the case in this study.

For this publication's CPRP, I uploaded *Parts I (Chapters 1, 2, and 3)*, *II (Chapters 4, and 5)*, and *III (Chapters 6)* in stages to a Google Drive folder shared with the collaborative peer reviewers. *Parts II and III* were released after I addressed feedback from *Part I*. To offer reviewers the opportunity to comment on the publication as a whole, the review process for *Part I* remained open until the entire review process ended. The CPRP has been successful. Some reviewers sent a few paragraphs or a bullet-point list. Others submitted a detailed, annotated document. I greatly appreciate the depth and diversity of the feedback I received and adopted suggested edits ~95% of the time during the review process.

---

[427] Wiley, "Types of Peer Review," accessed April 22, 2023, https://authorservices.wiley.com/Reviewers/journal-reviewers/what-is-peer-review/types-of-peer-review.html.

[428] Jae Yung Kwon et al., "Collaborative Peer Review Process as an Informal Interprofessional Learning Tool: Findings from an Exploratory Study," *Journal of Interprofessional Care*, 2017, https://doi.org/10.1080/13561820.2017.1358156.

[429] See *Table 1.5*.

[430] Elsevier, "Experimenting with Collaborative Peer Review (Reviewers' Update)," accessed April 22, 2023, https://www.elsevier.com/connect/archive/reviewers-update/experimenting-with-collaborative-peer-review.

[431] *ibid.*

Table 3.4 Pros and cons of the Collaborative Peer Review Process (CPRP) based on Elsevier's pilot study at journals Molecular Cell, Neuron, and Cell

Publication	Pros	Cons
Molecular Cell	▪ 17 of 24 reviewers responded and ~94% said they liked the discussion and would be willing to participate in a similar discussion in the future ▪ 5 of 10 authors responded to the survey and unanimously agreed that the interactive review process made it clearer to them how to revise their publication and the editor's summary of the discussions were helpful	▪ The process took longer than conventional peer review because of the additional discussion component ▪ Some reviewers expressed concern about the extra work ▪ Editors felt additional time was necessary to lead the discussions
Neuron	▪ The quality and extent of the discussions varied depending on whether reviewers believed the manuscript had the potential to be published ▪ The editors and reviewers felt the process was valuable in most cases	
Cell	▪ Responses were mixed: interest in interacting increased when reviewers had divergent views	

Source: Elsevier, "Experimenting with Collaborative Peer Review (Reviewers' Update)," accessed April 22, 2023, https://www.elsevier.com/connect/archive/reviewers-update/experimenting-with-collaborative-peer-review

3.3 Implementation

3.3.1 Iterative process

While previous sections in this chapter described the research process through a phase-based model, this study took a non-linear, iterative approach. This section describes in more detail the iterative research process based on Pineo et al.'s model of iterative transdisciplinary research in 2021[432].

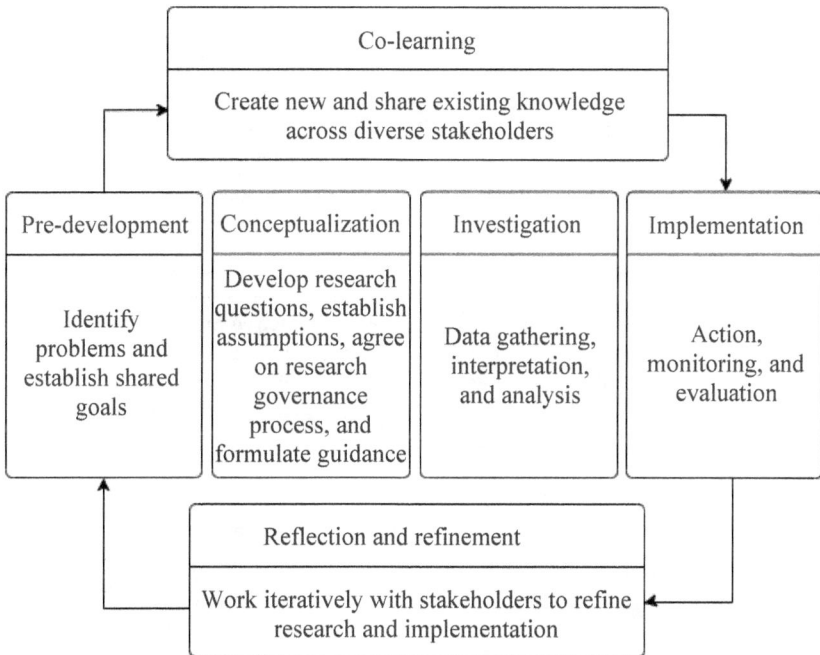

Figure 3.8 Model of transdisciplinary research by Pineo et al. in 2021

---

[432] Helen Pineo et al., "A New Transdisciplinary Research Model to Investigate and Improve the Health of the Public," *Health Promotion International* 36, no. 2 (April 15, 2021): 481–92, https://doi.org/10.1093/heapro/daaa125.

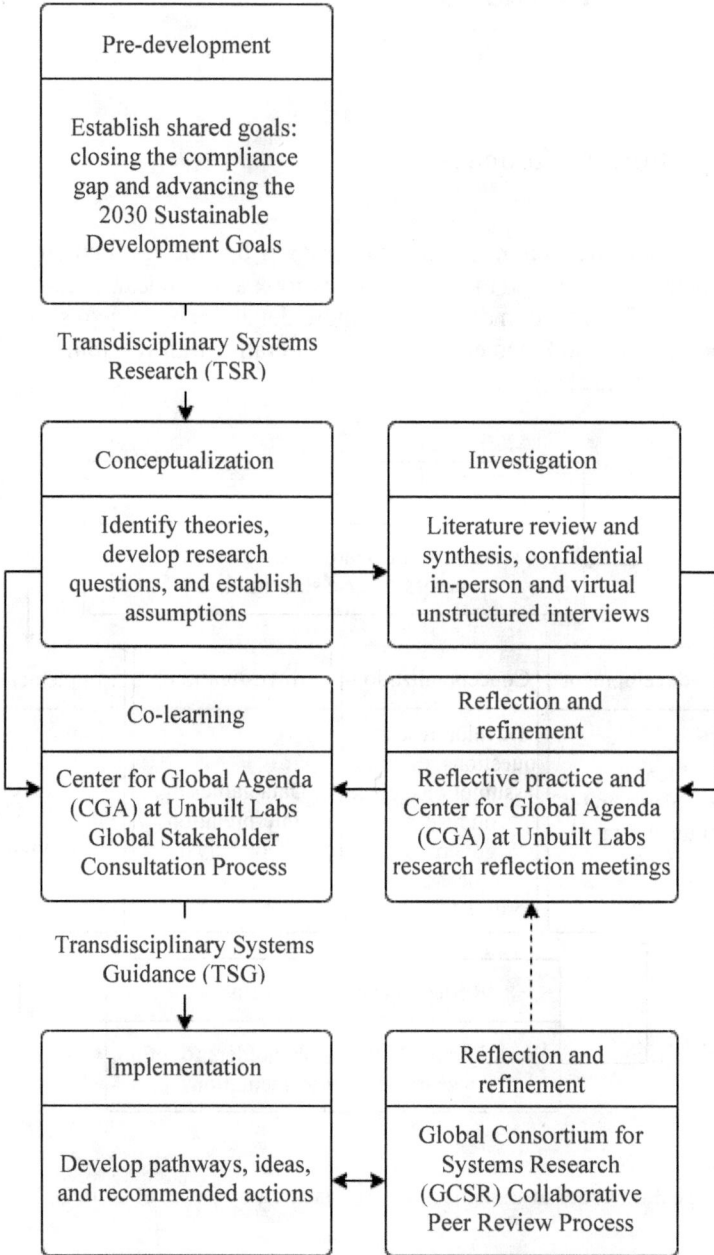

Figure 3.9 Iterative research process of this study

Although this study adopts Pineo et al.'s model, the workflow differs in several distinct ways as shown in *Figure 3.8*:

- The *pre-development* stage was pre-determined by international law (closing the compliance gap) and by global consensus (the 2030 Sustainable Development Goals). It is therefore not included within the iterative loop. The iterative process began with *conceptualization* (the development of theories in systems research and transdisciplinary research, and the assessment of their corresponding applicability in *Chapters 1* and *2*). The study then cycled through *investigation, reflection and refinement*, as well as *co-learning* as informed by the Transdisciplinary Systems Research (TSR) philosophy and methodology.

- The output of this global study on *implementation* is guidance based on evidence-gathered throughout the iterative process. Though I have implemented pilot studies of new initiatives based on gaps identified by this study, they are not the focus of this publication.

- The Collaborative Peer Review Process (CPRP) adds to the *reflection and refinement* process towards the end of the writing and synthesis. Even though this study uses an iterative research process, there are methodologies that are phase-dependent. For example, exploratory unstructured interviews are more helpful at the beginning of the research process, and a CPRP is not possible until there is some form of coherent written output. Consequently, while this study maintains the spirit of an iterative process i.e. all findings are subject to change during the research process (including research boundaries and the choice of the unit of analysis), there is still a beginning and an end to the project unlike the theoretical iterative loop presented by Pineo et al.

3.3.2 Challenges

Combining transdisciplinary research (TDR) and systems research to create Transdisciplinary Systems Research (TSR) has its benefits: for one, the synergy made this analysis possible. However, it also combined and amplified the challenges of the two fields.

In 2017, Fam, Smith, and Cordell identified some of the challenges of being a transdisciplinary researcher through semi-structured interviews with 14 leading and emerging transdisciplinary researchers and practitioners[433]. It is pivotal for TDR researchers to have:

- *Curiosity*: willingness to challenge the status quo and have a tolerance for uncertainty[434]
- *Commitment*: navigate political uncertainty and push through (mainstream academic) boundaries[435], especially because transdisciplinary research takes longer and is challenging to secure funding[436]
- *Critical awareness*: suspend judgment, question assumptions, listen, appreciate history (not reinvent the wheel), and be cautious of historical practices[437]
- *Creativity*: examine and re-imagine historical approaches, concepts, and narratives beyond disciplinary boundaries[438]
- *Communication*: encourage engagement and secure buy-in across diverse stakeholder groups[439]
- *Connectedness*: build trust and relationships with individuals, teams, communities, and disciplines[440]

In 2021, participant-observer Hamm published the challenges of systems research project at Pivot Projects: a group of several hundred volunteers from around the world connected virtually in the midst of a global pandemic and worked collaboratively to produce novel yet

---

[433] Dena Fam, Tanzi Smith, and Dana Cordell, "Being a Transdisciplinary Researcher: Skills and Dispositions Fostering Competence in Transdisciplinary Research and Practice," in *Transdisciplinary Research and Practice for Sustainability Outcomes*, ed. Dena Fam et al., Routledge Studies in Sustainability (London and New York: Routledge, 2017), 77–92. p. 78.
[434] *ibid*. p. 80-81.
[435] *ibid*. p. 81.
[436] *ibid*. p. 85.
[437] *ibid*. p. 82.
[438] *ibid*. p. 83.
[439] *ibid*. p. 84.
[440] *ibid*. p. 86.

practical recommendations to address global problems[441]. The team ultimately developed and presented proposals to policymaking bodies including the G20 and COP26[442]. Despite the very strong team, Hamm documented the challenges the team faced:

- *Outcome*: there was no assurance that the hundreds of volunteers would produce valuable insights and recommendations, and no assurance that the world's leaders would listen[443].
- *Buy-in*: involvement in Pivot Projects and people leading workstreams are on a voluntary basis, and people quietly disappear if they "didn't like what they saw after a few workstream meetings"[444].
- *Uncertainty*: the discovery process' uncertainty and the subsequent challenge of securing buy-in within a voluntary network led people to feel "afraid that people may start to lose interest and drift off"[445].
- *Funding*: it was "a perennial problem"[446]. At the Ecological Sequestration Trust, Head tried to raise $100 million from companies and foundations to pay for a ten-year program to develop data and modeling for interactions between humans and natural systems, but in the end, funding organizations were project-focused and "didn't want to pay for long-term planning and capacity planning"[447]. At Pivot Projects, funding was a challenge as well: "there really aren't funding streams for mobilization, collaboration, and systems thinking [...] the systems work and connecting things"[448]. Head secured eight funding prospects totaling $600,000 by May 2020, but funding failed to materialize: "By midsummer, still no money"[449]. Hamm concluded the book with "the future of Pivot Projects was in doubt"[450].

[441] Steve Hamm, *The Pivot: Addressing Global Problems Through Local Action* (New York and Chichester: Columbia University Press, 2021). p. 7.
[442] *ibid.* p. 5.
[443] Hamm, *The Pivot: Addressing Global Problems Through Local Action.* p. 8.
[444] *ibid.* p. 92.
[445] *ibid.* p. 95.
[446] *ibid.* p. 41.
[447] *ibid.* p. 41.
[448] *ibid.* p. 91.
[449] *ibid.* p. 91.
[450] *ibid.* p. 283.

3.3.3 Reflection

While I cannot speak to the Pivot Project's implementation as I have not been a participant, I have been involved in large volunteer research networks in the past and experienced similar challenges related to *outcome*, *buy-in*, *uncertainty*, and *funding* identified in the previous subsection. I can also attest to the challenges of conducting transdisciplinary research identified by Fam, Smith, and Cordell on *curiosity*, *commitment*, *critical awareness*, *creativity*, *communication*, and *connectedness* based on my experience with this research project.

Understanding other researchers' experiences implementing a research program with similar goals shaped the methodological choices and overall implementation. The Pivot Project's results influenced this project in several ways:

- I thought the Pivot Project's core team was highly qualified and committed. I trust the team's implementation and feel that repeating the same methods is unlikely to produce better results.
- Based on my experience with large volunteer research networks, I find current methods to structure systems research at scale resource-intensive and inefficient. TSR's approach to managing complexity (see *Section 3.2.3*) is a response to this demand. The collaboration approach is currently being replicated and tested at private sector R&D centers through the Venture Strategy Group (VSG) at Unbuilt Lab's Innovator in Residence (IIR) program.
- Based on Hamm's documentation, it appears that the Pivot Project's team did not secure funding. I felt that my project was unlikely to as well. As a result, I prioritized methodologies that are not cost-prohibitive: literature review, virtual workshop, online forum etc., and kept the core team small: on a day-to-day basis, I managed the full project. I appreciate the generous in-kind institutional support the project has received e.g. legitimacy, expertise, network, and outreach.
- My co-director at the Center for Global Agenda (CGA) at Unbuilt Labs, Dr. Marguerite Van Cook, and I have experience working with volunteers and public consultation processes – people have work, families, and social commitments, it is very difficult to secure commitment for long-term engagement. This is in line with the Pivot Project's learnings. As a result, I designed low-commitment

engagements such as one-off, self-contained workshops, requests for short (~500 words) statements and short (~10 minutes) presentations etc. to lower the barriers for people to engage. People who wished to participate in more than one engagement were welcome to do so, but was not required.

- I shared a similar concern with the Pivot Project about impact. The early engagement process was critical to assessing the likelihood of buy-in, adoption, and impact. Over the course of the project, I continuously examined the project's definition of and likelihood of success. I also conducted quarterly reviews of the project's viability based on the rapidly changing global landscape and new feedback. In the end, the project expanded in scope and took double the time expected, because of a combination of the pandemic, methodological innovations, challenging foresight questions, and competing commitments.

There is a critical challenge that Hamm's documentation does not address: the presentation of incomplete work products. Any meaningful iterative process will involve presenting in-process work products publicly for feedback. This is common practice in the private sector, and there is robust know-how on gathering actionable feedback in rapid iterative processes through user research, but it is less common in academia and the public sector. I ran basic tests for landing pages, email outreach campaigns, website information architecture etc. behind-the-scenes. These activities strengthened communications with diverse stakeholders and contributed greatly to the success of the project.

A challenge specific to using TSR is that the recommendations have to work both in theory and in practice. This was not an easy feat. It involved a significant amount of operational expertise and an understanding of the logics of different industries and stakeholder groups. The early engagement process and the global stakeholder consultation process were critical because they offered a chance to understand how different industries or stakeholder groups think as well as their sentiments on specific problems.

3.3.4 Limitations

There are some limitations to the project, mostly as a result of limitations to time, funding, and other resources. The project was conducted in English because of the inability to systematically translate research and documents conducted in multiple other languages. A future study that takes more languages into account can build on this study. Further, despite the many outreach channels and official venues to which I have access, more could have been done to encourage engagement. For example, I have been informed that participation can be difficult for historically underrepresented people and communities without dedicated funding. I did my best to accommodate, for example, by scheduling 1:1 meetings to listen to and understand their perspectives, but this is not as ideal as receiving a formal statement, which can then be included in the final publication. Time is a critical constraint given the *dynamic* nature of CAS[451]. The Center for Global Agenda (CGA) at Unbuilt Labs' website updates recommendations routinely.

---

[451] See *Table 1.1.*

Box 3-1: Transdisciplinary Systems Research (TSR) Q&A

Below is a Q&A from one of the weekly research reflection meetings at the Center for Global Agenda (CGA) at Unbuilt Labs between my Co-director Dr. Marguerite Van Cook and I.

Q: How would you start a Transdisciplinary Systems Research (TSR) project?

A: There is somewhat of a learning curve navigating so many moving parts, but *Part I* ought to provide enough theory for researchers and practitioners to conduct TSR. My project began by identifying a system as a unit of analysis (the global governance network) based on the project brief (to close the compliance gap and advance the 2030 Sustainable Development Goals). From there, I reviewed the project boundaries regularly and explored alternative solution conjectures. I would be happy to teach an interactive seminar in the future if there is interest. I would focus on reviewing literature through a TSR lens, and discuss how the lens can help researchers see around corners even within disciplinary boundaries.

Q: Can you answer stand-alone questions through Transdisciplinary Systems Research?

A: It is possible once you have done all of the groundwork analyzing a system, but I do not think it is possible to ask one stand-alone question, especially if we consider the properties of grand challenges (for example, see *Table 1.2 Properties of Wicked Problems*, Property 8. Every wicked problem is a symptom of another problem) and the importance of recognizing interconnections[452].

---

[452] See *Table 1.4.*

Q: *What outputs can I expect by following the TSR process?*

A: By definition, Transdisciplinary Systems Guidance (TSG) are outputs of TSR which can include policy recommendations, investment recommendations, and other recommended actions. There is no (maximum) limit to the TSR process' output, and I encourage future TSR researchers and practitioners to be creative, but at a minimum, there ought to be some form of written output that demonstrates a careful consideration of context and recommendations.

Q: *What is next for Transdisciplinary Systems Research?*

A: I am looking forward to understanding how TSR can be deployed at scale and foster collaboration within large research and practitioner teams. We have begun replicating TSR at private sector R&D centers and we have been looking to create self-sustaining research organizations through the Venture Strategy Group (VSG) at Unbuilt Lab's Innovator in Residence (IIR) program. I would be keen to develop a network of regional and thematic TSR labs to understand how we can better advance the 2030 Sustainable Development Goals. The Global Consortium for Systems Research (GCSR) may begin this work soon as well.

3.4 References

Center for Global Agenda (CGA) at Unbuilt Labs. "High Level
   Recommendations and Global Strategy." Unbuilt Labs, The Global
   Think Tank Ecosystem. Accessed February 13, 2024.
   https://unbuiltlabs.com/cga/high-level-recommendations-and-global-
   strategy.

Chaudhary, Anil. "Toward an Epistemology of Participatory Research." In
   *Participatory Action Research: International Contexts and
   Consequences*, edited by Robin McTaggart. Albany: State University of
   New York Press, 1997.

Chauhan, Rahul S. "Unstructured Interviews: Are They Really All That Bad?"
   Human Resource Development International 25, no. 4 (August 8, 2022):
   474–87. https://doi.org/10.1080/13678868.2019.1603019.

Cheung, Marvin. "A Theory on Transdisciplinary Systems Research (TSR)."
   Presented at the Future of Global Governance Series, Center for Global
   Agenda (CGA) at Unbuilt Labs, November 11, 2023.
   https://unbuiltlabs.com/a-theory-on-tsr.

———. "Keynote: What Can Systems Research Teach Us about Conducting
   Impactful Research for the 2030 Sustainable Development Goals."
   Presented at the Annual Innovation Conference, PatSnap, November 16,
   2023. https://unbuiltlabs.com/conducting-impactful-research-for-the-
   2030-sdgs.

Cohen, Sue, Tim Cole, Morag McDermont, and Angela Piccini. "Co-
   Production as Experimentation: The Research Forum as Method." In
   Imagining Regulation Differently: Co-Creating for Engagement, edited
   by Morag McDermont, Tim Cole, Janet Newman, and Angela Piccini.
   Bristol: Policy Press, 2020.

Cross, Nigel. "Research in Design Thinking." In *Research in Design
   Thinking*, edited by Nigel Cross, Kees Dorst, and Norbert Roozenburg.
   Netherlands: Delft University Press, 1992.

Cross, Nigel, Kees Dorst, and Norbert Roozenburg. "Preface." In *Research in
   Design Thinking*, edited by Nigel Cross, Kees Dorst, and Norbert
   Roozenburg. Netherlands: Delft University Press, 1992.

Dennett, Daniel. "Intentional Systems." *Journal of Philosophy* 68, no. 4
   (1971): 87–106. https://doi.org/10.2307/2025382.

———. "Intentional Systems Theory." In *Oxford Handbook of the
   Philosophy of Mind*, edited by Brian P. McLaughlin, Ansgar
   Beckermann, and Sven Walter. Oxford and New York: Oxford
   Handbooks Online, 2009.
   https://doi.org/10.1093/oxfordhb/9780199262618.003.0020.

———. *The Intentional Stance*. Cambridge, Massachusetts: MIT Press, 1989.

Elsevier. "Experimenting with Collaborative Peer Review (Reviewers'
   Update)." Accessed April 22, 2023.

https://www.elsevier.com/connect/archive/reviewers-update/experimenting-with-collaborative-peer-review.

Fam, Dena, Tanzi Smith, and Dana Cordell. "Being a Transdisciplinary Researcher: Skills and Dispositions Fostering Competence in Transdisciplinary Research and Practice." In *Transdisciplinary Research and Practice for Sustainability Outcomes*, edited by Dena Fam, Jane Palmer, Chris Riedy, and Cynthia Mitchell, 77–92. Routledge Studies in Sustainability. London and New York: Routledge, 2017.

Hamm, Steve. *The Pivot: Addressing Global Problems Through Local Action*. New York and Chichester: Columbia University Press, 2021.

Healy, Karen. "Participatory Action Research and Social Work: A Critical Appraisal." *International Social Work* 44, no. 1 (January 2001): 93–105. https://doi.org/10.1177/002087280104400108.

Keahey, Jennifer. "Sustainable Development and Participatory Action Research: A Systematic Review." *Systematic Practice and Action Research* 39 (2020): 291–306. https://doi.org/10.1007/s11213-020-09535-8.

Klein, Naomi. *This Changes Everything: Capitalism vs the Climate*. New York and London: Simon & Schuster Paperbacks, 2014.

Kwon, Jae Yung, Laura Yvonne Bulk, Zarina Giannone, Sarah Liva, Bubli Chakraborty, and Helen Brown. "Collaborative Peer Review Process as an Informal Interprofessional Learning Tool: Findings from an Exploratory Study." *Journal of Interprofessional Care*, 2017. https://doi.org/10.1080/13561820.2017.1358156.

Maher, Mary Lou, and Josiah Poon. "Modelling Design Exploration as Co-Evolution." *The Special Issues of Microcomputers in Civil Engineering on Evolutionary Systems in Design*, 1996.

Miles, Heather J. "Practising Difference across Geography: A Transdisciplinary and Deleuzian Approach to Intradisciplinary Thinking." *Environment and Planning F* 2, no. 4 (December 2023): 495–514. https://doi.org/10.1177/26349825231200607.

Mortari, Luigina. "Reflectivity in Research Practice: An Overview of Different Perspectives." *International Journal of Qualitative Methods* 14, no. 5 (December 9, 2015): 160940691561804. https://doi.org/10.1177/1609406915618045.

Norton, Richard K., Nina P. David, Stephen Buckman, and Patricia D. Koman. "Overlooking the Coast: Limited Local Planning for Coastal Area Management along Michigan's Great Lakes." *Land Use Policy* 71 (February 2018): 183–203. https://doi.org/10.1016/j.landusepol.2017.11.049.

Pain, Rachel, Sara Kindon, and Mike Kesby. "Participatory Action Research: Making a Difference to Theory, Practice and Action." In *Participatory Action Research Approaches and Method: Connecting People, Participation and Place*, edited by Sara Kindon, Rachel Pain, and Mike Kesby, 26–32. New York: Routledge, 2007.

Parkes, Margot, and Ruth Panelli. "Integrating Catchment Ecosystems and Community Health: The Value of Participatory Action Research." *Ecosystem Health* 7, no. 2 (2001): 85–106. https://doi.org/10.1046/j.1526-0992.2001.007002085.x.

Pineo, Helen, Eleanor R Turnbull, Michael Davies, Mike Rowson, Andrew C Hayward, Graham Hart, Anne M Johnson, and Robert W Aldridge. "A New Transdisciplinary Research Model to Investigate and Improve the Health of the Public." *Health Promotion International* 36, no. 2 (April 15, 2021): 481–92. https://doi.org/10.1093/heapro/daaa125.

Rittel, Horst W. J., and Melvin M. Webber. "Dilemmas in a General Theory of Planning." *Policy Sciences, Springer* 4, no. 2 (June 1973). https://doi.org/10.1007/BF01405730.

Tandon, Rajesh. "Social Transformation and Participatory Research." *Convergence: An International Journal of Adult Education* 21, no. 2–3 (1988): 5–18.

Turner, Jonathan. *Sociology: Studying the Human System*. 2nd ed. Santa Monica, California: Goodyear Publishing Company, 1981.

Wiley. "Types of Peer Review." Accessed April 22, 2023. https://authorservices.wiley.com/Reviewers/journal-reviewers/what-is-peer-review/types-of-peer-review.html.

Part 2

Findings & Discussions

4

Effecting Global Change: Navigating and Altering Constraints

4.0 Outline

After establishing system concepts and research methods in *Part I*, this chapter brings the analysis together to address system-wide transformation methods. *System-wide transformation methods* provide stakeholders with the means to navigate and alter the formal (i.e. laws and policies) and informal (i.e. cultural) constraints that limit progress towards closing the compliance gap and advancing the 2030 Sustainable Development Goals. To arrive at system-wide transformation methods, this chapter begins with a discussion of the history of global governance theory in *Section 4.1* since the contemporary global governance network is the system of interest. It then constructs a model of global change processes with reference to the compliance gap within the contemporary global governance network in *Section 4.2*. This chapter draws primarily from global governance theory, but it also uses Transdisciplinary Systems Research (TSR) to synthesize literature from *neo-institutionalist theory, intentional systems theory, organizational theory, social psychology*, and *socio-legal studies*. I reflect on the synthesis in *Section 4.3*.

4.1 History of Global Governance Theory

The first international organizations were established for the internationalization of norms in technical fields. For example, the Central Commission for the Navigation on the Rhine (1815 – Present)[453], the International Telegraph Union (1865 – Present)[454], the Universal Postal Union (1874 – Present)[455], and the International Bureau of Weights and Measures (1875 – Present)[456]. The League of Nations, the first international organization for preserving peace, was established in 1919 after World War I under the Treaty of Versailles "to promote international cooperation and to achieve peace and security"[457]. The Charter of the United Nations was signed in June 1945 and entered into force in October 1945[458] close to 80 years ago. As of April 1946, the League of Nations ceased to exist and handed all of its assets over to the United Nations[459].

Despite the history of multilateral cooperation, the concept of "global governance" and the question of global change only came to the fore around the 1990s[460]. In 1992, Rosenau defined *governance* as activities backed by shared goals that do not necessarily rely on sovereign or police powers to attain compliance[461]. In 1999, Hewson

---

[453] Central Commission for the Navigation of the Rhine, "Introduction," accessed May 3, 2023, https://www.ccr-zkr.org/11010100-en.html.

[454] International Telegraph Union, "History," ITU, accessed May 3, 2023, https://www.itu.int:443/en/about/Pages/history.aspx.

[455] Universal Postal Union, "About," accessed May 3, 2023, https://www.upu.int/en/Universal-Postal-Union.

[456] International Bureau of Weights and Measures, "Governance," accessed May 3, 2023, https://www.bipm.org/en/governance.

[457] United Nations, "Predecessor: The League of Nations," United Nations (United Nations), accessed May 3, 2023, https://www.un.org/en/about-us/history-of-the-un/predecessor.

[458] United Nations, "UN Charter," United Nations (United Nations), accessed May 4, 2023, https://www.un.org/en/about-us/un-charter.

[459] United Nations, "Predecessor: The League of Nations," United Nations (United Nations), accessed May 3, 2023, https://www.un.org/en/about-us/history-of-the-un/predecessor.

[460] Martin Hewson and Timothy J. Sinclair, "The Emergence of Global Governance Theory," in *Approaches to Global Governance Theory*, ed. Martin Hewson and Timothy J. Sinclair (Albany: State University of New York Press, 1999), 3–22. p. 3.

[461] James N. Rosenau, "Governance, Order, and Change in World Politics," in *Governance without Government: Order and Change in World Politics*, ed. James

and Sinclair identified the end of the Cold War in 1991 as one of the contributing factors to the renewed interest in the changing patterns of global governance[462]. As an extension of Rosenau's definition, *global governance* describes the complex global processes that enable stakeholders to commit to and act upon shared goals.

Contemporary global governance, or global governance in its form today, only began in the 1990s. Although extensive post-WWII decolonization in Africa, Asia, and the Middle East occurred[463] (80 former colonies have gained independence since the creation of the United Nations[464]), scholars generally agree that Cold War tensions "deeply affected the UN's security functions"[465]. The most visible mark of this new focus on global governance is the founding of the academic journal *Global Governance* in 1995[466]. *Global Governance* is published quarterly by Brill in association with the Academic Council on the United Nations System (ACUNS)[467].

Global governance theory was developed from the fields of international relations (IR) and international political economy (IPE). In 1988, Strange described the way IR started with the puzzling question: "why did nation-states continue to go to war when it was already clear that the economic gains made in war would never exceed the economic costs of doing so"[468]? Strange described the way IPE sought to address another puzzling question: why do states fail to regulate and stabilize the international financial system when experts agree more regulation is necessary[469]? In 1988, she observed the way markets are studied in economics with the assumption that they will not be disrupted by war, revolution, or other civil disorders[470]. She noted in 1996, "Anything as messy as power simply cannot be

---

N. Rosenau and Ernst-Otto Czempiel, Cambridge Studies in International Relations (Cambridge and New York: Cambridge University Press, 1992), 1–29. p. 4.

[462] Hewson and Sinclair, "The Emergence of Global Governance Theory." p. 3

[463] Jacques Fomerand, Cecelia M. Lynch, and Karen Mingst, "United Nations (UN) | Definition, History, Founders, Flag, & Facts," Britannica, May 4, 2023, https://www.britannica.com/topic/United-Nations.

[464] United Nations, "Decolonization," United Nations (United Nations), accessed May 4, 2023, https://www.un.org/en/global-issues/decolonization.

[465] Fomerand, Lynch, and Mingst, "United Nations (UN) | Definition, History, Founders, Flag, & Facts."

[466] Hewson and Sinclair, "The Emergence of Global Governance Theory." p. 19

[467] Academic Council on the United Nations System, "Global Governance Journal," accessed May 4, 2023, https://acuns.org/global-governance-journal/.

[468] Susan Strange, *States and Markets* (New York: Basil Blackwell, 1988). p. 11.

[469] *ibid.*

[470] *ibid.* p. 14.

included in an economic equation, or even a purely economic analysis"[471]. She also found it problematic that some economists narrowly define rationality as "action in pursuit of material gain or to avoid material loss, or costs"[472]. This is discussed in *Section 4.2*.

Since the end of WWII, the study of international relations has been predominantly guided by realism (i.e. the idea that states exist within an international system in which they are ultimately dependent on their own capabilities to further their national interests)[473]. In 1999, Hewson and Sinclair offered a more poignant understanding of realism: "politics is a power struggle"[474]. The influence of neorealism (i.e. states are rational actors that exist in a system where they have to fend for themselves) in the 1980s and 1990s was palpable[475]. Neorealism draws primarily from microeconomics, and critics have faulted neorealists "for neglecting the insights of history, sociology, and philosophy; for falsely claiming scientific validity; for failing to account for systemic transformations in international relations (including the end of the Cold War and the advent of globalization); and for an allegedly self-defeating analytical reductionism"[476]. Set against the backdrop of realism and neorealism, global governance theory sought to move beyond an economic globalization perspective with a focus on markets[477].

Global governance theory aims to offer a more comprehensive perspective on the politics of global change through the inclusion of non-state actors[478]. In 2003, Rosenau argued that micro-macro theories on how individuals and organizations (or parts and wholes) influence each other's behaviors have become more critical: enduring macro changes cannot occur if individuals withhold their support, and durable micro change is unlikely without altering macro support

---

[471] Susan Strange, *The Retreat of the State: The Diffusion of Power in the World Economy*, Cambridge Studies in International Relations (Cambridge and New York: Cambridge University Press, 1996). p. 20.

[472] Strange, *The Retreat of the State: The Diffusion of Power in the World Economy*. p. 20.

[473] "Realism | Definition, Theories, Examples, Problems, & Facts | Britannica," accessed May 7, 2023, https://www.britannica.com/topic/realism-political-and-social-science.

[474] Hewson and Sinclair, "The Emergence of Global Governance Theory." p. 4.

[475] Duncan Bell, "Realism | Definition, Theories, Examples, Problems, & Facts," Britannica, accessed May 7, 2023, https://www.britannica.com/topic/realism-political-and-social-science.

[476] *ibid.*

[477] Hewson and Sinclair, "The Emergence of Global Governance Theory." p. 5.

[478] *ibid.*

structures[479]. This can be understood intuitively as well: individuals want their organizations to be responsive to their goals, and leaders and organizations seek to influence people at the micro level[480]. In the past, researchers tended to view micro-level individual behavior as a consequence of macro-level historical, cultural, economic, and political structures with little regard for individuals' agency[481], but one is not necessarily more powerful than the other[482]. This mix of micro and macro is embedded within a broader intertwining of pervasive contradictions Rosenau calls *distant proximities*: the good and bad, global and local, public and private, decentralization and centralization, states and markets[483].

Beyond the focus on non-state actors, global governance scholars depart from IR, IPE, and other traditional approaches in several ways[484]. In 2005, Hoffmann and Ba argued that global governance theory moves "beyond 'high' politics to focus on issues such as the environment, human rights, labor, and intellectual property in addition to traditional security and political-economy issues"[485]. Despite vastly different views, beliefs, and concerns, global governance scholars tend to study rules and rule systems that constrain or influence actors' behaviors rather than a more traditional focus on power and unchecked state interactions[486]. Further, most global governance scholars adopt a *complex* and *dynamic[487]* worldview instead of a relatively static one in traditional approaches[488]. In 2014, Weiss and Wilkinson argued that global governance includes a normative dimension: it ought to encourage us to ask questions about "how the world is organized, how power and authority are exercised, and how adjustments (incremental, wholesale, or otherwise) can be made to make the world a better place"[489]. It is from this discourse that system-wide transformation methods emerge.

---

[479] James N. Rosenau, *Distant Proximities: Dynamics Beyond Globalization* (Princeton and Oxford: Princeton University Press, 2003). p. 22.
[480] *ibid*. p. 26.
[481] *ibid*. p. 24.
[482] Rosenau, *Distant Proximities: Dynamics Beyond Globalization*. p. XI-XII.
[483] *ibid*. p. 4-5.
[484] Matthew J. Hoffmann and Alice D. Ba, "Introduction: Coherence and Contestation," in *Contending Perspectives on Global Governance: Coherence, Contestation and World Order*, ed. Alice D. Ba and Matthew J. Hoffmann (London and New York: Routledge, 2005), 1–14. p. 5.
[485] *ibid*.
[486] *ibid*. p. 6.
[487] See *Table 1.1*.
[488] Hoffmann and Ba, "Introduction: Coherence and Contestation." p. 6.
[489] Thomas G. Weiss and Rorden Wilkinson, "Global Governance to the Rescue: Saving International Relations?," *Global Governance: A Review of*

Box 4-1: Q&A, Is there any cause for optimism?

This was a question I received from a climate change graphic novel artist. I get this question often, even from my colleagues at different United Nations agencies. 2030 is not that many years away, and our progress has been far too slow. To ask the question, is there any cause for optimism is akin to asking whether people have the capacity to change. History has always been won by a slim margin: a few votes, one "yes", or the first "no more". Implicit in the discussion on system-wide transformation methods is the assumption that individuals have the agency to overcome historical and sociological determinations[490]. We have to reject historical determinism, where history is made independent of an individual's actions, and pessimistic fatalism, where no desirable outcome is possible[491].

I am always inspired by and grateful for people who stand up for more sustainable and just practices. I am also inspired by the work of my colleagues. *A system-wide transformation can be achieved only when everyone takes a step forward together, like a puzzle that will be solved only when we turn all of the keys at the same time.* I hope you will support sustainable development however you can. We are living in difficult times with new wars and disruptions. We can only press on and hope that justice — and our compassion for each other — will prevail.

Multilateralism and International Organizations 20, no. 1 (August 19, 2014): 19–36, https://doi.org/10.1163/19426720-02001003. p. 31.
[490] Rodrigo Nunes, *Neither Vertical nor Horizontal: A Theory of Political Organisation* (London and New York: Verso, 2021). p. 105.
[491] Oxford Reference, "Historical Determinism," Oxford Reference, accessed November 17, 2021, https://doi.org/10.1093/oi/authority.20110803095938705.

4.2 Mechanisms for Institutional Change within the Contemporary Global Governance Network

System-wide transformation methods provide stakeholders with the means to navigate and alter the formal (i.e. international laws and policies) and informal (i.e. cultural) constraints that limit progress towards closing the compliance gap and advancing the 2030 Sustainable Development Goals. This definition is derived from neo-institutionalist theory. *Institutions* "include any form of constraint that human beings devise to shape human interaction"[492]. There are many definitions of *culture*[493], but I adopt the following as a working definition: "any set of shared, signifying practices – practices by which meaning is produced, performed, contested, or transformed"[494]. The theory on institutions has been embedded within global governance discourse. For example, Thakur and Van Langenhove in 2006 defined global governance as "The complex of formal and informal institutions, mechanisms, relationships, and processes [...] through which collective interests are articulated, rights and obligations are established, and differences are mediated"[495].

---

[492] Douglass C. North, *Institutions, Institutional Change, and Economic Performance*, The Political Economy of Institutions and Decisions (Cambridge ; New York: Cambridge University Press, 1990). p. 4.

[493] For example, as Vinson noted in 2021, some scholars define culture by enumerating a "laundry list of phenomena": norms, beliefs, values, rituals, artifacts etc. Others, as Lamont and Small observed in 2010, define culture by its function: culture as symbolic boundaries, frames, narratives, repertoires, cultural capital etc.

[494] Naomi Mezey, "Law As Culture," *Georgetown Law Faculty Publications and Other Works*, 2001, http://scholarship.law.georgetown.edu/facpub/317/. p. 42.

[495] Roberto Domínguez and Rafael Velázquez Flores, "Global Governance," in *Oxford Research Encyclopedia of International Studies*, by Roberto Domínguez and Rafael Velázquez Flores (Oxford University Press, 2018), https://doi.org/10.1093/acrefore/9780190846626.013.508. p. 3.

The rate of return for institutions rises as the complexity of society increases[496] because they "offer a stable (but not necessarily efficient) structure to human interaction"[497]. Without institutions, there would be tremendous confusion, danger, and high risks in exchanges[498]. They enable complex exchanges across time and space[499], and they affect the distribution of resources and power in society[500]. Consequently, they determine the relative cost of transacting as well as transformation for different actors[501]. Formal and informal constraints, together with how they are enforced, shape our daily lives[502].

In 1990, North argued that stability is created through hierarchy, where each level is more costly to change than the one before[503]. Institutions are therefore expensive to create and change[504]. Although institutions offer stability, they change continuously and alter the choices available to us[505]. Informal constraints tend to be more impervious to change and more difficult to measure[506]. Therefore, institutional changes are typically observed through the alterations of formal constraints[507], which can happen overnight as a result of political or judicial decisions[508]. These changes have historically been attributed to easily observable exogenous factors e.g. external crises, but endogenous processes e.g. actors within an institution, can also create change[509]. In 2011, Blyth argued that while exogenous factors can explain why a particular institution becomes unstable, it is the endogenous factors which determine the institution that emerges from the instability[510].

---

[496] North, *Institutions, Institutional Change, and Economic Performance*. p. 46.
[497] *ibid.* p. 6.
[498] John L. Campbell, *Institutional Change and Globalization* (Princeton, NJ: Princeton Univ. Press, 2004). p. 1.
[499] North, *Institutions, Institutional Change, and Economic Performance*. p. 83.
[500] Campbell, *Institutional Change and Globalization*. p. 1.
[501] *ibid.* p. 34.
[502] North, *Institutions, Institutional Change, and Economic Performance*. p. 83.
[503] *ibid.*
[504] Campbell, *Institutional Change and Globalization*. p. 13.
[505] North, *Institutions, Institutional Change, and Economic Performance*. p. 6.
[506] *ibid.*
[507] Sverrir Steinsson, "Rule Ambiguity, Institutional Clashes, and Population Loss: How Wikipedia Became the Last Good Place on the Internet," *American Political Science Review* 118, no. 1 (February 2024): 235–51, https://doi.org/10.1017/S0003055423000138. p. 235.
[508] North, *Institutions, Institutional Change, and Economic Performance*. p. 6.
[509] Steinsson, "Rule Ambiguity, Institutional Clashes, and Population Loss." p. 235.
[510] Mark Blyth, *Great Transformations: Economic Ideas and Institutional Change in the Twentieth Century*, 8. pr (Cambridge: Cambridge Univ. Press, 2011). p. 8.

There are three main theoretical approaches to explain why institutions change in neo-institutionalist theory — (1) *rational choice institutionalism*: actors use institutions to maximize their utility and institutions affect rational individual behavior[511], (2) *historical institutionalism*: actors' decision-making at critical junctures affect institutions because of *path dependency[512]*, and the decisions in turn shape social, political, and economic behavior[513], and (3) *sociological institutionalism*: shifts in actors' norms, values, and perceived social legitimacy of institutions create institutional change[514]. Historical and sociological institutionalism do not contradict the logic of Transdisciplinary Systems Research (TSR). They are also highly compatible with global governance theory. This chapter will review the literature from these approaches in greater detail.

However, I argue that rational choice institutionalism contradicts the logic of TSR[515]. Properties of wicked problems show there are *conflicting theories*, *no definitive formulations*, and *every wicked problem is essentially unique[516]*. As Geuss observed in 1981, only under the condition of perfect information with awareness of the full range of alternatives and relative costs will the "rational choice" assumption be credible[517]. This is impossible based on the properties of complex adaptive systems (CAS): CAS are *dynamic*, *non-linear*, and demonstrate *emergent behavior[518]*. As Blyth points out, the logic of rational choice's approach to "interests" produces dubious findings: "because they wanted to do it, they did it, and because we know they did it (assuming everyone acts on his or her own best interests), those show they wanted to do it."[519]. The circular manner in which research is pursued offers no satisfactory answer on why institutional change occurs[520].

---

[511] Blyth, *Great Transformations*. p. 28.

[512] See Table 1.1.

[513] Steinsson, "Rule Ambiguity, Institutional Clashes, and Population Loss." p. 236.

[514] James Patterson, Douwe L. De Voogt, and Rodolfo Sapiains, "Beyond Inputs and Outputs: Process-oriented Explanation of Institutional Change in Climate Adaptation Governance," *Environmental Policy and Governance* 29, no. 5 (September 2019): 360–75, https://doi.org/10.1002/eet.1865. p. 363.

[515] Different fields have refuted the rational choice assumption in social science. The most notable field is behavioral economics.

[516] See *Table 1.2*.

[517] *ibid*. p. 28.

[518] See *Table 1.1*.

[519] Blyth, *Great Transformations*. p. 28.

[520] *ibid*. p. 28.

To put this in more concrete terms, consider Wisdom et al.'s findings from a systematic review in 2014 of the theories and constructs in innovation adoption: "The same leadership variable (i.e., CEO's influence, champions, opinion leaders etc.), managerial and organizational support for innovation, and prior experience in adoption, are positively associated with adoption according to nine theoretical frameworks"[521]. This black box process tells us nothing about why actors would adopt an innovation. One can argue that people in senior management roles are hired for particular expertise, so the organization has already decided to invest in experimenting with the innovation. However, one can also argue that people in senior management would only stay with the organization if they believed their expertise would be valued. The positive association tells us nothing about why change happened or how to intervene.

Mechanisms are models of the processes through which actors influence an outcome[522]. The emphasis on mechanisms means moving beyond systematic covariation between variables or events[523] – which suggests the existence of a relationship, and towards an explanation[524] of why such a relationship exist[525]. In 1998, Elster described two types of mechanisms where quantitative modeling struggles: (1) *type A mechanisms* when an independent variable can trigger one of multiple incompatible reactions (for example, when a fight/ flight/ freeze response is triggered); and (2) *type B mechanisms* when an independent variable triggers two or more reactions in opposite directions which results in an indeterminate net effect[526]. In 1998,

---

[521] Jennifer P. Wisdom et al., "Innovation Adoption: A Review of Theories and Constructs," *Administration and Policy in Mental Health and Mental Health Services Research* 41, no. 4 (July 2014): 480–502, https://doi.org/10.1007/s10488-013-0486-4. p. 484.

[522] Peter Hedström and Richard Swedberg, "Social Mechanisms: An Introductory Essay," in *Social Mechanisms: An Analytical Approach to Social Theory*, ed. Peter Hedström and Richard Swedberg, Studies in Rationality and Social Change (Cambridge : New York: Cambridge University Press, 1998), 1–31. p. 6.

[523] *ibid.* p. 7.

[524] Thomas C. Schelling, "Social Mechanisms and Social Dynamics," in *Social Mechanisms: An Analytical Approach to Social Theory*, ed. Peter Hedström and Richard Swedberg, Studies in Rationality and Social Change (Cambridge : New York: Cambridge University Press, 1998), 32–44. p. 36.

[525] Hedström and Swedberg, "Social Mechanisms: An Introductory Essay." p. 8.

[526] Jon Elster, "A Plea for Mechanisms," in *Social Mechanisms: An Analytical Approach to Social Theory*, ed. Peter Hedström and Richard Swedberg, Studies in Rationality and Social Change (Cambridge : New York: Cambridge University Press, 1998), 45–73. p. 46.

Hedström and Swedberg described four core principles of the mechanism approach[527]:

1. *Action*: actors rather than variables *act*, macro-level changes ought to be conceptualized in terms of macro-micro, micro-micro, and micro-macro transitions[528]
2. *Precision*: a limited range phenomenon that can be found in many places in society[529]
3. *Abstraction*: a sharp focus on the central issue and the removal of irrelevant factors[530]
4. *Reduction*: the explanation narrows the gap between input and output, cause and effect[531]

The four core principles contribute to systems knowledge and transformation knowledge. I supplement these with a fifth principle to recognize the role of target knowledge and implementation knowledge in TSR[532].

5. *Implementation*: the explanation provides meaningful information for future actors to design targeted initiatives

The mechanism approach raises the thorny issue of causality. How do researchers know the mechanism is useful i.e. can be found in many places in society (*precise*), if CAS are constantly changing and unpredictable? How do researchers make any claims to knowledge if there are *emergent behaviors* or *non-linear*[533] outcomes? In 2004, Hulswit noted since the 17th century, the notion of causality have been characterized by at least two distinct conceptions: the Aristotelian-scholastic conception which recognizes causes as the "*active initiators of a change*" [534] and the scientific conception which emphasizes the "*inactive nodes in a law-like implication chain*" [535] e.g. the law of gravity[536]. This publication addresses both conceptions of causality through TSR with the support of two theories. The two theories can be understood as model assumptions specific to, but not exclusive to, the contemporary global governance network.

---

[527] Hedström and Swedberg, "Social Mechanisms: An Introductory Essay." p. 24.
[528] *ibid.*
[529] *ibid.*
[530] *ibid.*
[531] *ibid.* p. 25.
[532] See *Table 1.7.*
[533] See *Table 1.1.*
[534] James A. Coffman, "On Causality in Nonlinear Complex Systems," in *Philosophy of Complex Systems* (Elsevier, 2011), 287–309, https://doi.org/10.1016/B978-0-444-52076-0.50010-9. p. 288.
[535] *ibid.*
[536] *ibid.*

The first supporting theory is the neo-institutionalist theory described earlier in this section: although the contemporary global governance network is dynamic, the overarching *system of systems*[537] and the corresponding costs to change levels of the hierarchy create temporary stability[538]. Also recall the definition of complexity: *complexity* lies at the edge of chaos. There is insufficient agreement and certainty, but not so much disagreement that the system is considered completely random or chaotic[539]. Through the focus on mechanisms, this section identifies "law-like" processes that are more impervious to change. The behavior of CAS is *tightly coupled*[540] with its external environment, and consequently the research is both context- and time-sensitive. Expert judgment and collaborative research processes from TSR contribute towards understanding the credibility, stability, and precision of mechanisms.

The second supporting theory is Dennett's intentional systems theory introduced in *Section 3.2.1*. The Aristotelian-scholastic conception of causality identifies four casual categories per Coffman in 2011: "material (substances), efficient (mechanisms), formal (circumstances), and final (needs)"[541]. Intentional systems theory is a contemporary counterpart, with the physical stance (substances), the design stance (mechanisms), and the intentional stance (needs). Contextual details is beyond the scope of this book due to time and page count constraints. This conception of causality posits that the constituent actor groups within the contemporary global governance network, the mechanisms that facilitate or constrain change, and the goals of the network *cause* the network's behavior[542].

---

[537] See *Table 1.1*.

[538] North, *Institutions, Institutional Change, and Economic Performance*. p. 83.

[539] Paul E Plsek and Trisha Greenhalgh, "Complexity Science: The Challenge of Complexity in Health Care," *BMJ* 323 (September 15, 2001). p. 627.

[540] See *Table 1.1*.

[541] Coffman, "On Causality in Nonlinear Complex Systems." p. 288.

[542] This section focuses on *process tracing* research, a within-case study method for tracing causal mechanisms and how they manifest in an actual case. There is established literature on the causality tests for process tracing, see: David Collier, "Understanding Process Tracing," *PS: Political Science & Politics* 44, no. 4 (October 2011): 823–30, https://doi.org/10.1017/S1049096511001429.

4.2.1 *Physical Stance*: Definitions and Roles of Actor Groups

This subsection introduces the five key actor groups within the model of global change mechanism in the global governance network. It is important to differentiate between the term *actors* or *actor groups* which refer specifically to entities within the model constructed in this chapter, and *stakeholders* which refer to all individuals, social groups, organizations, or actors, who possess an interest, a legal obligation, a moral right, or other concern in the decisions or outcomes of the 2030 Sustainable Development Goals. The five actor groups are: (1) state actors, (2) IOs, NGOs, INGOs, (3) academia and civil society organizations, (4) MNCs, as well as (5) entrepreneurs and social entrepreneurs. This model does not include an exhaustive list of actors because of overlapping roles. Instead, it seeks to identify representative categories. For example, micro-, small and medium enterprises (MSMEs) are vital to the 2030 Sustainable Development Goals, but their roles in effecting global change for a system-wide transformation are similar to those of entrepreneurs and social entrepreneurs. The selection of actor groups is informed by Transdisciplinary Systems Research (TSR) processes as well as relevant literature discussed in the next few sections[543]. *Table 4.1* defines the key actor groups in this publication's model of the contemporary global governance network, and *Table 4.2* describes their roles.

The most important takeaway from *Table 4.2* is that each of the key actor groups has the capacity to advance sustainable development. Within this model, each of the key actor groups plays a different role in the contemporary global governance network. However, these roles are not exclusive in real life. As Kell observed in 1999, the increasingly globalized world has "blurred the boundaries between states and societies, domestic regulation and international commerce, public and private sector"[544].

---

[543] See *Table 3.4*.
[544] Susan K. Sell, "Multinational Corporations as Agents of Change," in *Private Authority and International Affairs*, ed. A. Claire Cutler, Virginia Haufler, and Tony Porter (Albania: State University of New York Press, 1999). p. 171.

Table 4.1 Definitions of key actor groups in this publication's model of the contemporary global governance network

Actor Group	Definition
State Actors	*State actors* are entities that act on behalf of a government body.
IOs, NGOs, and INGOs	*International organizations (IOs)* are groups with membership from at least three states, having activities in several states, and whose members are held together by a formal agreement.
	Non-governmental organizations (NGOs) are groups of individuals or organizations, usually not affiliated with any government, that is formed to provide services or to advocate for particular public policies.
	International non-governmental organizations (INGOs) are nonprofit groups that operate in global politics in different issue areas, often with a mission to protect a specific vulnerable population, a particular common, or a collective good.
Academia and Civil Society Organizations	*Academia* is the environment or community pursuing research, education, and scholarship.
	Civil society organizations are volunteer or nonprofit groups that perform a variety of services and humanitarian functions, communicate citizens' concerns to governments, examine policies, and encourage participation at the community level.
MNCs	*Multinational corporations (MNCs)* and transnational corporations are often used interchangeably. This chapter opts for the more contemporary term MNCs.
	Transnational corporations (TNCs) are incorporated or unincorporated enterprises which features parent enterprises and their foreign affiliates. A *parent enterprise* is an enterprise that controls assets of other entities in countries other than its home country, usually by owing a certain equity capital stake. A *foreign affiliate* is an incorporated or unincorporated enterprise in which an investor, who is a resident in another economy, owns a stake that permits a lasting interest in the management of that enterprise (an equity

stake of 10% for an incorporated enterprise, or its equivalent for an unincorporated enterprise).

Entrepreneurs and Social Entrepreneurs	*Entrepreneurs* are people who organize, manage, and assume the risk of new ventures. This includes *business entrepreneurs* with the goal of generating profits, *policy entrepreneurs* with the goal of influencing policy outcomes, *institutional entrepreneurs* with the goal of creating new institutions or transforming existing ones, and *norm entrepreneurs* with the goal of changing social norms and shared standards.
	Social entrepreneurs are people who organize, manage, and assume the risk of new ventures with the goal of addressing social problems while generating profits.

Sources: Law Insider, "State Actor Definition," accessed June 6, 2023, https://www.lawinsider.com/dictionary/state-actor; Karen Mingst, "International Organization | Definition, History, & Facts," Britannica, April 13, 2023, https://www.britannica.com/topic/international-organization; Margaret P. Karns, "Nongovernmental Organization (NGO)," Britannica, May 3, 2023, https://www.britannica.com/topic/nongovernmental-organization; Valeria Bello, "International Nongovernmental Organizations," *Oxford Bibliographies*, 2012, https://doi.org/10.1093/obo/9780199743292-0051. Introduction; United Nations, "Higher Education Sustainability Initiative | Department of Economic and Social Affairs," accessed March 4, 2024, https://sdgs.un.org/HESI; United Nations, "About Us," United Nations Civil Society (United Nations), accessed March 4, 2024, https://www.un.org/en/civil-society/page/about-us; Brian Roach, "A Primer on Multinational Corporations," in *Leviathans: Multinational Corporations and the New Global History*, ed. Alfred D. Chandler, Jr. and Bruce Mazlish (Cambridge: Cambridge University Press, 2005), 19–44. p. 24; UNCTAD, "World Investment Report 2012: Methodological Note" (UNCTAD, 2012), https://unctad.org/system/files/official-document/WIR2012MethodologicalNote_en.pdf. p. 3; Daniel Costa, "Entrepreneurship | Definition, Historical Theorists, & Facts," Britannica Money, June 2, 2023, https://www.britannica.com/topic/entrepreneurship; United Nations, *World Youth Report 2020: Youth Social Entrepreneurship and the 2030 Agenda*, World Youth Report (UN, 2020), https://doi.org/10.18356/248b499b-en. p. 1.

Table 4.2 Roles of key actor groups in this publication's model of the contemporary global governance network

Actor Group	Roles
State Actors	States possess the greatest range of rights and obligations under international law. These are outlined in the *Montevideo Convention on Rights and Duties of States (1934)*.
IOs, NGOs, and INGOs	Abbott and Snidal in 2001, Cupitt, Whitlock, and Whitlock in 2001, and Gutner in 2017 suggest IOs: (a) act as representatives of states, (b) work as a vehicle for pooling activities, assets, or risks, (c) influence the capabilities and interests of state by promoting norms and practices among states, (d) transmit new ideas for international governance as epistemic communities, (e) provide a stable negotiating forum and allow a fast response to sudden developments, (f) overcome bargaining deadlocks by reducing transaction costs and improving information about preferences, (g) provide ad-hoc panels and more permanent institutions for dispute resolution, (h) issue legally blinding decisions with the consent of member states, (i) influence state behavior through agenda setting and compliance monitoring, and (j) try individuals accused of war crimes or crimes against humanity, promote reconciliation, and bring justice. NGOs and INGOs often work closely with IOs to effect global change. Spiro in 1998, Dai in 2013, Gutner in 2017 suggest NGOs and INGOs can: (a) legitimize human rights initiatives, suggest focal points for oppositional movements, and provide a forum for continuing mobilization of human rights activism, (b) indirectly provide support by disseminating advice and practices, or help define terms like human rights and refugees, and (c) engage in productive cross-border collaborations between NGOs. For example, an NGO in one state can foster political will by supplying information regarding abuses to an IO or NGO in another state and put pressure on domestic practices with the financial support of foundations.
Academia and Civil Society Organizations	The United Nations Department of Economic and Social Affairs (DESA) Higher Education Sustainability Initiative suggests academia can: (a) create a community of shared learning and facilitate knowledge transfer,

	(b) rethink criteria for assessment of performance, (c) support curricula updates and promote careers that support the Goals, and (d) align academic publishing with the Goals.
	The United Nations Civil Society Unit suggests civil society organizations can: (a) provide analysis and expertise, (b) serve as early warning mechanisms, (c) help monitor and implement international agreements, including Agenda 2030 and the Sustainable Development Goals, and (d) focus world attention on important issues facing humanity.
MNCs	In 2009, Wettstein described the growing influence of MNCs: an increasing number of people spend over 75% of their active time (time awake) under the direct rule and supervision of corporations. MNCs have access to resources unmatched by most other actor groups and subsequently shape formal and informal constraints through their operations. Dunning in 1997, Hall and Sassen in 2004, Jones in 2015, Wettstein in 2009 suggest MNCs can: (a) support the diffusion of management practices, values, and lifestyles through management consultancies, advertising agencies, hotels, and food companies, (b) influence academia due to the close connection between education and employment, and (c) pursue their interests through state structures.
Entrepreneurs and Social Entrepreneurs	UN resolutions recognized the role of entrepreneurship in A/Res/67/202 in 2012, A/Res/71/221 in 2016, and A/Res/73/225 in 2018. Entrepreneurs can: (a) improve social conditions and address environmental challenges through the introduction of new climate change mitigation and adaptation technologies and resilience measures, (b) prompt environmentally sustainable practices and consumption patterns, and (c) develop new technologies and innovative business models that enable high, sustained, inclusive and equitable economic growth while protecting workers' rights.
	UN resolutions recognized the role of social entrepreneurship in A/Res/71/221 in 2016, and A/Res/73/225 in 2018. Social entrepreneurs can create alternative sustainable models of (a) production, (b) finance and (c) consumption to respond to social, economic and environmental issues, while generating value.

Sources: Kenneth W. Abbott and Duncan Snidal, "Why States Act Through Formal International Organizations," in *The Politics of Global Governance: International Organizations in an Interdependent World*, ed. Paul F. Diehl, 2nd ed. (Boulder and London: Lynne Rienner Publishers, 2001). p. 32; Kenneth W. Abbott and Duncan Snidal, "Why States Act Through Formal International Organizations," in *The Politics of Global Governance: International Organizations in an Interdependent World*, ed. Paul F. Diehl, 2nd ed. (Boulder and London: Lynne Rienner Publishers, 2001), 9–43. p. 17, 19, 20, 24, 30, 31; Xinyuan Dai, "The 'Compliance Gap' and the Efficacy of International Human Rights Institutions," in *The Persistent Power of Human Rights: From Commitment to Compliance*, ed. Thomas Risse, Stephen C. Ropp, and Kathryn Sikkink (Cambridge: Cambridge University Press, 2013), 85–102. p. 97; Tamar Gutner, *International Organizations in World Politics* (Los Angeles and London: CQ Press, 2017). p. 46; Peter J. Spiro, "Nonstate Actors in Global Politics," *American Journal of International Law* 92, no. 4 (October 1998): 808–11, https://doi.org/10.2307/2998158. p. 809; Geoffrey Jones, "Multinationals from the 1930s to the 1980s," in *Leviathans: Multinational Corporations and the New Global History*, ed. Alfred D. Chandler, Jr. and Bruce Mazlish (Cambridge: Cambridge University Press, 2005), 81–104. p. 92-93; Florian Wettstein, *Multinational Corporations and Global Justice: Human Rights Obligations of a Quasi-Governmental Institution* (Stanford, California: Stanford Business Books, 2009). p. 214, 238; Saskia Sassen, "The State and Globalization," in *The Emergence of Private Authority in Global Governance*, ed. Rodney Bruce Hall and Thomas J. Biersteker, Cambridge Studies in International Relations (Cambridge and New York: Cambridge University Press, 2004), 91–114. p. 94; Rodney Bruce Hall and Thomas J. Biersteker, "Private Authority as Global Governance," in *The Emergence of Private Authority in Global Governance*, ed. Rodney Bruce Hall and Thomas J. Biersteker, Cambridge Studies in International Relations (Cambridge and New York: Cambridge University Press, 2004), 203–22. p. 203; John H. Dunning, *Alliance Capitalism and Global Business*, Routledge Studies in International Business and the World Economy (London and New York: Routledge, 1997). p. 171-173. United Nations, "Higher Education Sustainability Initiative | Department of Economic and Social Affairs," accessed March 4, 2024, https://sdgs.un.org/HESI; United Nations, "About Us," United Nations Civil Society (United Nations), accessed March 4, 2024, https://www.un.org/en/civil-society/page/about-us; Evangelia Petridou and Jörgen Sparf, "For Safety's Sake: The Strategies of Institutional Entrepreneurs and Bureaucratic Reforms in Swedish Crisis Management, 2001–2009," *Policy and Society* 36, no. 4 (October 2, 2017): 556–74, https://doi.org/10.1080/14494035.2017.1369677. p. 558-559.

4.2.2 *Intentional Stance*: Priorities

This component of the model identifies current priorities and concepts within the contemporary global governance that are gaining traction.

I.   *2030 Sustainable Development Goals*

"Transforming our world: the 2030 Agenda for Sustainable Development" (A/Res/70/1) outlines 17 Sustainable Development Goals and 169 targets. It "seek to build on the Millennium Development Goals and complete what they did not achieve [... and] to realize the human rights of all and to achieve gender equality and the empowerment of all women and girls"[545]. Please consult the Resolution for the complete list of goals and targets.

II.   *Annual UN Climate Change Conference (COP)*

UN Climate Change conferences (or COPs) take place every year and are the only multilateral decision-making forum on climate change, with almost complete membership of all countries. During the COP, delegates negotiate agreements to address the climate crisis, such as limiting global temperature rise to 1.5 degrees Celsius and helping vulnerable communities adapt to the effects of climate change[546].

III.   *2024 UN Summit of the Future multilateral solutions for a better tomorrow*

Following *Our Common Agenda* in 2021 by the Secretary-General, the General Assembly adopted resolution A/Res/76/307 in 2022. It "*Decides* that the Summit of the Future has an important role to play in reaffirming the Charter of the United Nations, reinvigorating multilateralism, boosting implementation of existing commitments, agreeing on concrete solutions to challenges and restoring trust among Member States"[547]

---

[545] A/Res/70/1, Preamble
[546] UNFCCC, "About COP 28 | UNFCCC," accessed March 16, 2024, https://unfccc.int/process-and-meetings/conferences/un-climate-change-conference-united-arab-emirates-nov/dec-2023/about-cop-28#Why-is-COP28-important.
[547] A/Res/76/307, ¶ 1

IV.   *Global Commons and Global Public Goods*

In 2021, *Our Common Agenda: Report of the Secretary-General* described global commons and global public goods:

- *Global commons* "usually refer to natural or cultural resources that are shared by and benefit us all"[548]. Four conventionally understood commons include "the high seas, the atmosphere, Antarctica and outer space"[549]
- *Public goods* "are understood as those goods and services provided to and benefiting all of society, which at the national level may include street lighting, [and] fire departments"[550]
- *Global public goods (GPGs)* are public goods that are "global in nature, in that they cannot be adequately provided by any one State acting alone, and they concern the welfare of humanity as a whole"[551] e.g. "global health, information, global economy, healthy planet, science, peace, digital, and more"[552]

In 2022, the High-level Advisory Board on Effective Multilateralism established by the Secretary-General described GPG principles:

- *Principle of universality*: "the difference between international (concerning relations between States) and global (without reference to States) suggests that GPGs should be about people rather than States [… and] they should be global across time and space, accounting for the benefits and risks of today's actions on people everywhere and everywhen"[553]
- *Principle of inclusion*: "inclusion can be the participation of smaller States in decision-making, a greater role for the private sector in some processes, and/or a set of processes to involve marginalized communities in a global process"[554]
- *Principle of equity*: "This can be described in access terms: [...] all people benefit from the eradication of polio. But it can also be described in terms of rights: all people have a right to breathable air"[555]

---

[548] António Guterres, *Our Common Agenda: Report of the Secretary-General* (United States: United Nations, 2021). p. 48.
[549] *ibid.*
[550] *ibid.*
[551] *ibid.* p. 48.
[552] *ibid.* p. 50.
[553] United Nations University Centre for Policy Research, "Framing Paper: Definitions, Principles and Objectives" (High-level Advisory Board on Effective Multilateralism (HLAB), 2022). p. 7.
[554] United Nations University Centre for Policy Research, "Framing Paper: Definitions, Principles and Objectives." p. 7.
[555] *ibid.*

4.2.3 *Design Stance*: Processes for Change

What are the processes to navigate and alter formal (i.e. laws and policies) and informal (i.e. cultural) constraints that limit sustainable development? This necessitates the introduction of the abstract notion of "an individual" i.e. a person within the global governance network. Examining processes for change solely at the level of groups and organizations without considering individuals would yield a circular analysis i.e. if smaller groups influence bigger groups, who influences smaller groups? Individuals from different actor groups will face different constraints and participate differently within the contemporary global governance network. By focusing on the mechanisms and the way various actor groups interact, this component of the model shows the means to navigate and alter constraints for individuals from different actor groups, to close the compliance gap and advance the 2030 Sustainable Development Goals.

I.   *Navigating and altering formal constraints*

This section focuses on Carpenter's macro-level norm-setting mechanism *across* the contemporary global governance network in 2014, and Steinsson's micro-level norm emergence mechanism *within* an organization in 2024.

Carpenter found that despite concerns raised in 2004 by the academic community over fully automated weapon "killer robots", no NGO had the item formally on the agenda until the President of the International Committee of the Red Cross (ICRC) acknowledged the problem in late 2011[556]. After the Human Rights Watch (HRW) published a report in 2012 calling for a ban, nine other human security organizations joined the steering committee for a new campaign, leading to the convening of thirty NGOs at a conference and a growing list of signatories[557]. Carpenter found the same norm-setting process in child soldiering, conflict diamonds, and landmines. Except when there is the support of a state actor or extreme sensitivity over the issue, such as allegations against the highest-level decision-making bodies, mainstream INGO's institutional power is almost always a pre-requisite[558]. The mechanism is shown in *Figure 4.1*.

---

[556] Charli Carpenter, *"Lost" Causes: Agenda Vetting in Global Issue Networks and the Shaping of Human Security* (Ithaca: Cornell University Press, 2014). p. 1.
[557] *ibid.* p. 2.
[558] *ibid.*

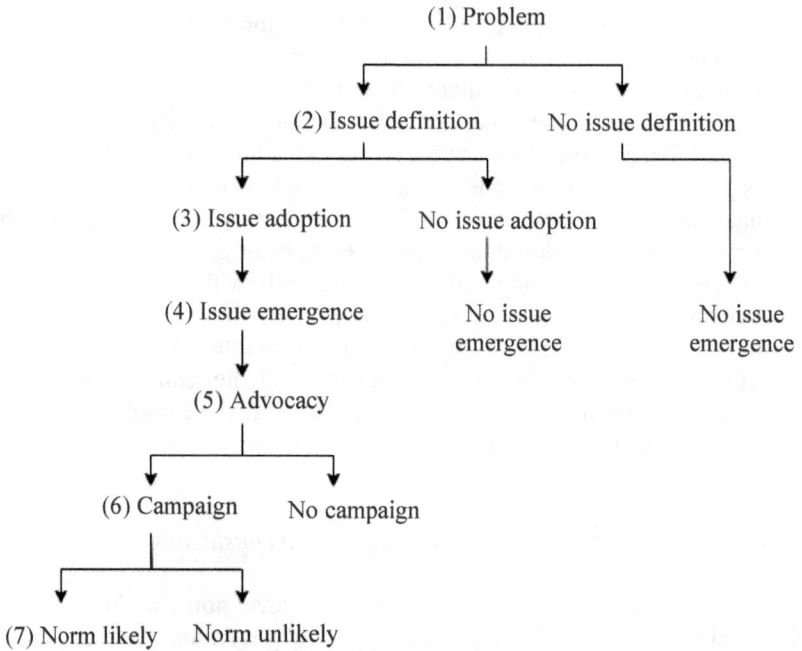

Figure 4.1 Norm-setting mechanism across the contemporary global governance network by Carpenter in 2014

1. First, a *problem* is identified by an individual or group. This is then escalated to a small NGO, or a research facility within an academic institution. The vetting process by institutions depends on not just the merits of the claim, but also the organization's network and ability. The organization has to ask whether it has the ability to realize the projects' goals.

2. The organization then initiates the *issue definition* process. This involves an iterative process of identifying responsible parties, demonstrating how a situation is not natural or accidental, and proposing solutions. In 2021, Hernández described the importance of *knowledge diplomacy* in transformation throughout the issue definition process[559]. This includes efforts to produce knowledge with non-academic stakeholders[560] and equitable access to knowledge resources[561].

3. *Issue emergence* occurs when a leading INGO within the issue cluster incorporates the issue into their official agenda. These major players have the largest budgets, the greatest name recognition, the most access, and the densest network. These gatekeepers, though small in comparison to the state actors they wish to influence, can offer or deny institutional power, and their denial can significantly compromise rights-based claims.

4. *Advocacy* by a leading INGO involves signaling their concern to stakeholders, smaller NGOs, and state actors. This will then trigger donor attention as well as material resources and increase the visibility of the issue further. Coordination of specialized expertise also occurs at this stage.

5. *Campaigns* to create new norms are initiated at this stage with other non-state actors.

6. If successful, this results in *norm setting* at the highest-level decision-making bodies domestically such as the Supreme Court, or internationally such as the United Nations Environment Assembly. State actors are heavily involved in these decision-making bodies.

---

[559] Ariel Macaspac Hernández, *Taming the Big Green Elephant: Setting the Motion for Transformation towards Sustainability*, Globale Gesellschaft Und Internationale Beziehungen (Wiesbaden: Springer VS. Springer Fachmedien Wiesbaden GmbH, 2021). p. 18.
[560] *ibid.* p. 90.
[561] *ibid.* p. 87-88.

Steinsson's norm-emergence mechanism within an organization complements Carpenter's norm-setting mechanism across the contemporary global governance network. Steinsson's mechanism is shown in *Figure 4.2*. It is derived from a study on the gradual reinterpretation of the Neutral Point of View (NPOV) guideline in English Wikipedia across 63 representative articles[562]. It involves four steps:

1. The necessarily ambiguous nature of institutional rules and norms creates spaces for multiple interpretations and disputes
2. A small group of actors begins to apply new interpretations as a result of the rule ambiguity
3. The new interpretation is validated in some way, which alters the balance of power
4. Frequent application and adoption of the new interpretation shape organizational norms and transform the institution[563]

In the case of the NPOV guideline, the reinterpretation of the rule led to exits by people who supported the original interpretation, and the population loss led to significant endogenous institutional change[564].

The mechanisms described by Carpenter and Steinsson demonstrate the events necessary for long term changes to occur, but *how* might an individual push for norms that can close the compliance gap and advance the 2030 Sustainable Development Goals? What can individuals do to increase their chances of success? Brysk in 2013 described the importance of "mobilizing political will to transform the power structures that are the source of abuse or neglect"[565]. *Table 4.3* considers the different types of power in the contemporary global governance network.

---

[562] Steinsson, "Rule Ambiguity, Institutional Clashes, and Population Loss." p. 235-236.
[563] *ibid.* p. 237-238.
[564] *ibid.* p. 235.
[565] Alison Brysk, *Speaking Rights to Power: Constructing Political Will* (Oxford: Oxford University Press, 2013). p. 1.

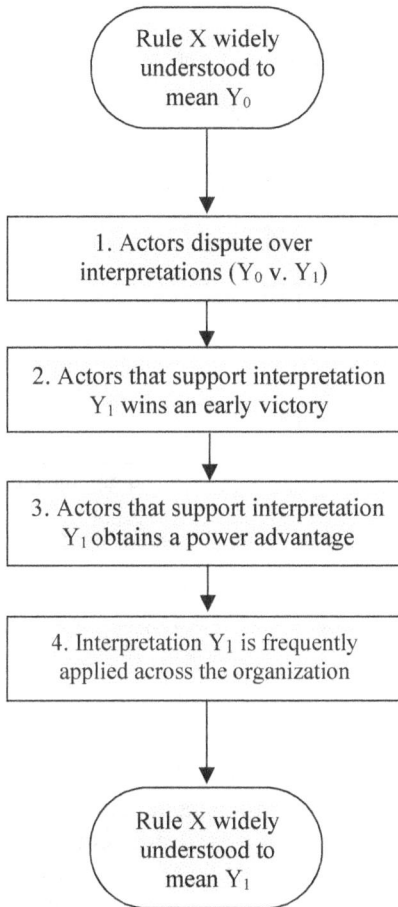

Figure 4.2 Norm-emergence mechanism within an organization by Steinsson in 2024

Table 4.3 Types of power in the contemporary global governance network

Type of Power	Definition (Exert influence through…)
Physical	Use of or threats to use physical force
Economic	Use of material resources such as money or goods
Structural	Use of the actor's position in the structures of society
Institutional	Use of rules and decision-making procedures
Moral	Use of rights-based claims and claims of justice
Expert	Use of credibility
Discursive	Use of language and communication
Network	Use of personal relationships

Source: Moon, Suerie. "Power in Global Governance: An Expanded Typology from Global Health." *Globalization and Health* 15, no. 1 (November 2019): 1–9. https://doi.org/10.1186/s12992-019-0515-5. p. 5-7.

While an individual who flags out an injustice possesses different degrees of expert, discursive, moral, and network power, the increasing demands for economic and structural power as demonstrated by Carpenter's model in *Figure 4.1* mean one *must* organize to respond to existing power structures fully[566]. *Organizing* involves "creating the conditions for that coming together" [567]. There is a minimum threshold that has to be met to differentiate between an organization and people occupying the same physical or digital space. From a social psychology point of view, a *group* has some foundation for a collective bond that is meaningful to the individual members e.g. a shared common experience or characteristic[568].

---

[566] Nunes, *Neither Vertical nor Horizontal: A Theory of Political Organisation*. p. 37.
[567] *ibid.* p. 20.
[568] Van Bavel, Jay J., and Dominic J. Packer. *The Power of Us.* New York: Little, Brown Spark, 2021. p. 14.

In 2021, Nunes' study of the Occupy movement revealed the challenges of "horizontal" and "leaderless" mass mobilizations during the advocacy and campaigning stages[569]. Horizontal mobilizations tend to demand a large amount of time and energy with little progress, fail to pivot or scale when pressures increase, and collapse in on themselves as they run out of steam[570]. He argued that some form of leadership is necessary despite historical trauma associated with different power structures[571] — while concrete action proposals can be bids for control, no movement has ever fully corresponded to "the myth of a multitude of unconnected individuals joining together all at once, like a crowd in a musical magically breaking into song" [572]. Ultimately, the degree of organization has to be proportional to the ambition of the movement[573].

II.   *Navigating and altering informal constraints*

In 1996, Melucci offered insights on *movements*: a fragmented phenomenon that contains a multitude of differentiated meanings with different historical roots, forms of action, and modes of organization[574]. These often consume a large part of their energies to bind such differences together[575]. Individuals in movements draw from *culture as repertoires*, which offers them various perspectives and courses of action to navigate different situations[576]. Movements are not merely an aggregation of individuals[577], but rather the outcome of a complex process of negotiation between individual and collective identities, contradictory pressures, as well as changing environments[578]. They signal a transformation in the logic and processes that guide society, give shape to an emerging force[579], and challenge the legitimacy of power[580].

---

[569] See *Figure 4.1*.
[570] Nunes, *Neither Vertical nor Horizontal: A Theory of Political Organisation*. p. 1.
[571] *ibid*. p. 37.
[572] *ibid*. p. 122.
[573] *ibid*.
[574] Alberto Melucci, *Challenging Codes: Collective Action in the Information Age* (Cambridge: Cambridge University Press, 1996). p. 5.
[575] *ibid*. p. 13.
[576] Lamont and Small, "How Culture Matters: Enriching Our Understanding of Poverty." p. 82.
[577] Melucci, *Challenging Codes: Collective Action in the Information Age*. p. 18.
[578] *ibid*. p. 75.
[579] *ibid*. p. 1.
[580] *ibid*. p. 30.

If movements consume such large amounts of energy to come together and start out highly dependent on reciprocity[581], how can one emerge? Melucci argued that it is the group's collective identity that ensures the continuity and permanence of the movement [582]. A *collective identity* is a process through which individuals interact to create a shared sense of identity[583]. This is created through *culture as symbolic boundaries*, which provide conceptual distinctions between objects, people, and practices[584]. There are three conditions for a *collective identity*[585]:

1. The legitimate and justifiable limits of the group with respect to its social environment.
2. Some regulation on group membership with conditions for joining: a group without a boundary would not be differentiable from the social environment.
3. A criteria by which its members recognize themselves and are recognized e.g. through names, symbols, motifs, colors, and logos.

One of the ways to enable a *collective identity* to emerge is to organize around a well-researched and well-articulated theory of change. A robust theory of change leads to better coordination and more opportunities for evaluation[586]. Burchett et al. in 2024 defined a *theory of change* as a theory that describes the causal mechanisms at work, and sets out how the guidance offered may lead to a shared goal[587]. It can also be understood as a summary of the work product produced in the issue definition stage. Blyth in 2011 described this more broadly as *ideas*. They provide actors with an interpretive framework to explain the cause and urgency of a problem, suggest preferred initiatives[588], challenge existing institutions, and serve as a blueprint for their replacements[589]. Ideas mobilize *culture as narratives* which people use

[581] Nunes, *Neither Vertical nor Horizontal: A Theory of Political Organisation*. p. 128.
[582] Melucci, *Challenging Codes: Collective Action in the Information Age*. p. 75.
[583] Angie Andriot and Timothy J. Owens, "Identity," obo, accessed March 12, 2024, https://www.oxfordbibliographies.com/display/document/obo-9780199756384/obo-9780199756384-0025.xml.
[584] Lamont and Small, "How Culture Matters: Enriching Our Understanding of Poverty." p. 85.
[585] *ibid*. p. 75.
[586] Melucci, *Challenging Codes: Collective Action in the Information Age*. p. 75.
[587] Helen Elizabeth Denise Burchett et al., "Developing a Theory of Change – the Importance of Rich Process Data and Authors' Insights into Context, Implementation and Mechanisms," *Global Health Promotion*, March 4, 2024, 17579759241232387, https://doi.org/10.1177/17579759241232387. p. 1.
[588] Blyth, *Great Transformations*. p. 11; also see *Table 1.2*.
[589] *ibid*. p. 259.

to make sense of their lives[590], and *culture as cultural capital*, social assets through which individuals and groups distinguish themselves from others[591]. Consistent with Steinsson's mechanism, Nunes found that small victories and partial reforms in line with the theory of change "act as proof of concept for activists and supporters, intensify collective enthusiasm, and create steppingstones towards higher objectives"[592].

This is not to say that a collective identity will appear just by having an idea or a theory of change. *Collective identity* and consequent *collective actions* are the outcomes of "complex processes of interaction mediated by certain networks of belonging"[593]. These include partnerships, hidden networks, meeting points, and organizations supporting a similar cause[594]. Though connected by the circulation of information and personnel, individuals and networks operate entirely independently of the movement until brief moments of collective mobilization, before they "submerge again in the fabric of daily life"[595]. There are two main implications to Melucci's observations. First, it is important to create the physical or digital space for organizing and engagement. Second, movements that are compatible with and inseparable from members' personal identities outside of the movement are more likely to succeed[596].

Empirical research by Tajfel in 1974 clarified the relationship between collective identity and collective action. Specifically, he found that research subjects *categorize*: they simplify the social environment by grouping individuals in ways that are meaningful to the subject, bringing together other individuals and events that align with the subject's actions, attitudes, and system of belief[597]. Through *culture as frames*, individuals develop normative conceptions about what is good and bad, as well as cognitive conceptions about what is perceived as

---

[590] Lamont and Small, "How Culture Matters: Enriching Our Understanding of Poverty."' p. 84.
[591] *ibid*. p. 86.
[592] Nunes, *Neither Vertical nor Horizontal: A Theory of Political Organisation*. p. 221.
[593] Melucci, *Challenging Codes: Collective Action in the Information Age*. p. 18.
[594] *ibid*. p. 18.
[595] *ibid*. p. 115.
[596] *ibid*.
[597] Tajfel, Henri. "Social Identity and Intergroup Behaviour." *Social Science Information* 13, no. 2 (April 1974): 65–93. https://doi.org/10.1177/053901847401300204. p. 69.

real[598]. Social identity and social reality are subsequently developed based on the knowledge of the group or groups they belong to and the emotional significance attached to their membership[599]. Individuals, wanting to achieve a satisfactory concept or image, would advance the interests of the group, even when they derive no direct benefit[600]. Research by Van Zomeren, Postmes, and Spears in 2008 found that *injustice*, "group-based inequality or deprivation"[601], catalyzes collective action.

Over time, collective identity and actions *become* the unified empirical actor that can be understood as a *social movement*[602]. Collective actors gradually develop familiarity with the organizational structure and the capacity to resolve challenges in an increasingly hostile environment[603]. Redundant roles in the early stages counteract possible defections and provide access as well as network density[604]. The organizational structure is then streamlined as the demands of the movement and individual commitment become clearer, slowly crystallizing into an organizational form with a system of rules and leadership relationship[605]. This system of rules and leadership functions still exist in decentralized organizations or horizontal organizational structures: rather than being fixed, the role circulates and is never fully stabilized[606]. These relationships, however, will be subjected to contradictory pressures as the movement matures[607]. The original group can restructure around a new direction, divide into smaller groups, or breakdown as a result of irreconcilable differences[608].

---

[598] Lamont and Small, "How Culture Matters: Enriching Our Understanding of Poverty." p. 80.

[599] *ibid.*

[600] Tajfel, Henri. "Social Identity and Intergroup Behaviour." *Social Science Information* 13, no. 2 (April 1974): 65–93. https://doi.org/10.1177/053901847401300204. p. 69.

[601] Van Zomeren, Martijn, Tom Postmes, and Russell Spears. "Toward an Integrative Social Identity Model of Collective Action: A Quantitative Research Synthesis of Three Socio-Psychological Perspectives." *Psychological Bulletin* 134 (August 1, 2008): 504–35. https://doi.org/10.1037/0033-2909.134.4.504. p. 506.

[602] Melucci, *Challenging Codes: Collective Action in the Information Age*. p. 75.

[603] *ibid.* p. 75.

[604] *ibid.* p. 114.

[605] *ibid.* p. 72.

[606] Nunes, *Neither Vertical nor Horizontal: A Theory of Political Organisation*. p. 180.

[607] Melucci, *Challenging Codes: Collective Action in the Information Age*. p. 75.

[608] *ibid.* p. 75.

While setting new norms for powerful actors e.g. state actors, IOs, or MNCs, to advance the 2030 Sustainable Development Goals may seem distant, it is possible. In the past two decades, non-state actors, particularly norm-setting International Organizations (IOs), have been understood as both a *stage* or a proxy of powerful states, and *actors* in their own right[609]. Scholars using a state-centric method of analysis have focused on how non-state actors extend the power of states and their inability to exert influence over state behavior[610]: Even though IOs have relative autonomy, they may use it to reinforce existing power instead of challenging it[611]. Other scholars have argued that IOs can become "intended and accidental agents of inclusion and empowerment"[612] since states and non-state actors are only willing to support IO activities so far as they are perceived to be legitimate[613].

There are ways to intervene MNCs behavior as well. Current conceptions of modern corporations as the ultimate rational actors driven by profits alone fail to capture their complexity[614]. Scholarship points to a much wider range of motivating factors such as (a) market share, (b) funding, (c) risk management, (d) reputation, (e) organizational learning, and (f) values-based concerns[615]. Haufler in 2010 argued that while corporations can respond to new demands by stonewalling, campaigns to impose direct costs on undesirable behavior by state and non-state actors have been successful at influencing corporations[616]. Initiatives can be designed to address corporation's motivating factors. For example, by prompting shifts in consumer behavior (loss of market share), leading shifts in investor priorities with increased risk awareness (loss of funding)[617], and offering incentives for acquiring sustainable development knowledge (gains in organizational learning).

---

[609] Tamar Gutner, *International Organizations in World Politics* (Los Angeles and London: CQ Press, 2017). p. 48.

[610] Spiro, "Nonstate Actors in Global Politics." p. 809.

[611] Michael Barnett and Raymond Duvall, "International Organization and the Diffusion of Power," in *International Organization and Global Governance*, ed. Thomas G. Weiss and Rorden Wilkinson (Abingdon and New York: Routledge, 2014). p. 50.

[612] *ibid.* p. 48.

[613] Barnett and Duvall, "International Organization and the Diffusion of Power." p. 50.

[614] *ibid.* p. 106.

[615] *ibid.*

[616] Virginia Haufler, "Corporations in Zones of Conflict: Issues, Actors, and Institutions," in *Who Governs the Globe*, ed. Deborah D. Avant, Martha Finnemore, and Susan K. Sell, Cambridge Studies in International Relations (Cambridge and New York: Cambridge University Press, 2010), 102–30. p. 113.

[617] *ibid.*

For people who are skeptical of an individual's ability to effect change at a global scale, Brysk's remark in 2013 offers some reassurance: if "campaigns and appeals were purely symbolic, or meaningless modernist myths, or false consciousness, abusive regimes worldwide would not work so hard to ban, subvert, and contest them"[618]. While each of the key actor groups plays different roles in institutional change, this component of the model highlights some commonalities: (1) the importance of organizing to change formal constraints, and (2) the possibility of altering informal constraints by mobilizing culture as symbolic boundaries, frames, narratives, repertoires, and cultural capital.

4.2.4 Implications on Closing the Compliance Gap and Advancing the 2030 Sustainable Development Goals

As MNC's motivating factors show, the boundary between formal and informal constraints is more nuanced in practice. Emerging literature from sociolegal studies describes law and culture as *co-constitutive* i.e. law is both constituted by and being constituted by culture[619]. One interpretation is to view constraints from law and culture as a spectrum with two distinct ends. For example, values-based concerns would appear to lie more towards the cultural end of the spectrum. Another interpretation, however, is to see them as entangled[620] i.e. culture as law and law as culture. For example, culture gives rise to *frames* and *narratives* around social identity, but they can also be shaped by laws. Some collective identities gain legitimacy through legal processes or are actively shaped by the legal arguments that are considered legitimate[621]. More broadly, law provides a *repertoire* for the collective political imagination and

---

[618] Brysk, *Speaking Rights to Power: Constructing Political Will.* p. 7.
[619] Mezey, "Law As Culture." p. 46-47.
[620] Amanda Perry-Kessaris, "Making the 'Constitutive Idea' Empirically, Conceptually and Normatively Available Through Sociolegal Design," *SSRN Electronic Journal*, 2023, https://doi.org/10.2139/ssrn.4498328. p. 1.
[621] Abigail C. Saguy and Forrest Stuart, "Culture and Law: Beyond a Paradigm of Cause and Effect," *The ANNALS of the American Academy of Political and Social Science* 619, no. 1 (September 2008): 149–64, https://doi.org/10.1177/0002716208320458. p. 154.

defines concepts such as civil rights or civic duty[622]. These interpretations highlight the importance of informal constraints.

Box 1-2 described global diplomacy as a set of topics that converge around *interactions*. The synthesis in this chapter shows the importance of interactions to the emergence of informal constraints — they allow stakeholders to contest norms' interpretations and adapt new meanings. Two types of interactions are of particular importance:

1. *Focused social interactions* at a micro-level: dialogue with a mutual focus of attention, and a mutual appreciation of each other as unique individuals beyond social roles[623]. This is in contrast to *social attention* (i.e. one-way interaction, colloquially known as "people watching") and *unfocused social interactions* (i.e. two-way, role-based interactions such as purchasing a ticket at a ticket booth)[624].

2. *Sustained and iterative engagements* at a micro-macro-level: repeated dialogue between organizations and stakeholders that demonstrate *reciprocity* (i.e. responsiveness to feedback), which is a condition for knowledge co-creation[625].

The importance of interaction to the emergence of informal constraints, have profound implications on closing the compliance gap and advancing the 2030 Sustainable Development Goals. While the idea of formal and informal constraints come intuitively at a national level, the lack of enforcement mechanisms for formal constraints at a global level means the global governance network *depends* on strong informal constraints to function. Common arguments for culture at a global level, such as creativity, diversity, and heritage, fail to take into account the significance of culture as the means to facilitate commitment to international agreements. In this sense, culture ought to be considered a global public good alongside digital and information. Herein lies the challenge: the Goals seek to influence individual and group behavior at a global level, but current

---

[622] Hajar Yazdiha, "The Relationality of Law and Culture: Dominant Approaches and New Directions for Cultural Sociologists," *Sociology Compass* 11, no. 12 (December 2017): e12545, https://doi.org/10.1111/soc4.12545. p. 3.

[623] Jeffrey A Hall, "When Is Social Media Use Social Interaction? Defining Mediated Social Interaction," *New Media & Society* 20, no. 1 (January 2018): 162–79, https://doi.org/10.1177/1461444816660782. p. 163-164.

[624] *ibid*.

[625] Kim A. Johnston and Anne B. Lane, "Communication with Intent: A Typology of Communicative Interaction in Engagement," *Public Relations Review* 47, no. 1 (March 2021): 101925, https://doi.org/10.1016/j.pubrev.2020.101925. p. 6.

infrastructure does not even allow effective communication with those whose priority they seek to influence. The United Nations, which seeks to coordinate action across the contemporary global governance network, is designed to communicate with governments and not with individuals[626]. Certainly, the prevailing approach to issue imperatives[627] *as if* there were enforcement mechanisms to support formal constraints has to be rethought.

Consequently, what is necessary to close the compliance gap is not only communication infrastructure, but culture as infrastructure. *Culture as infrastructure* describes the culture and cultural organizations that allow stakeholders to contest norms' interpretations and adapt informal constraints in line with the goals of the global community given the absence of enforcement mechanisms at a global level for formal constraints (i.e. laws and policies). To be clear, this publication is *not* recommending centralization. The operationally and managerially independent parts that make up the global governance network[628] provide highly desirable checks and balances. What it is recommending, however, are global initiatives that empower individuals to participate in building this infrastructure. This is discussed in *Chapter 6*.

---

[626] See *Section 5.1.5.*
[627] See *Section 1.2.3.*
[628] See *Section 1.2.1.*

4.3 Reflection on Transdisciplinary Systems Research (TSR)

This chapter was perhaps the most challenging to write, because Transdisciplinary Systems Research (TSR) imposes stringent constraints. In an ideal case, there would be a change mechanism for each actor group, but this is an area with limited literature and limited data at a global scale. TSR compensates for this limitation by validating these mechanisms through collaborative research processes. *Chapter 5*, the next chapter, has informed the contents of this chapter, but I have structured them separately for readability. Concepts from Transdisciplinary Systems Research (TSR) have been embedded within this chapter. *Table 4.4* reflects on this chapter with reference to the common elements of contemporary systems thinking.

Table 4.4 Reflection on systems thinking in *Chapter 4*

Element	Reflection
1. Recognizing interconnections	*Section 4.2.3* covered this aspect by considering the mechanisms through which actors interact.
2. Identifying and understanding feedback	*Section 4.2.3* discussed the mechanisms through which actors interact and provide feedback to each other. However, there is limited literature on the amplifying or dampening effects of feedback loops within actor groups in the contemporary global governance network.
3. Understanding system structure	*Section 4.2.3* addressed this aspect.
4. Identifying and understanding non-linear relationships	The mechanisms in *Section 4.2.3* identified critical junctures that are vital to change within the contemporary global governance network.
5. Understanding dynamic behavior	The overarching system of systems and the corresponding costs to change levels of the hierarchy create temporary stability. *Section 4.2.3* identified "law-like" processes that are more impervious to change.
6. Reducing complexity by modelling systems conceptually	*Section 4.3* presented a model of change processes.
7. Understanding systems at different scales	*Section 4.2.3* described two mechanisms, one for norm emergence within a network of actor groups across the contemporary global governance network, and one for norm emergence within an organization.
8. Understanding goals, priorities, and intentions	*Sections 4.2.1* and *4.2.2* considered this aspect.

Note: see description of elements in *Table 1.4*.

4.4 References

Abbott, Kenneth W., and Duncan Snidal. "Why States Act Through Formal International Organizations." In *The Politics of Global Governance: International Organizations in an Interdependent World*, edited by Paul F. Diehl, 2nd ed., 9–43. Boulder and London: Lynne Rienner Publishers, 2001.

Academic Council on the United Nations System. "Global Governance Journal." Accessed May 4, 2023. https://acuns.org/global-governance-journal/.

Andriot, Angie, and Timothy J. Owens. "Identity." obo. Accessed March 12, 2024. https://www.oxfordbibliographies.com/display/document/obo-9780199756384/obo-9780199756384-0025.xml.

Barnett, Michael, and Raymond Duvall. "International Organization and the Diffusion of Power." In *International Organization and Global Governance*, edited by Thomas G. Weiss and Rorden Wilkinson. Abingdon and New York: Routledge, 2014.

Bell, Duncan. "Realism | Definition, Theories, Examples, Problems, & Facts." Britannica. Accessed May 7, 2023. https://www.britannica.com/topic/realism-political-and-social-science.

Blyth, Mark. *Great Transformations: Economic Ideas and Institutional Change in the Twentieth Century*. 8. pr. Cambridge: Cambridge Univ. Press, 2011.

Brysk, Alison. *Speaking Rights to Power: Constructing Political Will*. Oxford: Oxford University Press, 2013.

Burchett, Helen Elizabeth Denise, Rebecca S. French, Sally Griffin, Málica De Melo, Joelma Joaquim Picardo, and Dylan Kneale. "Developing a Theory of Change – the Importance of Rich Process Data and Authors' Insights into Context, Implementation and Mechanisms." *Global Health Promotion*, March 4, 2024, 17579759241232387. https://doi.org/10.1177/17579759241232387.

Campbell, John L. *Institutional Change and Globalization*. Princeton, NJ: Princeton Univ. Press, 2004.

Carpenter, Charli. *"Lost" Causes: Agenda Vetting in Global Issue Networks and the Shaping of Human Security*. Ithaca: Cornell University Press, 2014.

Central Commission for the Navigation of the Rhine. "Introduction." Accessed May 3, 2023. https://www.ccr-zkr.org/11010100-en.html.

Coffman, James A. "On Causality in Nonlinear Complex Systems." In *Philosophy of Complex Systems*, 287–309. Elsevier, 2011. https://doi.org/10.1016/B978-0-444-52076-0.50010-9.

Collier, David. "Understanding Process Tracing." *PS: Political Science & Politics* 44, no. 4 (October 2011): 823–30. https://doi.org/10.1017/S1049096511001429.

Costa, Daniel. "Entrepreneurship | Definition, Historical Theorists, & Facts." Britannica Money, June 2, 2023. https://www.britannica.com/topic/entrepreneurship.

Dai, Xinyuan. "The 'Compliance Gap' and the Efficacy of International Human Rights Institutions." In *The Persistent Power of Human Rights: From Commitment to Compliance*, edited by Thomas Risse, Stephen C. Ropp, and Kathryn Sikkink, 85–102. Cambridge: Cambridge University Press, 2013.

Domínguez, Roberto, and Rafael Velázquez Flores. "Global Governance." In *Oxford Research Encyclopedia of International Studies*, by Roberto Domínguez and Rafael Velázquez Flores. Oxford University Press, 2018. https://doi.org/10.1093/acrefore/9780190846626.013.508.

———. "Global Governance." In *Oxford Research Encyclopedia of International Studies*, by Roberto Domínguez and Rafael Velázquez Flores. Oxford University Press, 2018. https://doi.org/10.1093/acrefore/9780190846626.013.508.

Dunning, John H. *Alliance Capitalism and Global Business*. Routledge Studies in International Business and the World Economy. London and New York: Routledge, 1997.

Elster, Jon. "A Plea for Mechanisms." In *Social Mechanisms: An Analytical Approach to Social Theory*, edited by Peter Hedström and Richard Swedberg, 45–73. Studies in Rationality and Social Change. Cambridge : New York: Cambridge University Press, 1998.

Fomerand, Jacques, Cecelia M. Lynch, and Karen Mingst. "United Nations (UN) | Definition, History, Founders, Flag, & Facts." Britannica, May 4, 2023. https://www.britannica.com/topic/United-Nations.

Guterres, António. *Our Common Agenda: Report of the Secretary-General*. United States: United Nations, 2021.

Gutner, Tamar. *International Organizations in World Politics*. Los Angeles and London: CQ Press, 2017.

Hall, Jeffrey A. "When Is Social Media Use Social Interaction? Defining Mediated Social Interaction." *New Media & Society* 20, no. 1 (January 2018): 162–79. https://doi.org/10.1177/1461444816660782.

Hall, Rodney Bruce, and Thomas J. Biersteker. "Private Authority as Global Governance." In *The Emergence of Private Authority in Global Governance*, edited by Rodney Bruce Hall and Thomas J. Biersteker, 203–22. Cambridge Studies in International Relations. Cambridge and New York: Cambridge University Press, 2004.

———. "The Emergence of Private Authority in the International System." In *The Emergence of Private Authority in Global*

Governance, edited by Rodney Bruce Hall and Thomas J. Biersteker. Cambridge Studies in International Relations. Cambridge and New York: Cambridge University Press, 2004.

Haufler, Virginia. "Corporations in Zones of Conflict: Issues, Actors, and Institutions." In *Who Governs the Globe*, edited by Deborah D. Avant, Martha Finnemore, and Susan K. Sell, 102–30. Cambridge Studies in International Relations. Cambridge and New York: Cambridge University Press, 2010.

Hedström, Peter, and Richard Swedberg. "Social Mechanisms: An Introductory Essay." In *Social Mechanisms: An Analytical Approach to Social Theory*, edited by Peter Hedström and Richard Swedberg, 1–31. Studies in Rationality and Social Change. Cambridge : New York: Cambridge University Press, 1998.

Held, David, and Mathais Koenig-Archibugi. "Introduction." In *Global Governance and Public Accountability*, edited by David Held and Mathais Koenig-Archibugi. Massachusetts and Oxford: Blackwell Publishing, 2005.

Hernández, Ariel Macaspac. *Taming the Big Green Elephant: Setting the Motion for Transformation towards Sustainability*. Globale Gesellschaft Und Internationale Beziehungen. Wiesbaden: Springer VS. Springer Fachmedien Wiesbaden GmbH, 2021.

Hewson, Martin, and Timothy J. Sinclair. "The Emergence of Global Governance Theory." In *Approaches to Global Governance Theory*, edited by Martin Hewson and Timothy J. Sinclair, 3–22. Albany: State University of New York Press, 1999.

Hoffmann, Matthew J., and Alice D. Ba. "Introduction: Coherence and Contestation." In *Contending Perspectives on Global Governance: Coherence, Contestation and World Order*, edited by Alice D. Ba and Matthew J. Hoffmann, 1–14. London and New York: Routledge, 2005.

International Bureau of Weights and Measures. "Governance." Accessed May 3, 2023. https://www.bipm.org/en/governance.

International Telegraph Union. "History." ITU. Accessed May 3, 2023. https://www.itu.int:443/en/about/Pages/history.aspx.

Johnston, Kim A., and Anne B. Lane. "Communication with Intent: A Typology of Communicative Interaction in Engagement." *Public Relations Review* 47, no. 1 (March 2021): 101925. https://doi.org/10.1016/j.pubrev.2020.101925.

Jones, Geoffrey. "Multinationals from the 1930s to the 1980s." In *Leviathans: Multinational Corporations and the New Global History*, edited by Alfred D. Chandler, Jr. and Bruce Mazlish, 81–104. Cambridge: Cambridge University Press, 2005.

Karns, Margaret P. "Nongovernmental Organization (NGO)." Britannica, May 3, 2023. https://www.britannica.com/topic/nongovernmental-organization.

Lamont, Michèle, and Mario Luis Small. "How Culture Matters: Enriching Our Understanding of Poverty." In *The Colors of Poverty: Why Racial and Ethnic Disparities Persist*, edited by Ann Chih Lin and David R. Harris. The National Poverty Center Series on Poverty and Public Policy. New York: Russell Sage Foundation, 2010.

Law Insider. "State Actor Definition." Accessed June 6, 2023. https://www.lawinsider.com/dictionary/state-actor.

Melucci, Alberto. *Challenging Codes: Collective Action in the Information Age*. Cambridge: Cambridge University Press, 1996.

Mezey, Naomi. "Law As Culture." *Georgetown Law Faculty Publications and Other Works*, 2001. http://scholarship.law.georgetown.edu/facpub/317/.

Mingst, Karen. "International Organization | Definition, History, & Facts." Britannica, April 13, 2023. https://www.britannica.com/topic/international-organization.

Moon, Suerie. "Power in Global Governance: An Expanded Typology from Global Health." *Globalization and Health* 15, no. S1 (November 2019): 74. https://doi.org/10.1186/s12992-019-0515-5.

Moury, Catherine, and Mafalda Escada. "Understanding Successful Policy Innovation: The Case of Portuguese Drug Policy." *Addiction* 118, no. 5 (May 2023): 967–78. https://doi.org/10.1111/add.16099.

Nations, United. "Decolonization." United Nations. United Nations. Accessed May 4, 2023. https://www.un.org/en/global-issues/decolonization.

North, Douglass C. *Institutions, Institutional Change, and Economic Performance*. The Political Economy of Institutions and Decisions. Cambridge ; New York: Cambridge University Press, 1990.

Nunes, Rodrigo. *Neither Vertical nor Horizontal: A Theory of Political Organisation*. London and New York: Verso, 2021.

Oxford Reference. "Historical Determinism." Oxford Reference. Accessed November 17, 2021. https://doi.org/10.1093/oi/authority.20110803095938705.

Patterson, James, Douwe L. De Voogt, and Rodolfo Sapiains. "Beyond Inputs and Outputs: Process-oriented Explanation of Institutional Change in Climate Adaptation Governance." *Environmental Policy and Governance* 29, no. 5 (September 2019): 360–75. https://doi.org/10.1002/eet.1865.

Perry-Kessaris, Amanda. "Making the 'Constitutive Idea' Empirically, Conceptually and Normatively Available Through Sociolegal Design." *SSRN Electronic Journal*, 2023. https://doi.org/10.2139/ssrn.4498328.

Petridou, Evangelia, and Jörgen Sparf. "For Safety's Sake: The Strategies of Institutional Entrepreneurs and Bureaucratic Reforms in Swedish Crisis Management, 2001–2009." *Policy and Society* 36, no. 4 (October 2, 2017): 556–74. https://doi.org/10.1080/14494035.2017.1369677.

Plsek, Paul E, and Trisha Greenhalgh. "Complexity Science: The Challenge of Complexity in Health Care." *BMJ* 323 (September 15, 2001).

Roach, Brian. "A Primer on Multinational Corporations." In *Leviathans: Multinational Corporations and the New Global History*, edited by Alfred D. Chandler, Jr. and Bruce Mazlish, 19–44. Cambridge: Cambridge University Press, 2005.

Rosenau, James N. *Distant Proximities: Dynamics Beyond Globalization.* Princeton and Oxford: Princeton University Press, 2003.

———. "Governance, Order, and Change in World Politics." In *Governance without Government: Order and Change in World Politics*, edited by James N. Rosenau and Ernst-Otto Czempiel, 1–29. Cambridge Studies in International Relations. Cambridge and New York: Cambridge University Press, 1992.

Saguy, Abigail C., and Forrest Stuart. "Culture and Law: Beyond a Paradigm of Cause and Effect." *The ANNALS of the American Academy of Political and Social Science* 619, no. 1 (September 2008): 149–64. https://doi.org/10.1177/0002716208320458.

Sassen, Saskia. "The State and Globalization." In *The Emergence of Private Authority in Global Governance*, edited by Rodney Bruce Hall and Thomas J. Biersteker, 91–114. Cambridge Studies in International Relations. Cambridge and New York: Cambridge University Press, 2004.

Schelling, Thomas C. "Social Mechanisms and Social Dynamics." In *Social Mechanisms: An Analytical Approach to Social Theory*, edited by Peter Hedström and Richard Swedberg, 32–44. Studies in Rationality and Social Change. Cambridge : New York: Cambridge University Press, 1998.

Sell, Susan K. "Multinational Corporations as Agents of Change." In *Private Authority and International Affairs*, edited by A. Claire Cutler, Virginia Haufler, and Tony Porter. Albania: State University of New York Press, 1999.

Sergeyev, Yuriy. "Sergeyev's Letter," November 24, 2021.

Spiro, Peter J. "Nonstate Actors in Global Politics." *American Journal of International Law* 92, no. 4 (October 1998): 808–11. https://doi.org/10.2307/2998158.

Steinsson, Sverrir. "Rule Ambiguity, Institutional Clashes, and Population Loss: How Wikipedia Became the Last Good Place on the Internet." *American Political Science Review* 118, no. 1 (February 2024): 235–51. https://doi.org/10.1017/S0003055423000138.

Strange, Susan. *States and Markets.* New York: Basil Blackwell, 1988.

———. *The Retreat of the State: The Diffusion of Power in the World Economy.* Cambridge Studies in International Relations. Cambridge and New York: Cambridge University Press, 1996.

Tajfel, Henri. "Social Identity and Intergroup Behaviour." *Social Science Information* 13, no. 2 (April 1974): 65–93. https://doi.org/10.1177/053901847401300204.

UNCTAD. "World Investment Report 2012: Methodological Note." UNCTAD, 2012. https://unctad.org/system/files/official-document/WIR2012MethodologicalNote_en.pdf.

UNFCCC. "About COP 28 | UNFCCC." Accessed March 16, 2024. https://unfccc.int/process-and-meetings/conferences/un-climate-change-conference-united-arab-emirates-nov/dec-2023/about-cop-28#Why-is-COP28-important.

United Nations. "About Us." United Nations Civil Society. United Nations. Accessed March 4, 2024. https://www.un.org/en/civil-society/page/about-us.

———. "Higher Education Sustainability Initiative | Department of Economic and Social Affairs." Accessed March 4, 2024. https://sdgs.un.org/HESI.

———. "Predecessor: The League of Nations." United Nations. United Nations. Accessed May 3, 2023. https://www.un.org/en/about-us/history-of-the-un/predecessor.

———. "UN Charter." United Nations. United Nations. Accessed May 4, 2023. https://www.un.org/en/about-us/un-charter.

———. *World Youth Report 2020: Youth Social Entrepreneurship and the 2030 Agenda*. World Youth Report. UN, 2020. https://doi.org/10.18356/248b499b-en.

United Nations University Centre for Policy Research. "Framing Paper: Definitions, Principles and Objectives." High-level Advisory Board on Effective Multilateralism (HLAB), 2022.

Universal Postal Union. "About." Accessed May 3, 2023. https://www.upu.int/en/Universal-Postal-Union.

Van Bavel, Jay J., and Dominic J. Packer. *The Power of Us*. New York: Little, Brown Spark, 2021.

Van Zomeren, Martijn, Tom Postmes, and Russell Spears. "Toward an Integrative Social Identity Model of Collective Action: A Quantitative Research Synthesis of Three Socio-Psychological Perspectives." *Psychological Bulletin* 134, no. 4 (July 2008): 504–35. https://doi.org/10.1037/0033-2909.134.4.504.

Vinson, Alexandra H. "Culture as Infrastructure in Learning Health Systems." *Learning Health Systems* 5, no. 3 (July 2021): e10267. https://doi.org/10.1002/lrh2.10267.

Weiss, Thomas G., and Rorden Wilkinson. "Global Governance to the Rescue: Saving International Relations?" *Global Governance: A Review of Multilateralism and International Organizations* 20, no. 1 (August 19, 2014): 19–36. https://doi.org/10.1163/19426720-02001003.

Wettstein, Florian. *Multinational Corporations and Global Justice: Human Rights Obligations of a Quasi-Governmental Institution.* Stanford, California: Stanford Business Books, 2009.

Wisdom, Jennifer P., Ka Ho Brian Chor, Kimberly E. Hoagwood, and Sarah M. Horwitz. "Innovation Adoption: A Review of Theories and Constructs." *Administration and Policy in Mental Health and Mental Health Services Research* 41, no. 4 (July 2014): 480–502. https://doi.org/10.1007/s10488-013-0486-4.

Yazdiha, Hajar. "The Relationality of Law and Culture: Dominant Approaches and New Directions for Cultural Sociologists." *Sociology Compass* 11, no. 12 (December 2017): e12545. https://doi.org/10.1111/soc4.12545.

5

Global Stakeholder Consultation Process

5.0 Outline

Chapter 5 considers emerging perspectives on the 2030 Sustainable Development Goals as part of target knowledge in Transdisciplinary Systems Research (TSR). It presents documentation from the public access Global Stakeholder Consultation Process coordinated through the Center for Global Agenda (CGA) at Unbuilt Labs. *Section 5.1* contains the Future of Global Governance Series Proceedings. *Section 5.2* contains featured statements from a wide range of stakeholders who submitted a written statement in response to a draft framework. The final iteration of the framework has been included in *Section 6.2*. Together, *Sections 5.1* and *5.2* present diverse perspectives on system-wide transformation methods to close the compliance gap and advance the 2030 Sustainable Development Goals. *Section 5.3* summarizes and reflects on the Global Stakeholder Consultation process.

5.1 Center for Global Agenda (CGA) at Unbuilt Labs Future of Global Governance Series Proceedings with Excerpts

5.1.1 *Workshop*: Nature and Natural Objects as Actors in Everyday Lives

I. *Abstract*

自然をつくる国日本 (Japan: Nation Building Nature) and the Center for Global Agenda (CGA) at Unbuilt Labs co-hosted a workshop to examine our relationship with nature and natural objects. This has profound implications for sustainable development and global governance in the age of climate crises. How might we reimagine historic narratives around the conquest of nature and the consumption of natural resources? What are the agentic contributions of natural objects like forests, oceans, and rivers, to our everyday lives? How might it affect our attitudes towards environmental personhood, the idea that natural objects should be holders of legal rights and have legally recognized worth and dignity? How might we manifest the desire to coexist with nature?

This 2-part workshop invited participants to use practice-based research, in particular photo-elicitation, as a tool to record and investigate nature and natural objects as actors in our everyday lives. What socio-political and personal meanings do we attribute to nature? How might our expertise and lived experience affect our interpretation of each other's artifacts? We welcomed everyone — artists, academics, students, and private as well as public sector actors, to join us in reconceptualizing nature and natural objects.

Part 1: 13 August 2022, 9am-10:30am Eastern Time (Online, Zoom)

The first part of the workshop began with a presentation by Joachim Nijs based on his research in *Japan: Nation Building Nature* (nai010 Publishers, 2021), in which he showed how idealized images of nature in Japan are to a certain extent modern productions. He demonstrated that the Japanese views of nature also take shape in a concrete reality, reflecting – and responding to – demands of daily life. He drew on literature from the arts, politics, and science, to show the ways in which Japan's earthquake ecology, monsoon ecology, post-nuclear ecology, and island ecology have made an observable impact on the urban environment. In so doing, Joachim revealed how the conception of nature impacts our socio-political realities, and provided a conceptual framework for analyzing images.

We then opened the floor to guest speakers Julien Isoré (Alan Tod, forest artist) and Peggy Cyphers (Professor of Painting, Pratt Institute). We also provided a brief introduction to digital photography for the everyday person so that public participants could engage in their own explorations. We asked participants to upload their photographs together with one or two paragraphs describing their findings to the Public Forum for the Recommended UN Action Plan to Close the Compliance Gap (CCG) on the SDG16 Hub, a portal hosted by the UNDP Oslo Governance Centre, before Part 2 of the workshop in a week.

Part 2: 20 August 2022, 9am-10:30am Eastern Time (Online, Zoom)

The second part of the workshop presented an opportunity for participants to share and discuss their photographs in the form of a studio discussion. We sought to gather participants from different continents and all walks of life. We strongly recommended historically underrepresented people and communities to participate in the process.

II.   *Highlights*

- To deliver a longer term impact on nature-related initiatives, it is important to go beyond "more greenery" and introduce thoughtful cultural practices as well. Simultaneously, with the rise of eco-distress and eco-anxiety, great care has to be taken when communicating and introducing nature-related cultural practices to avoid extreme behaviors.
- There is greater disaster preparedness in areas that have historically been prone to earthquakes, and to different degrees "an earthquake culture" where earthquake preparedness and readiness are integrated into local culture. This includes risk-aware building practices, art, legends, rites and rituals, narratives of survivors, poems, as well as

disaster education and training. Given the drastic changes in climate we expect to see in the near future, it is vital to engage the culture industry and develop adaptive practices. These practices demand active effort, building, and long-term commitment.

- We currently attribute value to man-made objects with limited appreciation for wildlife itself. This is unhelpful to the cause of preserving nature. In certain cultures, natural forests are considered monuments and vital cultural property. We have to re-examine ways to advocate for the cultural value of nature to create the desire to co-exist with nature, both at a grass-roots level such as social media advocacy, and at a policy level.
- The toxicity of art materials and waste generated in the process of creating cultural products, whether at art schools or in industries, would benefit from further investigation. It is important to research and develop materials as well as practices that are more sustainable.

III.   *Participants*

- Amparo Elisa Rojas Ramirez (Project Leader, SIU Ventures Miami part of SIU at Educative Group San Ignacio de Loyola – Peru)
- Arthur Wandzel (Founder, Delta Capture)
- Cathleen Zeippen (Individual)
- Dr. Swati Bute (Associate Professor, Jagran Lakecity University, Bhopal-India)
- James Romberger (Artist and Professor, School of Visual Arts)
- Lee Cherry (NC State University College of Design)
- Louise O'Boyle (Associate Dean (Academic Quality & Student Experience), Ulster University)
- Nabiha Miskini (Chief Service, National Institute of Statistics)
- Rashida Atthar (Educationist, NGOs and Institutes)
- Sarah Johnson (PhD Candidate, Kingston School of Art)

We are also pleased to receive an expert statement from Peter Kennard, Professor of Political Arts, Royal College of Art (RCA). The statement is available in *Section 5.2.7.*

5.1.2 *Global Consortium for Systems Research (GCSR) Keynote*: System Science, Jim Hall, FREng (Professor of Climate and Environmental Risks; Director of Research, School of Geography and the Environment, University of Oxford)

I.   Abstract

Session at UN General Assembly Science Summit (SSUNGA77) co-convened by the Center for Global Agenda (CGA) at Unbuilt Labs on the 29ᵗʰ of September 2022.

The Global Consortium for Systems Research (GCSR) announced the GCSR 2022-2023 10ᵗʰ Anniversary Strategic Plan during the session including the new mandate "We study, forecast, and guide systems change to solve grand challenges". GCSR invited Jim Hall, FREng to deliver a keynote presentation on system science.

II.   *Excerpts from Keynote Presentation*

Excerpts have been edited for clarity.

Jim Hall, FREng (Professor of Climate and Environmental Risks and Director of Research at the School of Geography and the Environment at the University of Oxford):

JH: Hello, Marvin. Hello, colleagues. It is a great pleasure and an honour to be here this afternoon, this afternoon in England at least and to say a few words on this topic of systems, and in particular, how systems analysis are applied or not applied in policy and government settings.

JH: Let me just begin with a few words about what is understood by a system: a focus on systems means a focus on interactions — not dwelling obsessively from a reductive point of view at the individual entities and seeking to understand them in all of their detail, but instead looking at how the entities within the system interact with one another, and how those interactions then lead to and help to explain the things that we observe. The properties we observe at a macro scale (emergent properties through complex interactions) in many different ways shape the world in which we are living. The biggest problems we face are system problems.

JH: If we think about climate change, for example, we recognize vast numbers of interactions, both leading to carbon emissions and emissions of other greenhouse gases, but also how the Earth system responds to those carbon emissions with interactions between the Earth's surfaces, ecosystems, the oceans, the atmosphere, and the cryosphere. In a sense, climate is an emergent property of those interactions. If we look at energy (which is the greatest contributor to carbon emissions) to understand how we are going to get carbon emissions down based on how we produce and use energy, we need to understand energy as a system. So what are the sources of energy (the majority of them being hydrocarbons at the moment), and how do those sources transform? For example, how is gas turned into electricity in gas turbines; what is the demand for or use of energy?

JH: In order to understand the energy crisis we face at the moment, we have to understand the position of Russia and the countries which consume fossil fuels produced in Russia, how those interact with each other spatially, or what the effect of the shock of conflict on that system ends up being. If we are going to decarbonize the power system, that requires a system view as well. For example, why would we be interested in hydrogen? If you are going to use it to heat your house, it does not make much sense at all. One has to electrolyze water to create hydrogen, pump hydrogen around, and then burn it again in your house — it would make much more sense just to heat your house with electricity. But if one understands all of the multiple potential uses of hydrogen not just for heating, but as an energy storage medium — as a means of propulsion in ships and possibly aeroplanes, as an industrial feedstock for a number of industries which are difficult to decarbonise, like the steel industry; if you put that system together, then you begin to understand the motivation for why hydrogen is such an interesting product. And it is only by understanding things as a system that you can make that case.

JH: Let me just say a few brief words about the 2030 Sustainable Development Goals because, in many senses, they are a system par excellence. I am not saying they are perfect, but they are in a sense the best we have of a complete description of what the world collectively has said that it wants. It is that attempt at completeness that I really love about the 2030 SDGs and all of their flaws. But then as soon as we begin thinking about the implementation of the

2030 SDGs, again, we begin to see a whole host of interactions that these individual goals and targets cannot be attacked on their own. Indeed we have plenty of opportunities to do multiple beneficial things at the same time by adopting strategies that span across the 2030 SDGs, and tackling those points of leverage, those points of system intervention where we might have the opportunity for the most benefit.

JH: So how does all of that then play into the role of government? The short answer there would be to say with difficulty that governments all over the world struggle with coordination problems. They are created as hierarchies. Of course, everywhere has a leader of some shape or form and from that cascades a hierarchy and almost inevitably a series of silos. Governments inevitably struggle with systems challenges and the response, which is coordination across government is something I think it would be true to say every government struggles with.

JH: The first thing I would say about that is not to agonize too much because this is a challenge that every government faces and is addressing more or less imperfectly. The second thing is that if you can address a problem in a silo then why not? That is by far the easiest way to do it. Give your silo a target and tell that silo to get on with it, and so in that way, if we can narrow down the number of truly cross cutting issues that we are dealing with, then that makes the challenge of government a bit easier. The third point to make is that if interdependences are inevitable, and they are, of course, then there are ways in which we can appeal to self-organization whilst having some sense of problem ownership. I think that is needed. But sometimes there is a kind of knee-jerk reaction when a cross cutting problem is identified to create another cabinet committee with another minister in charge of it, and those things usually run out of steam and then end up getting abolished. Whereas if people can be empowered to self-organize their systems problems, maybe they are more enduring. The fourth point to make, and this is in the sense, a classic systems remark is be open to learning an adaptation. Recognize that mistakes are going to be made and create structures which can monitor, understand what is going on, learn from that monitoring, and can adapt very quickly. In many governments across the world, the COVID pandemic forced government to learn and to adapt and to create new ways of working incredibly rapidly and on many occasions incredibly creatively.

JH: Actually, I have just been at a government committee meeting today, and many of the officials there the night before had been at a big celebration of party. Really, covid related parties have gotten a bad reputation in this country, but this was an official one in which the civil service had brought together hundreds of civil servants who had worked incredibly hard to adapt and change the way in which they work in order to manage the covid crises. One of the points of discussion is well what can we learn from this? What can we build in, from the way in which we did adapt in order to address systems problems in a better way in the future? But I think there is also another sense from that gathering: we do not want to do this again very soon and unfortunately we seem to be living in a world where dramatic shocks are happening very frequently because following covid we now have an energy crisis and accompanying cost of living crisis right away across the world. But amongst this we have to really put a premium value on stability because a lot of things that I am talking about are extremely difficult to achieve during turmoil. So this is a question of balancing that lesson to make mistakes, learn, adapt, and sprint from time to time with a need to value stability within systems.

JH: I am conscious of time, but I just wanted to make two more remarks. One is on the role of system models in their broader sense, and that includes computer models. There are many domains in which one would not embark upon a water resource management plan or an energy system decarbonization without a model. These days one has to be cautious about the role of models. But what do they do? The first thing is that even though they are all wrong, they give a sense of proportion, they tell you how things add up and that is really important. They provide a boundary around which different actors within the system ideally can congregate and develop a shared understanding of that system to explore possible futures and scenard — not to predict the future — I do not think that is possible but to explore the future and to understand sensitivities and intervention points.

JH: The final point I want to make, however, is around alienation versus participation. A lot of what I am talking about either turns people off or they find it completely inaccessible or both. Part of my research program has been around developing so called system of systems model but I have been told very firmly that the terminology system of systems just does not work for policymakers. Members of the general public for the most part have not got a clue what it is getting at. We have to be extremely careful about elitism in this context. Think very carefully about how we can make that type of discourse accessible. I think a big part of that is around the articulation of purpose and creating narratives around how systems can achieve that purpose for people. And that, I think, is about the best we can do.

5.1.3 *Venture Strategy Group (VSG) at Unbuilt Labs Presentations*: Innovators in Residence (IIR) program

I.   *Abstract*

Session at UN General Assembly Science Summit (SSUNGA77) co-convened by the Center for Global Agenda (CGA) at Unbuilt Labs on the 29th of September 2022.

The Venture Strategy Group (VSG) at Unbuilt Labs launched the Innovators in Residence (IIR) pilot program between 2021 and 2022 where founders looking to set up solutions-oriented research organizations to solve grand challenges receive 1 year of support through monthly 1:1 advising sessions.

VSG invited two of the IIRs to present their findings on emerging issues. We are pleased to welcome Dennis Larsen and Shady El Damaty, Ph.D.

II.   Excerpts from Presentations

Excerpts have been edited for clarity.

Dennis Larsen (Co-Founder and Director, Initiative for Global Sustainable Economies (IGSE); University Lecturer, BI Norwegian Business School)

Presentation 1: Initiative for Global Sustainable Economies (IGSE)

DL: The Initiative for Global Sustainable Economies (IGSE) was developed out of the foundational concept that we have to make more informed business and political decisions with a stronger awareness of long termism and not only the current needs of society and stakeholders, but also future stakeholder, societal, planetary, and ecological needs. I think back to the Norwegian previous Prime Minister, Gro Harlem Brundtland, who was part of the United Nations. Of course, the Brundtland Commission was named after her, and she was one of the godmothers of sustainability, if you will. The Brundtland Commission defines sustainability as meeting the needs of the present without compromising the ability of future generations to meet their own needs. This is what we have to start to embrace and embody in our economic modeling and in our business and political decision-making. I want to bring to life five overarching points that led us to focus on this initiative. I will end with a bit of detail around the initiatives that we are looking at exploring.

DL: We see changes in the field of economics. We have to re-explore what economics is becoming and how it can inform better decision-making. We see increased polarization, populism, and short termism in decision making, which can be seen to be halting progress towards more sustainable and circular economic systems. We are also starting to see increased fatigue in concepts such as ESG, kind of overused terms — we have heard about green washing. We see a bit of fatigue setting in around the concepts in the political and media discourse. We also see that reporting standards are evolving both internationally as well as from an EU and even the SEC, looking more at how companies should be reporting on climate impacts, but also other ESG material issues that can have both positive and negative impacts on true sustainable business models.

Finally, we see increased anti-greenwashing activism on the part of NGOs. Some business leaders are shirking away from taking bold action and indeed are being more careful in their claims, given the potential counterreaction that they will be facing.

DL: Economics is changing as a field of study, as a field of science, but also as a concept. We are moving much more towards circularity, regenerative economics, donut economics, organic, more systems approaches. When I studied economics back in the 90s there was this concept of a homo economicus like this rational all-knowing being that governs all the economic models and decision making course — an impossible concept. We are starting to see in the field of economics more infusion of sociology, psychology, more of the empathy and emotional concepts as well, as well as an understanding that there are boundaries, upward boundaries in terms of what the climate can hold, that need to be factored into economic decision making.

DL: Second, we have seen enhanced or increased polarization over the last few years. We started studying this from a language and communication perspective to see what some of the terms and concepts are that can better frame the discussion around environmental recycling and global warming as opposed to the phrase "climate change". We did some research in the United States and started looking at what would work to bridge the divide politically and socially to foster a common purpose and attention on this extremely important topic. We found some interesting results. Highlights here include moving towards concepts such as reuse, repurpose, recycle, focusing on a future environment for all as opposed to the term climate change, which can in itself be polarizing. We are looking at how learnings from this research program apply globally as well.

DL: Third, as I mentioned, ESG fatigue. We are seeing reporting from international news media being a little bit more cynical in the last quarter or so. Investment in ESG funds have dropped significantly, a near 60% drop in Q1 of this year compared to last year. Fatigue is setting in both from the financial markets perspective where we had a positive ripple effect initially when Larry Fink heralded a new age of companies being forced or at least expected to focus much more on purpose and on sustainability, and moving from shareholder to stakeholder capitalism. But we are now seeing a bit of a pendulum shift towards the other side again towards short termism and financial capitalism and not paying enough attention to longer term negative externalities and impacts on societies.

DL: Regulations change and we want to be part of this dialogue. There are currently consultations underway in the EU with the Corporate Reporting Sustainable Reporting Directive. The European Sustainable Reporting Standards (ESRS) which are entering into force, are expected to standardize how companies of a certain size report on issues that are deemed to be material not only in terms of how they would impact the companies, but also how they would impact society. The concept of double materiality is gaining traction, which offers great opportunities for companies to not only pick up the issues that are going to be most impactful to their future operating successes, but also to start to communicate in a better and more standardized way to their stakeholders how they are having a positive impact on important sustainability issues.

Shady El Damaty, Ph.D. (President, Opsci; Co-Founder, Holonym)

Presentation 2: OpSci Society – Infrastructure for Distributed Research Coordination

SED: My name is Shady El Damaty, Ph.D. I am a neuroscientist, and over the past year, Marvin has been watching our decentralized science movement. Today I will be speaking about the infrastructure we have been building for distributed research coordination, which is a very historically challenging problem. I want you to try putting yourself in the shoes of an undergraduate. They have a background in neuroscience and they might know a family member who has been diagnosed with Alzheimer's. They decide: "hey, I am going to go to grad school and research this, and perhaps have some impact since this is so close to me". If you load up the widest reaching search engine for academic knowledge, artifacts, and dimensions of AI, and put in a search term like amyloid beta oligomers, or perhaps just Alzheimer's disease, you are going to be completely overwhelmed with search results. It is very difficult to figure out where to get started and what an actual source of truth is. So it is quite clear that we have tons of knowledge out there. But how much knowledge actually exists, and where can we identify that wisdom?

SED: I believe it has been validated over time that better coordination mechanisms are necessary to manage this information overload.

Journals have been exceptionally important in the past for curating and helping us wade through information. They sit in the middle of this cycle between funders and knowledge creators, where scientists are generating knowledge and submitting that to journals for dissemination by other scientists. All the while the journals are collecting metrics to see which scientists are working together, which ones are publishing together — perhaps they are collecting other metrics like impact metrics or h-indices that tell us a little bit about how scientists are using each others' works. So an important part of the publication process is the scientists themselves: they are outsourced labor for the journals, and they peer review each others' works; they sit on the advisory boards and editorial boards. You have a closed loop cycle where research evaluation relies on journals that produce metrics driven by business models, based on knowledge curation done by experts that are not reimbursed or perhaps recognized for that work. This system has worked for about half century. It has been in existence, but it is far from perfect.

SED: In 2006, the crystal structure of the amyloid beta star 56 protein was allegedly identified as a great target for drugs to address or treat cognitive decline associated with early onset Alzheimer's. Rodent models have proposed that dementia-like symptoms seem to be related to the presence of this protein in large amounts from the brain. The team behind this basically accelerated into academic stardom and started receiving millions and millions of dollars in grants to further explore this drug and collect data that could be used for clinical trials and the creation of new medicines. The PI behind this drug, Sylvain Lesné — his h-index is absolutely through the roof because of the results of this work. But it was not until just about the last couple of months that the data that was underlying AB 56, or amyloid beta 56 likely includes falsified data.

SED: So you have to ask yourself, is the h-index really tracking the impact that we seek to see in the product of scientific research? How could it be that millions and millions of dollars of taxpayer funding is channeled directly into falsified or non reproducible science? If you dig up the numbers and see what the reproducibility rates are for scientific findings, they are pretty dismal. About 10% of data collected by publicly funded research or taxpayer funded research in the US is published alongside the papers, and over 70% of researchers across fields have trouble replicating these results — it is not just a neuroscience thing — it is also across fields such as physics and psychology. I think the lack of data and lack of coordination are to blame there.

SED: We can ask some follow-up questions. What does a scientific society configured around open science practice, data-sharing, the sharing of research findings, and collaboratively working towards actual impact look like? How do we create systems with mechanisms that drive behavior towards specific objectives such as reproducible practice or training? We asked this question to about 700 members of our community and they consider these conditions critical to open science and reproducible research whether it is for researchers at an institution as independent discoverers, independent investigators, or in industry roles. Number one: time and time again it is low hassle funding. That is followed really closely by recognition and compensation for scientists' contributions whether it is working for a journal or working in a lab, or other types of collaborations. The last two that kind of really stuck out to us are the need for global community collaboration and connection. Scientists often feel very isolated and siloed in the work that they do. It is important that they are able to tap into the wealth of data that is being generated.

5.1.4 *CGA Panel Discussion*: Engaging Young Leaders — 2030 Sustainable Development Goals, Climate Literacy, and Education

I. *Abstract*

Session at UN General Assembly Science Summit (SSUNGA77) co-convened by the Center for Global Agenda (CGA) at Unbuilt Labs on the 29ᵗʰ of September 2022.

We are pleased to engage panelists on the subject of the 2030 Sustainable Development Goals, Climate Literacy, and Education.

II.   *Excerpts from Panel Discussion and Q&A*

Excerpts have been edited for clarity.

Inez Harker-Schuch, Ph.D. (Co-founder, The Planet Academy; Researcher and Environmental Scientist):

IHS: Systems thinking allows us to — as we have the SDGs, put the SDGs into a concept that we can understand and interpret. We can also interpret them regionally, culturally, internationally, nationally, and in all these different ways. I think that is very important: this idea of how we see ourselves, because climate and sustainable issues of climate change is different for everybody. Someone who is living, let us say, in America you call them hurricanes, elsewhere they are called cyclones. In these areas, cyclones and hurricanes have a social dimension and they are associated with climate change. But for people in Europe, there is no association with that whatsoever. In fact, they do not realize that cyclones and hurricanes are some of the worst environmental disasters that we will experience as their frequency and magnitude increase.

IHS: I have had some major inroads on climate literacy and engaging young leaders during my career, looking at how we communicate sustainability issues. Very frequently, instead of actually looking at the system itself, we have been looking at fear appeals and we have been looking at impacts — we have been trying to get people emotional about the issue, and then we have been very upset when they have reacted emotionally to this problem. The communication efforts have all included these very strong emotive responses — we are all going to die. In almost every media outlet when they are portraying climate change, they are talking about a hopeless future. How could that possibly motivate young people to become engaged with the issue of climate change when they have the basic response to fight or flight?

IHS: One of the things we have to do is remove the fear from the climate literacy area and put more of a rationale into that. We have to explain the climate problem as a system and not just discuss the impacts, but also discuss the physical mechanisms that describe it before we start thinking about anthropogenic change. When I think about education, which has been a constant theme throughout here, I think about the idea of democratizing knowledge. We assume that knowledge is shared equally and we assume that democracy is somehow something we have in our civil society that everybody has access to. But democracy only takes place when we all have information to the same quality of education. If we do not have the same access, we do not have the same rights as citizens in order to express ourselves or vote or make decisions. That is one of the underlying things for all of the different topics at the session today.

Lowell Clare, MA, MLA (Independent Researcher):

LC: I took some notes — something that I underlined is how important it is to democratize visions of the future and how important it is to create opportunities for people from diverse backgrounds to be able to imagine themselves or place themselves in the future. Because when we talk about educating people and bringing more stakeholders into the process of organized global climate action, it is not just about capturing the attention of people in the present, it is about capturing and channeling their empathy for people in the future. A really great way to do that is by bringing futures literacy or bringing future thinking into the classroom and even into the professional sphere. But really, my background as a designer has taught me how important it is to be able to show people what you are talking about. A lot of what you do as a designer — you show people the future because most people are not able to see something that does not exist yet. So when we talk about how to empower not just students, but people generally — and to get them to engage with some very complicated, very big picture thinking that addresses topics at enormous scales that most people are just not comfortable thinking in or dealing with – pictures, infographics, visualizations diagrams, these are all tools that can really help us to broaden the conversation. It is not just creating those images and showing them to people, but bringing as many people from around the world as possible into the generation of those images. Because it is so important that everybody, everybody has the opportunity to see themselves in the future.

5.1.5 *CGA Panel Discussion*: Health Policy, Research Infrastructure, and Health for All

I.   *Abstract*

Session at UN General Assembly Science Summit (SSUNGA77) co-convened by the Center for Global Agenda (CGA) at Unbuilt Labs on the 29th of September 2022.

We are delighted to welcome an esteemed panel to discusses topics including (1) data privacy, (2) engagement with civil society, and (3) the future of clinical research.

II.   *Excerpts from Panel Discussion and Q&A*

Excerpts have been edited for clarity.

Steve MacFeely (Director of Data and Analytics, World Health Organization (WHO))[629]

SM: I am coming to you from Paris. In fact, I am just leaving a meeting at UNESCO, where we are talking about these very issues. From a World Health Organization perspective (WHO), obviously, we deal with a lot of sensitive information. As official statisticians, our job is to ensure that we do not breach confidentiality either inadvertently or deliberately obviously. Health data is particularly sensitive. As an example, AIDS or hepatitis in some countries may be taken as an indicator of sexual preference, and that in itself then may be illegal. So we have to be really, really careful about the use of and access to data.

SM: But more globally, then, the WHO is part of the UN system. I just had a meeting today where we were discussing a forthcoming Summit in 2024 called the Summit of the Future. A large measure of that Summit will deal with data issues and in particular, data governance.

---

[629] Steve MacFeely was a co-lead on the Data Strategy of the Secretary-General for Action by Everyone, Everywhere 2020 – 2022, and a lead author of the 2020 System-wide Roadmap for Innovating UN Data and Statistics. He has also recently authored the article "Towards an International Data Governance Framework". MacFeely submitted a statement to the Center for Global Agenda (CGA) at Unbuilt Labs ahead of the panel discussion, this has been included in *Section 5.2.8.*

The issue of privacy as a whole, the human rights aspects of data — in fact, whether even access to your own data should become a human right. These are all types of issues that we are discussing, and trying to balance data privacy without restricting the opportunities that data presents. You read out that piece from my submission where I said: data can be a tool, but it can also be dangerous[630]. That is where we are trying to strike a balance between the two — we do not want to limit opportunities that data can provide, but we want to restrict or try and mitigate against the worst misuses and abuses of data, and try to protect individuals and communities.

SM: It is a great question — effective ways to engage with civil society, and I wish I had a good answer. It is the thing that is actually keeping us awake at night. As we sit there discussing at the UN different kinds of data governance models, the kind of realization is that the traditional UN model was to engage with member states. But when we are talking about data governance, discussing it with member states alone is not going to cut it. So we need to engage with private sector, which is challenging because that itself is a homogeneous or heterogeneous group. But the biggest challenge is how do we engage with civil society, how do we engage with the individuals? Because every individual is being impacted by the development from the data world. And it is a real challenge because the UN is not really geared up for communicating with individuals. It is really designed to communicate with governments. And this is a big challenge.

SM: So here we are on one hand discussing data governance kind of in the abstract, trying to formulate good policies. But when we go to do the consultation piece, how do we do it? We can organize regional sessions and that will be important because there will be different cultural views. And I could spend a lifetime just talking about what Rachele had said a few minutes ago, because I think that was really interesting. But that is still not enough. We are looking at online options, we are looking at all sorts of things. But honestly, I do not know. This is the big challenge. How do you communicate effectively with 8 billion people, a billion of whom at least do not even have a legal identity. And how do we talk to them about having an identity and having data? Because that is the reality that we face.

SM: Now, we all have multiple identities. We do not even know how many we have. Like as a thought experiment, could you imagine if you woke up tomorrow morning and all of the databases for your data

---

[630] See *Section 5.2.9*.

exist were just white? It would be a great book. So you wake up in the morning, nothing works. So here I am. I physically exist, but in every other sense of the word, I would not exist anymore. So this is what we are trying to grapple with. What I would do is I turn around the question to the rest of the panel and say, if anybody's got any good ideas, I would love to hear them because this is the piece that is really worrying us. How do we have this discussion with 8 billion people?

Ivy Kwan Arce (President, Treatment Action Group (TAG); Research in Action Award (RIAA) Honoree)[631]

IKA: I am interested in the equality of access to data. Data is really important, but I think about the impact of what we consider data protection here, and the impact of what that does in different countries as well. What makes you vulnerable when you are a commodity of information? Data can help solve a lot of issues, but then that same commodity can put you in danger as well. So those are the kinds of concerns as active as humans, especially when you are tasked with a certain issue, whether it is a virus in your body or mobilizing a community. What does that look like when data is important? Is the only place in clinical trials? You have to have some kind of infrastructure where the person whose data is being extracted has an understanding that it is happening and is able to establish some kind of boundary.

IKA: One of the things that would be interesting to work through in the future is who are the governors, who are the good people, who is really guarding data privacy? For example, you are genetically testing your heritage. The transfer and acquisition of data and business is something nobody really monitors. So you think it was Facebook, or you are trying to find your heritage, that is one company, in a couple of years, the data gets sold, and it is the same way when we update our phone, we have to say yes, otherwise we cannot really go to the next phase. So it really does not give any sense of ownership of your own data, and the processes in place are so easily bypassed. That is also bypassed by certain governors of elections in different countries — every four years especially in the US, things can change. Whatever the understanding was four years ago may not hold today. Other countries have more longevity in terms of building things and fixing things, but I think the future, especially when we have the younger generations born into culture where accepting the terms and conditions is

---

[631] Ivy Kwan Arce was featured at the recent Whitney Biennale: "Activism for Global Pandemic Equity", she was also recently interviewed by the National Aids Memorial: "Ivy Kwan Arce -Women and AIDS - Surviving Voices".

mandatory — I mean, even the whole exchange of Apple now saying on their website, do you really want to share this or go under and personalize that? Most people do not do that. It is written in a way that you just say yes. So the governance of data — who you think is good or who dictates the terms are the safekeepers. It is a huge issue that needs to be defined.

IKA: What I found interesting was to watch Covid play out after being HIV positive for 32 years. For most diseases where clinical trials happen, most communities do not know who the participants are, versus in HIV. We adamantly shape those clinical trials and force the government to be part of that planning with us rather than just having pharmaceutical companies draw out their goals. We drew our goals and we summoned each other to come to participate in that. We summoned ourselves to know when side effects were too much and changed the safety program. Covid has a little of that history mixed in because some of the people working on that have also worked on HIV challenges. Unless you have active participation from communities, clinical research can be very disassociated. It goes back to bigger companies taking whatever, determining the product, designing the clinical trial and their outcomes, without the participation of patients, individuals, and communities. That is the part that for me has been really hard — to stay in community and to tell the story — that one needs to participate in, even with a short four-year timeframe in this country, if you do not have that, you really lose the little control that you have as a consumer and as somebody who could even be on a path for health recovery.

IKA: The only way I have seen civil society engagement work is when the higher ups and the people on the ground participate. Either end of this balance has never shown to work. Many models where patients are included take time when you are talking to people. The people on the ground need the space and the time to learn, to be able to participate at the table, and then you have to create the table for them to come to you. That is the reflection from HIV especially here in New York. At one point the people living with the challenges of HIV do not have to navigate their daily lives with all this heavy policy of how you are supposed to behave in a workspace. The person who is dealing with the illness needs the right tools and very specific education. When we say be educated, education has to be very, very specific — you have to be very militant about learning and exploring challenges in order to participate. Without that, it just looks like what always seems very separate — a separate project that does not consider the person or their conditions. These methods are old science already. We are at a time when medications are personalized. Therefore, policymakers and researchers can only function more efficiently when patients are educated enough to participate in and help shape those clinical trials. And that time and time has been the success of HIV treatment. You can see it in different parts of population globally: when they are in environments where the patient is educated enough, that becomes incredibly valuable to policymakers and researchers. That is when clinical research works best. Thank you.

Shady El Damaty, Ph.D. (President, Opsci; Co-Founder, Holonym)[632]

SED: I just wanted to chime in a little bit because actually a lot of what I do has to do with cryptography and identity. Self-sovereign identity is a key cornerstone for how we think of intellectual ownership as well as patient and data privacy. I think if you work meaningfully with data, trying to transform it or use it to make decisions or analyze it, you end up finding that provenance is really important. If you follow the branches of provenance: the history of data to its roots, it always goes down to an identity. There always has to be an identity that commits that data, transforms that data, and signs off that data. So data and identity seem, at least in my mind, completely intertwined and very difficult to dissociate if you are trying to build resilient systems that are private and self-owned.

Rachele Hendricks-Sturrup, DHSc, MSc, MA (Research Director, Real World Evidence, Duke-Margolis Institute for Health Policy)[633]

RHS: My name is Dr. Rachele Hendrick Sturrup, the Research Director of Real World Evidence at the Duke-Margolis Institute for Health Policy in Washington, DC. I am really happy to talk about data privacy within the context of real world data and also in the broader context of big data, which many argue is quite different. Real world data is largely applied to the regulatory context. So think about the U.S. Food and Drug Administration (FDA), the European Medicines Agency, Health Canada, and others that oversee or regulate medical

---

[632] Shady El Damaty, Ph.D. contributed as a member of the audience.
[633] Rachele Hendricks-Sturrup, DHSc, Msc, MA was a co-author of FDA User Fee Reauthorization and the Value of Real-World Evidence, as well as a moderator and presenter at the 2022 Duke-Margolis Convening on the State of Real-World Evidence Policy.

products. They consider data from a variety of different sources, whether it is from a healthcare system, Fitbit Watch, the internet, social media, your email, whatever that might be. Those fall under the bucket of our definition of real world data. Big data — data that is outside of the regulatory context, has additional real world and broader implications.

RHS: Given that data comes from a variety of sources, it may or may not be deidentified or identifiable. And given that the data can travel at the speed of light across oceans and across time zones within seconds, the data can be transferred to different legal jurisdictions. As an example, we can think about the United States and the state of our privacy policy landscape, then compare that to the European landscape, which many argue is a bit more robust and protective over data privacy and discretion. As we think about privacy, there are a lot of implications here. There are many different levels. We can think about protecting the discretion of the data itself, protecting the system in which the data is collected or exchanged, and then also thinking about the ways in which the data can be engineered or re-engineered to obscure the identities of the data subjects.

RHS: When we think about identity, going back to my comment about levels, I think there are two key layers to this, at least within the human experience and this context — we have the right to be individuals and a right to have that identity. With that come ideals around individualism. There are community level considerations that certainly have privacy implications as well, such as protecting the identity of a community, such that the community has sovereign rights as an identifiable and self-identifying community. The privacy of that community and the discretion of their data should therefore be acknowledged within the broader policy context. But then, to Ivy's point about commoditizing data, whether it is data about an individual or data about a population or a subpopulation, we also have to think about what was the basis for creating identity. Ultimately, it boils down to the fact that identity is a way of creating order within a system. With that order came the ability to protect assets within that system. It is arguably paternalistic, but at the end of the day, there is a financial or asset management component to that. We see that with companies as well. To Ivy's point, whereas a company like direct-to-consumer genetic testing company cannot acquire an individual's genetic data in exchange for a genetic profile about that person. So really appealing to that person's desire to be understood as an individual. They have commoditized that. Separately, they have figured out a way to also use the data that they acquire to not only conduct generalizable research, but also engage in further commoditizing of the data to serve a financial purpose. A financial purpose that is solely owned by that company's or solely within that company's interest. That data can be used to create new drugs, it can be sold to drug companies. Those are just two examples.

RHS: I think what Steve just highlighted is that we live in this grey area of identity in the 21st century. We obviously have our physical identity, whether it is legal or illegal, and we also have a digital identity. Quite frankly, not having a digital identity these days as an adult is very dangerous. In fact, you can quickly fall behind. There are some people who might disagree with that in one way or another, but the fact of the matter is that today, in order to navigate our world and its complexities, and in order to navigate day to day living, you have to have some form of digital identity, whether it is minuscule or maximum. And then obviously, again, with that comes this huge grey area that one has to choose to live in on a certain spectrum. That is certainly up to the individual. It is certainly not up to them if they are born somewhere where having a digital identity is mandatory. That introduces an entirely different level of human rights that we have to consider. We are still in the process of disentangling all of that, especially from a policy standpoint, and then also trying to build in some of the cultural aspects that accompany one sense of identity as well. Trying to reconcile digital identity with community identity or individual identity. There are some cultural contentions even within that. In some places, having an individual or having an individualistic, I would say, perspective of oneself is not quite welcome, whereas it is the community's identity that you need to be more concerned about. So we have not even figured it out as human beings, but now we have added in the 21st century, again, another layer to understanding what identity means by creating a digital world that we must live in in order to survive.

5.2 Featured Statements

5.2.1 Benjamin Hanussek (Director, Polish-Japanese Academy of Information Technology (PJAIT) Game Lab)

Video Games and their potential to contribute to advance the 2030 Sustainable Development Goals

BH: Video Games have always been able to capture the Zeitgeist of the era in which they have been developed. Looking back at the Arcades of the 70s we can clearly see how video game content thematized The Space Race. Video games have become since then far more sophisticated in the ways they communicate complex ideas and allow us to interact with them.

BH: Today, video games have become an immersive portal through which we learn about history, identity and increasingly about the impacts of climate change. Games are essentially simulations that allow us to experience and experiment with whatever they contain. And that autonomy that players are given, to feel and to impact the environment that they are interacting with is what makes video games so much more powerful than other forms of media.

BH: Sid Meier's Civilization 6 allows players to create and develop a society by means of science, culture, military, diplomacy and religion. However, in the game our decision to boost for example the production of our civilization by industrial means has a direct impact on the climate which can lead to rising water levels, droughts and other environmental catastrophes, ultimately leading to the destruction of our planet and our society. The game has sold today almost 10 million copies worldwide and has been praised by the press and its players who were especially excited and intrigued by how the game operationalized and thematized climate change, leading to an individual and memorable experience for each player.

BH: More games, such as Stubby Games' The Entropy Centre, where players must reverse the destruction of the planet caused by climate change, are being released every year that help not just raise awareness but also allow players to develop a critical and individual relationship to the issues of climate change.

BH: This trend in gaming is yet on one hand heavily underfunded while on the other hand going unnoticed by educators that wish to engage young people with the topic of climate change in a less intimidating and threatening way. News media and social media have a tendency to perpetuate a doom-and-gloom climate narrative that discourages engagement and paralyze readers.

BH: I see a huge potential for video games to contribute to the advancement of the 2030 Sustainable Development Goals. But to yield this potential game developers and designers require better financial incentives to thematize the topic and eventually even include scientists in the development of impactful and informative video games on climate change. Also, to unfold their impact, games on climate change should be used as supplementary materials in schools. For that educators should receive training by developers and experts in game-based learning to ensure an effective deployment of these games in classrooms.

BH: The impact of video games on young people is rarely questioned — why not take the opportunity to make a positive impact? Why not use this fantastic medium to engage new generations to care about our planet and its climate?

5.2.2 Brent M. Shea, Ph.D. (Professor of Sociology, Emeritus & Adjunct, Sweet Briar College)

BMS: Sustainable Development Goal 3 proposes to "ensure healthy lives and promote well-being for all at all ages", and includes universal health care[634]. The final report of the WHO Council on the Economics of Health for All provides an assessment of the production and distribution of health and well-being across economies: "Alongside a healthy and sustainable environment, human health and wellbeing must be the ultimate goal of economic activity. This goal requires investment and innovation by all actors in the economy, which can also help steer the rate and direction of economic growth. Growth not for growth's sake but for people and planet."[635]

BMS: Interventions to achieve health for all cannot be guided by the linear assumption that more is better, even if economic growth occurs. Whether the example is nutrition, antibiotics, pain killers, radiation, or surgery, blood pressure or blood sugar levels, a curvilinear pattern is evident, with no or low intervention often equalling or surpassing aggressive intervention in its positive effect on health. The well-being of the individual is of increasing interest now, given the ability to aggressively treat incurably ill people. Increasingly sensitive scanning technology is capable of detecting tiny abnormalities that can be treated unnecessarily in relation to their effect on how long an individual lives, resulting in debilitating side effects with negative effects on health and well-being. The legacy of over-diagnosis and over-treatment is the hundreds of thousands of false positives that should have been ignored rather than treated because of the deleterious side effects of treatment. Most population-based screening that affects primary care (and secondary and tertiary care as well) has not been adequately evaluated scientifically, including oral, skin, testicular, thyroid, and esophageal cancer. That is not to say targeted screening is not appropriately done when symptoms or risk factors are present, as in the case of smokers or those exposed to side-stream smoke being screened for lung cancer, the leading type of cancer-related deaths in the world and a major cause of both heart disease and stroke.

BMS: In the US, infant mortality rates are higher and life expectancy is shorter than in the other prosperous countries, even though much

---

[634] United Nations, "Health," *United Nations Sustainable Development* (blog), accessed April 7, 2024, https://www.un.org/sustainabledevelopment/health/.
[635] Mazzucato, "Preface," in *Health for All - Transforming Economies to Deliver What Matters* (World Health Organization, 2023).

more money is spent on each patient in the US than in any other country. LMICs face similar scenarios as they become prosperous enough to begin to consider taxes on cigarettes or alcohol, enforcement of seat belt, helmet, or child car seat laws, or direct to consumer advertising of prescription drugs, for example. What no longer is possible in the US, like marketing of tobacco products to children, is now likely to occur in the LMICs with fewer regulations, resulting in lifetime use of a highly addictive substance causally related to the development of NCDs like cancer and cardiovascular disease and responsible for one of every ten deaths worldwide.

BMS: As targets of the SDGs are pursued between now and 2030, universal health coverage remains a worthy goal. In contrast, the unintended outcomes of health care delivery that include over-diagnosis and overtreatment are not worthy goals, despite their probable contribution to economic growth.

5.2.3 Christina Ntulo (Country Director, StrongMinds Uganda)

Working to utilize cross-sectoral partnerships to benefit global mental health

CN: In 2018, the Lancet Commission on Global Mental Health issued a call for collective action to align mental health with the Sustainable Development Goals (SDGs), recognizing that mental health and development are intrinsically linked. The report called for broader mental health investments, including preventative care (especially for children and adolescents) and improved quality of care. Since then, we have seen NGOs, governments, and the private sector understanding that good mental health is the foundation of thriving individuals, families, and communities, yet, despite this and other calls to action, global investment in mental health has lagged far behind other development initiatives. Mental health still accounts for less than one percent of public health expenditures in low- and middle-income countries (LMICs).

CN: In 2022, The World Health Organization's Global Mental Health Report affirmed the connection between mental health and all seventeen of the SDGs and called for innovative, cost-effective solutions to comprehensively address mental health as a critical part of global development. Partnerships between NGOs and government agencies ensure that mental health is addressed comprehensively at multiple levels, such as primary healthcare settings, schools, and communities. When institutions cooperate across sectors, we shift the conversation about mental health: stigma and misconceptions are eliminated, and people who need help can better access available mental health resources.

CN: Research on mental health in Africa has been thin to date. At StrongMinds, we believe that prevalence studies of mental health disorders significantly undercount depression rates in sub-Saharan Africa. While official figures suggest that depression rates for adults hover around 5% in Africa, StrongMinds mobilizers conducting door-to-door screening in Uganda and Zambia see depression rates as high as 20-30%.

CN: However, research shows that mental health has a bi-directional relationship with many of the African continent's significant challenges. For example, mental health disorders such as depression can put people — particularly adolescent girls — at greater risk of HIV infection while inhibiting the ability of those living with HIV to adhere to or seek treatment. Poverty, poor nutrition, and lack of education can exacerbate depression, while depression can also interfere with an individual's ability to earn a stable income, achieve food security, or finish school.

CN: We know from our work that when you treat depression in a single individual, the world around them starts to change. Our clients report that they are able to work more frequently, send their kids to school more regularly, and feed their families more meals daily. Overall, family well-being improves.

CN: No one organization can meet the needs for mental health access alone. We need cross-sectoral collaboration to fully assess the impact of mental health disorders on human well-being in sub-Saharan Africa and across the continent.

5.2.4 Domenico Dentoni (Full Professor and Co-Director of the Chair COAST (Communication and OrgAnizing for Sustainable Transformations), Montpellier Business School)

DD: In our role of academic organization striving to connect with organisations across sectors and society as a whole, we propose insights into the meanings, roles and formats of systems mapping - as visual interfaces to apply systems thinking and to ultimately trigger or support systems change[636] - for three fundamental reasons. First, the language of systems change has been growing in popularity as a process to address wicked problems across multiple interconnected scales; yet, across these scales, recent global trends suggest problems are becoming more wicked, not less, over time. Second, narratives on the necessity of transformation across multiple spheres to address wicked problems have been proliferating, yet direction and pace of socio-ecological transformations seems all but desirable. Third, urgent calls for building cross-scale systems coherence as an underlying necessity to steer these transformations have been multiplying; yet, we experience living in an increasingly polarised world. Connecting these facts from a problem-centric perspective, we would conclude that we are still fundamentally missing something in the way we currently think of social innovation, enact narratives of transformation, and launch calls for cross-scale systems coherence[637].

DD: Because of these reasons, in our role as engaged scholars, we first propose to our stakeholders to collectively reflect on how to use systems mapping to meaningfully support and build coherence towards systems transformations. Specifically, we propose to use systems mapping as a tool, as an event or as a (dialectic or experimentation) process over time depending on the goals and timing of the desired transformation. Second, on the basis of the principle that complex problems and socio-ecological systems are two sides on the same coin[638], we propose a specific approach that combines the use of

---

[636] Domenico Dentoni et al., "Systems Thinking, Mapping and Change in Food and Agriculture," *Bio-Based and Applied Economics* 11, no. 4 (May 3, 2023): 277–301, https://doi.org/10.36253/bae-13930.

[637] Sylvia Grewatsch, Steve Kennedy, and Pratima (Tima) Bansal, "Tackling Wicked Problems in Strategic Management with Systems Thinking," *Strategic Organization* 21, no. 3 (August 2023): 721–32, https://doi.org/10.1177/14761270211038635.

[638] Peter M. Senge et al., "Collaborating for Systemic Change," *MIT Sloan Management Review*, 2007.

two maps: causal loop diagrams and value network maps[639]. The combined use of these maps pragmatically supports multi-stakeholder groups to collectively understand how complex problems and social systems relate to each other, and to collectively envision how they can address these problems coherently through systems change[640].

5.2.5 Emma Leiken (Chief of Programs, Omidyar Network)

On youth engagement as a strategic imperative in the responsible technology movement and considerations for funders

EL: Globally, there is consensus that technology is both positively transforming society, and at the same time, exacerbating existing harms and presenting new risks. Big tech, in particular, is increasingly under scrutiny for its harmful effects on young people — children, teens, and young adults. Whether amplifying divisive and objectively harmful content that promotes self-harm or disinformation, surveilling and then monetizing young people's data without informed consent, or otherwise deploying dark patterns, or design elements that deliberately obscure and mislead people into making unintended and possibly harmful online choices to maximize profit and engagement at the expense of user safety and privacy — our global technology ecosystem is broken. Many of those who face the brunt of its backlash are young people themselves.

EL: At the same time, there is reason to be optimistic. There is increasing momentum around the idea that young people's experiences of technology are unique, and worthy of attention, particularly in the realm of policy. Given they experience the harms of big tech acutely and will be creating and governing the technology of our future, their meaningful inclusion in technology

---

[639] Dentoni et al., "Systems Thinking, Mapping and Change in Food and Agriculture."

[640] **DD**: More information available at: https://www.montpellier-bs.com/international/faculty-and-research/faculty-departments/centers-chairs/the-coast-chair/

policy and advocacy is not a "nice-to-have," but rather, a strategic imperative when it comes to building the coalitions, narratives, and solutions needed to move towards a more equitable and accountable technology future. Here are some lessons I have come across while working to amplify youth voices in the responsible technology movement.

EL: Intergenerational partnerships are critical. Youth-led organizations are some of the most scrappy and effective entities when it comes to policy, advocacy and narrative change work. At the same time, many youth-led organizations face infrastructural, relational and cultural barriers that impede their ability to achieve maximum impact. These barriers can take the shape of a lack of operational capacity and know-how to register as a 501(c)3 is or 501(c)4 organization and therefore receive sustainable funding, the natural leadership churn that arises when students in leadership positions have competing obligations such as schoolwork, which results in the loss of institutional memory, or otherwise a lack of durable networks in policy spaces. For these reasons, meaningful partnership with adult-led organizations can have a transformative impact on youth-led organizations. Youth leaders can benefit from the networks, operational expertise and mentorship of adult leaders, and adult leaders can benefit from the creativity, expertise, and unique lived experience young people bring to the table. One of many examples of successful youth-adult collaboration in the technology policy arena was the advocacy around the California Age Appropriate Design Code. Intergenerational partnerships can strategically navigate inside and outside game tactics when it comes to policy and advocacy, convey compelling stories, and build toward more sustainable structures.

EL: It is time to embrace intersectionality across issue areas. A disconnect exists between how young leaders and funders (most of which are not Gen-Z) discuss and parse out issues adjacent to the responsible technology movement. Youth communities are much more likely to view technology, education, mental health, climate, economic, and social policy issues as intertwined and interdependent. For example, youth-led organization Gen-Z for Change's advocacy around reproductive rights bled into technology policy advocacy when, in attempting to combat online misinformation, the team wrote a script that allowed users to spam Crisis Pregnancy Centers' Yelp reviews to inform people that these centers do not actually perform abortion services, though they purported to do so. After meeting directly with the Gen-Z For Change team, Yelp agreed to join forces with the teenage influencers by adding consumer notices to crisis pregnancy centers to more clearly distinguish them from the clinics actually providing abortion services. In contrast to the intersectionality youth groups often bring to issues adjacent to technology, funders almost unanimously view these issues as distinct, carving out separate funding portfolios for education, healthcare, civic engagement, and technology policy. This disconnect implicates the foundation ecosystem's ability to effectively support youth-led organizations looking at issues holistically. For example, while unmitigated algorithms are exacerbating the youth mental health crisis with significant implications for educational outcomes, some education-focused funders suggest that technology policy is out of scope. This narrow way of thinking about issues limits philanthropic support for youth-driven initiatives that might talk about issues differently than their adult-led counterparts but are broadly values aligned in their view of the problem and the solutions.

EL: Invest in building leadership pipelines early. Companies, organizations, governance bodies, and multilateral institutions may seek to engage young people as a way to strategically enhance their narrative, economic, and policy currency and incorporate cutting-edge perspectives to ensure organizational competitiveness. But it's a long-term play, as much as a short-term one. By investing in young people early, these organizations will also create and strengthen the pipeline of advocates who will eventually be leading and governing companies, civil society organizations, and public institutions themselves.

5.2.6 Jerome Glenn (CEO, The Millennium Project)

JG: An international assessment of how to govern the potential transition from Artificial Narrow Intelligence (ANI) to potential Artificial General Intelligence (AGI) is needed. If the initial conditions of AGI are not "right," it could evolve into the kind of Artificial Super Intelligence (ASI) that Stephen Hawking, Elon Musk, and Bill Gates have warned the public could threaten the future of humanity via the future globally connected Internet of Things (IoT).

JG: There are many excellent centers studying values and the ethical issues of ANI, but not potential global governance models for the transition to AGI.

JG: The distinctions among ANI, AGI, and ASI are usually missing in these studies.

JG: Current work on AI governance is designed to catch up with the artificial narrow intelligence proliferating worldwide today. Meanwhile, investment into AGI development is forecast to be $50 billion by 2023. Expert judgments about when AGI will be possible vary. Some working to develop AGI believe it is possible to have AGI in as soon as ten years. It is likely to take ten years to: 1) develop ANI to AGI international or global agreements; 2) design the governance system; and 3) begin implementation. Hence, it would be wise to begin exploring potential governance approaches and their potential effectiveness now. We need to jump ahead to anticipate governance requirements for what AGI could become. Beginning now to explore and assess rules for governance of AGI will not stifle its development, since such rules would not be in place for at least ten years. (Consider how long it is taking to create a global governance system for climate change.)

5.2.7 Lowell Clare, MA, MLA (Independent Researcher)

LC: Our Common Agenda was released on the 75th anniversary of the United Nations (2020) as a framework for accelerated implementation of existing agreements. It features Twelve Key Proposals that emphasize the role of scientific diplomacy and strategic foresight in achieving the Sustainable Development Goals for 2030. Our Common Agenda and the Sustainable development goals both rely on increased interest, action and collaboration between the widest array of stakeholders possible. A strategy for increasing engagement and active participation in meeting the seventeen SDGs within the rubric of science diplomacy would be to incorporate more imagery into reports and assessments.

LC: Climate Outreach was founded in 2004 as the first English non-profit to focus solely on communicating climate change. They use peer reviewed social science to create, collate and disseminate imagery that not only describes climate change but encourages action in viewers. Their 2015 Climate Visuals: Seven Principles for Visual Climate Change Communication report by lays out a useful foundation for generating and deploying imagery to effectively turn passive audiences into active stakeholders as described in the ACO and SDGs. The Seven Key Takeaways are: (1) show 'real people' not staged photo-ops, (2) tell new stories, (3) show climate causes at scale, (4) climate impacts are emotionally powerful, (5) show local (but serious) climate impacts, (6) be very careful with protest imagery and (7) understand your audience. Their research shows that not only are images a useful tool to communicate the effects of climate change but that the most effective ones help to tell the stories about people living with series effects of climate change in specific places.

LC: Rigorously produced graphics and visualizations of environmental changes add a currently lacking element to vital documents. Visuals that focus on how people currently or use or might inhabit places altered in the future by the climate crises would help translate the immense scale of the climate crises into tangible vignettes. We need to encourage specialists with the skills to accurately represent environments under a variety of climate scenarios at a time when they need to be more accessible to as many stakeholders as possible. We should also encourage artists and designers to engage with data from the Intergovernmental Panel on Climate Change (IPCC) to bring a human perspective together with critical research. Easily understandable graphics can support climate literacy.

5.2.8 Peter Kennard (Professor of Political Art, Royal College of Art (RCA))

PK: In August this year the Intergovernmental Panel on Climate Change (IPCC) released their report. Their findings, prepared by 234 scientists from 66 countries, warn that human activity has warmed the climate to a point that is unparalleled by anything in the last 2,000 years and that by 2019 atmospheric CO_2 concentrations were higher than at anytime in at least 2 million years. The United Nations Secretary-General Antonio Guterres said the IPCC report was the 'code red for humanity, the alarm bells are deafening and the evidence is irrefutable'. Hence the title for this installation which I've made specifically for the public space of Trongate 103 where the entrance to Street Level Photoworks is located.

PK: The empty words issuing from the mouths of government leaders worldwide on the climate crisis continue to be backed up and supported by corporate profit for the good of share prices rather than human beings. The military-industrial complex is eating up the earth, spitting out the poorest people and waging war on them. The countries from which refugees flock have often been destroyed by the rapacious policies and weaponry of the very same countries that are refusing them entry.

PK: Through photomontage I'm trying to turn my outrage into image. In Code Red a recurring image I use and abuse is the beautiful photo of the whole earth taken by the Apollo astronauts in 1972. I cut it up, tear it, pummel it, add industrial chimneys, oil refineries exploding, polluted dust, gas masks, parched earth and floods. But I also show a montage of the earth surrounded by a clock, symbolising climate/nuclear destruction, its hands being pulled back from midnight by climate protesters. There is also an image of planet earth transformed into a seed sprouting a tree. Photos can become entwined through photomontage so that the increasing destruction of the natural world can be envisaged and revealed not as inevitable but the result of human activity. The resulting montage can then be used a visual arm of the struggle for climate justice.

PK: In a photomontage two clicks of the camera shutter can be brought together to reveal a third meaning. What is shown in Code Red is that oil is still flowing freely out of the ground, the chimneys are still belching out their pollutants and luxury yachts are growing longer by the day. E.M Forster's dictum 'only connect' applies equally to making montages connecting the catastrophe that is climate destruction and its relationship to military power. They are both existentially and physically deeply connected. The U.S military is the largest single consumer of petroleum in the world.

PK: We're living in a time of absolute emergency. We're tottering through the rubble of the rampant free market. It's a time in which images can open up a critical space that can jolt assumptions and break through denial. The poet Shelley wrote that 'we must imagine what we know'. By picturing the result of extracting wealth out of the ground by every means possible I'm trying to picture what we know will happen if we don't stop this plunder.

5.2.9 Steve MacFeely (Director of Data and Analytics, World Health Organization (WHO))

A Global Data Convention

SM: Data. The single word that defines our age. Easily shared, duplicated and traded, the glue that binds and drives the digital economy, the cloud, blockchain, the Internet-of-Things, and even our politics. They offer promise but also peril – they are a tool for liberation, but also potentially a weapon for exploitation.

SM: Data transcend borders, challenge national sovereignty and are increasingly being thought of as a new form of capital. While some countries and regions have begun to try and tackle the challenge of how to regulate the collection and use of data, such a piecemeal, fragmented approach risks creating barriers to production, trade, innovation and cooperation.

SM: Given the importance of data for the modern digital economy, for surveillance, for AI, there will be few more important geopolitical issues in the coming years. Hence the chief statisticians of the international statistical system are calling for a **Global Data Compact**.

SM: A **Global Data Compact** would constitute an integrated set of data principles and standards that unite national governments, public institutions, private sector, civil society organizations and academia. These would include elements such as: privacy of personal data; data accessibility; data exchange; data interoperability; and transparency, to name a few.

SM: A **Global Data Compact** would help avoid a fragmentation where each country or region adopts their own solution by promoting common objectives. This would give individuals and enterprises confidence that data relevant to them carries similar protections and obligations no matter where they are collected or used.

SM: Building upon the existing canon of international human rights and other conventions, laws and treaties that set out useful principles and compliance mechanisms and build upon them, a **Global Data Convention** could move beyond establishing ethical principles and create a global architecture that also includes standards and incentives for compliance. Such an architecture could be the foundation for rethinking the data economy, promoting open data, encouraging data exchange, and facilitating trade mechanisms.

5.2.10 Stuart RF King (Research Culture Manager, eLife, UK) and Damian Pattinson (Executive Director, eLife, UK)

SRFK & DP: Sustainable development led by evidence-based decision-making requires a strong international research ecosystem. Science and innovation not only provide new solutions to address global challenges; the scientific method itself can also help evaluate the impact of actions and success towards advancing the 2030 Sustainable Development Goals.

SRFK & DP: For this to happen, however, stakeholders at every point along the research-to-action pipeline must have barrier-free access to scientific findings – to keep pace with the rapidly changing global landscape – as well as trustworthy indicators that convey the merits and limitations of specific studies.

SRFK & DP: The recent boom in the use of preprints, particularly within the life and medical sciences, has provided unprecedented levels of access and profoundly changed the pace of scholarly scientific communication. Researchers can now rapidly disseminate their findings to a wider audience than ever before, free of charge, and without the delays and inefficiencies incumbent in pre-publication peer review.

SRFK & DP: Peer review – the act of researchers reading, thinking carefully about, and commenting on their colleagues' work – is nevertheless an integral part of science. Researchers and readers of research alike appreciate it as an important quality control process. While peer review has typically been tied up within traditional journal publishing and used to gatekeep which articles are published in which venues, fortunately, this no longer needs to be the case. Technology already exists to bring the scrutiny of peer review to findings published as preprints and make the peer reviewers' assessments publicly available to all interested in the work. Uncoupled from journals in this manner, people from historically under-represented communities can also become more involved in the peer review process.

SRFK & DP: The remaining barrier to the widespread adoption of this "preprint-first" model is not technological but cultural. Researchers keen to break away from the outdated and wasteful systems of pre-publication peer review must trust that they will not be penalised in terms of their funding and careers.

SRFK & DP: This calls for individual and collaborative efforts from stakeholders across the industry – including funders, research institutions and publishers – to ensure that researchers who participate in current challenges and respond to sustainable development demands through timely preprint-first publishing are recognised and rewarded.

SRFK & DP: In October 2022, eLife announced that it will eliminate "accept/reject" decisions after peer review and instead focus on preprint review and assessment. For all preprints peer-reviewed by eLife, reviewers and editors will prepare a public assessment of the work to accompany the preprint and transform it into a Reviewed Preprint. Every eLife assessment will use a common vocabulary to summarise the significance of the findings and the strength of the evidence reported in the preprint, allowing a nuanced appraisal of the work in a clear and consistent manner. A group of 10 funders and other research organisations have since committed to including reviewed preprints from eLife and others involved in preprint review in their evaluation processes. Among these supporters are the Gates Foundation, Howard Hughes Medical Institute, Knut and Alice Wallenberg Foundation, and Wellcome.

5.2.11 Umberto Fracassi (Research Scientist, Istituto Nazionale di Geofisica e Vulcanologia (INGV))

UF: Natural hazards and anthropogenic factors interact in multiple ways and across various scales, close or afar, in time and space. They lay out a web of complexities that can appear overwhelming to the citizens of contemporary societies – even in the ones statistically affluent and educated. There comes the role of natural, earth and space sciences – from oceanography to high-atmosphere physics, and from seismology to space exploration. They carry transformative instruments to decipher and help protecting planet Earth for its most precious and fragile content: life.

UF: These science avenues study nature for what it is – with all its grand and miniature dimensions, its seemingly slow processes that unveil sudden effects, the complex interactions among forces and bodies, across distances and time. Science as a whole – and especially these particular branches – can deliver precious intellectual templates in accepting and challenging first-order complexities rising at the intersection among the physical world, the biosphere, and the intellectual landscape of scholarly thought.

UF: Seemingly immaterial yet overarchingly concrete, and drawing on a diverse knowledge, the latter one can – and should – distill guidelines and best practices to be routed towards societies, to assist them in building tools to proactively adapt to a world at times perceived by contemporary societies as inscrutable, increasingly richer in risks and poorer in resources.

UF: Therefore, the tools of yesterday's intellectual quests can prove instrumental to decipher today's and tomorrow's societal issues, such as:
- The long records of natural events (hazards)
- Far-flung origins (our solar system and the universe)
- Far-reaching effects (feedback, periodicity, and recurrence times)
- The need to forecast (or at least account for) the irregular behaviors of modern phenomena.

UF: The knowledge of compounded risks of natural origin provides an outlook on where and what to call for enduring communities. This applies also to risks resulting from interaction among natural events and anthropogenic components. Since natural phenomena embed complexities due to multiple variables and intrinsic feedback, interaction among natural and non-natural ones brings novel issues, requiring a remarkably broad outlook – global and beyond. The natural consequence is then to envision natural risks against population distribution, spatial extents of natural resources, size, and time window of induced effects.

5.3 Reflection on Global Stakeholder Consultation Process

The Global Stakeholder Consultation Process has been successful overall, as it has solicited a wide range of perspectives. Proactively initiating discussions, designing low-commitment engagements, and publishing select statements in full have contributed to the success of the process. However, there is always more that can be done. Indeed, as *Chapter 4* suggests, the early stages of developing ideas are highly dependent on reciprocity. Not every invitation to participate was successful, whether that was due to participants' time, financial, or other types of limitations. There were also some contributions that unfortunately did not make it to the final publication after rounds of reviews[641]. I have included every contribution where possible within the parameters of Transdisciplinary Systems Research (TSR), including those whose views do not necessarily align with my own. *Table 5.1* presents a summary of discussions.

Table 5.1 Summary of discussions from the Global Stakeholder Consultation Process

Section	Summary
5.1.1	To deliver a lasting impact in nature-related initiatives, it is important to go beyond "more greenery" and introduce thoughtful cultural practices as well. Further, given the drastic changes in climate we expect to see in the near future, it is vital to engage the culture industry and develop adaptive practices. These practices demand active effort, building, and long-term commitment. However, with the rise of eco-distress and eco-anxiety, great care has to be taken when communicating and introducing nature-related cultural practices to avoid extreme behaviors.
5.1.2	Hall discussed the challenges of applying systems research in policy and government settings: (a) governments have hierarchies that inevitably create silos, but silos are not inherently unproductive because a silo with a target can be quite effective, (b) creating new committees for cross-cutting

---

[641] See *Chapters 2* and *3*.

	problems may not be as enduring as empowering existing structures to adapt, (c) the terminology of system of systems is too esoteric for policymakers and the general public: it would be helpful to create accessible narratives around the purpose of taking a systems approach and how it would achieve people's goals.
5.1.3	Larsen's research in the United States suggested a strong buy-in on concepts focusing on a future environment for all e.g. concepts such as reuse, repurpose, and recycle. El Damaty's research described the three most important factors to open science and reproducible research: (1) low hassle funding, (2) recognition and compensation for scientists' contribution, (3) global collaboration and connection.
5.1.4	Harker-Schuch challenged the use of emotive language in climate change communications: "we have been trying to get people emotional about the issue and then we have been very upset when they have reacted emotionally to this problem". She points to the importance of explaining the climate as a system and discussing the mechanisms, not just the impacts. Knowledge-sharing through climate literacy provides everyone with the ability to express our ideas and make informed decisions. Clare discussed the challenges of presenting big picture ideas at enormous scales in sustainable development. Designers can play a role in facilitating communications – through pictures, infographics, and visualizations, to help people from diverse backgrounds imagine themselves in the future: "Because it is so important that everybody, everybody has the opportunity to see themselves in the future."
5.1.5	MacFeely described the difficulty in engaging effectively with civil society: the traditional UN model was designed to engage with member states. How do you communicate effectively with 8 billion people, a billion of whom at least do not even have a legal identity. And how do we talk to them about having an identity and having data? Kwan Arce discussed the importance of equal access to data and data governance. She pointed to the commoditization of data and the poor monitoring of the transfer and acquisition of individuals' personal data. She advocated for the importance of education: "The people on the ground need the space and the time to learn, to be able to participate at the table, and then you have to create the table for them to come to you."

El Damaty discussed the idea of data provenance: tracking the history of data to its roots always returns to an identity. "There always has to be an identity that commits that data, transforms that data, and signs off that data."

Hendricks-Sturrup observed the difficulty of reconciling digital identity with community identity or individual identity. To navigate day-to-day living, it is now necessary to have some form of digital identity. Some people can choose to live on a spectrum from a minimum to a maximum digital footprint, but the option is not available to those who are born somewhere where a digital identity is mandatory. Identity can help create order and protect assets, but a lack of privacy can impede individuals' and communities' abilities to have an identity.

| 5.2.1 | Hanussek described the value of video game's immersive experience: the "autonomy that players are given, to feel and to impact the environment that they are interacting with is what makes video games so much more power than other forms of media". He advocated for the inclusion of scientists in developing informative video games on climate change, and providing training to educators on game-based learning. The impact of video games on young people is rarely questioned, purposefully designed games can have the opportunity to deliver a positive impact. |

| 5.2.2 | Shea discussed the nuances of the Health for All target. While universal health coverage remains a worthy goal, over-diagnosis and overtreatment can be problematic despite their potential contributions to economic growth. He also drew attention to the rise of non-communicable diseases (NCDs) in developing countries. |

| 5.2.3 | Ntulo made a call for cross-sectoral collaborations to fully assess the impact of mental health disorders on human well-being in sub-Saharan Africa and across the continent. The Lancet Commission on Global Mental Health in 2018 recognized the intrinsic connection between mental health and development, and the WHO's Global Mental Health Report in 2022 affirmed the connection between mental health and all 17 of the 2030 Sustainable Development Goals. However, the prevalence of mental health disorders is likely under-reported. While official figures hover around 5% in Africa, StrongMind's door-to-door screening in Uganda and Zambia saw depression rates as high as 20-30%. |

| 5.2.4 | Dentoni recognized the gap between the realization that a system change is necessary, and the transformation that has actually taken place. He advocated for the use of causal loop |

	diagrams and value network maps to collectively envision systems change initiatives.
5.2.5	Leiken advocated for youth engagement in the responsible technology movement. Youth-led organizations can bring creativity, expertise, and unique lived experience, and would benefit from the networks and mentorship from established organizations. She also pointed to the importance for funders to embrace intersectionality across issue areas: "Youth communities are much more likely to view technology, education, mental health, climate, economic, and social policy issues as intertwined and interdependent. [...] In contrast to the intersectionality youth groups often bring to issues adjacent to technology, funders almost unanimously view these issues as distinct, carving out separate funding portfolios for education, healthcare, civic engagement, and technology policy."
5.2.6	Glenn noted the lack of a distinction between Artificial Narrow Intelligence (ANI), Artificial General Intelligence (AGI), and Artificial Super Intelligence (ASI) at centers studying values and ethical issues of ANI. He advocated for an international assessment on how to govern the potential transition from ANI to AGI. He argued that AGI policies is likely to take at least ten years to develop considering the time it took for the global governance network to respond to climate change, so proactive engagement would be beneficial.
5.2.7	Clare advocated for the inclusion of designers in developing climate scenarios to increase accessibility. Artists and designers can be encouraged to engage with data from the IPCC to bring a human perspective to critical research. Easily understandable graphics can support climate literacy.
5.2.8	Kennard's site-specific installation for Street Level Photoworks to coincide with the 2021 UN Climate Change show how photography can be used to bring politics to a wider audience. He argued: "It's a time in which images can open up a critical space that can jolt assumptions and break through denial."
5.2.9	MacFeely advocated for a Global Data Compact, which would constitute an integrated set of data principles and standards that unite all stakeholders. It would give individuals and organizations that data carry similar protections and obligations no matter where they are collected or used through standards and incentives for compliance. It would also include elements such as: privacy of personal data, data accessibility, data exchange, data interoperability, and transparency, to name a few.

5.2.10	King and Pattinson advocated for barrier-free access to scientific findings and the use of a "preprint-first" model. In October 2022, eLife began exclusively reviewing papers already published as preprints, and publishing Reviewed Preprints with public versions of peer review assessments and an eLife assessment. This model moves beyond an "accept/reject" decision, captures the valuable dialogue between authors and reviewers, and offers an assessment of the research content in a language that is accessible to a non-expert reader. Among the supporting funders are the Gates Foundation, Howard Hughes Medical Institute, Knut and Alice Wallenberg Foundation, and Wellcome.
5.2.11	Fracassi discussed the complex intersections between natural hazards and anthropogenic factors. It is therefore important to examine and communicate how the burden of risks from disasters will be distributed within the population.

5.4 References

Dentoni, Domenico, Carlo Cucchi, Marija Roglic, Rob Lubberink, Rahmin Bender-Salazar, and Timothy Manyise. "Systems Thinking, Mapping and Change in Food and Agriculture." *Bio-Based and Applied Economics* 11, no. 4 (May 3, 2023): 277–301. https://doi.org/10.36253/bae-13930.

Grewatsch, Sylvia, Steve Kennedy, and Pratima (Tima) Bansal. "Tackling Wicked Problems in Strategic Management with Systems Thinking." *Strategic Organization* 21, no. 3 (August 2023): 721–32. https://doi.org/10.1177/14761270211038635.

Mazzucato. "Preface." In *Health for All - Transforming Economies to Deliver What Matters*. World Health Organization, 2023.

Senge, Peter M., Benyamin B. Lichtensetin, Katrin Kaeufer, Hilary Bradbury, and John S. Carroll. "Collaborating for Systemic Change." *MIT Sloan Management Review*, 2007.

United Nations. "Health." *United Nations Sustainable Development* (blog). Accessed April 7, 2024. https://www.un.org/sustainabledevelopment/health/.

WHO Council on the Economics of Health for All. *Health for All - Transforming Economies to Deliver What Matters*. World Health Organization, 2023.

Part 3

Conclusion & Recommendations

6

System-wide Transformation Guidance

6.0 Outline

This final chapter develops actionable recommendations through the approach of *Transdisciplinary Systems Guidance (TSG)*. TSG draws on implementation knowledge to assess and produce context-dependent guidance, e.g. policy recommendations, investment recommendations, and other recommended actions. In so doing, it produces *system-wide transformation guidance*, advice that is grounded in implementation knowledge, and formulated to help stakeholders achieve a *system-wide transformation*[642]. Based on Maher and Poon's model of the co-evolution of problem space and solution-space in 1996[643], *Section 6.1* reviews the considerations in *Chapters 1* to *5* to construct a narrowed down solution space of viable alternative solution conjectures in *Section 6.2*. This is in the form of a framework of pathways from global diplomacy. *Section 6.3* discusses 5 ideas from global diplomacy that emerged and 9 interconnected recommended actions. It focuses in particular on actions with a target implementation period between the short (up to 1 year) and medium (up to 3 years) terms. *Section 6.4* reflects on the recommendations with reference to the properties of grand challenges. *Section 6.5* concludes the book with an executive summary.

---

[642] See *Section 1.2.1.*
[643] See *Section 3.2.3.*

6.1 Considerations from *Chapter 1* to *5*

The publication began by considering some broad perspectives on systems in *Chapter 1*. It then clarified concepts such as systems, system-wide transformation, and grand challenges to define the abstract challenge of a system-wide transformation. *Chapters 2* and *3* discussed ways of reconciling these challenges through Transdisciplinary Systems Research (TSR). This enabled the construction of a model for global change processes within the contemporary global governance network in *Chapter 4*. Finally, *Chapter 5* broadened the discussion by considering emerging topics and perspectives. Considerations from each of the chapters help narrow down the solution space. The *solution space* consists of the collection of viable alternative solution conjectures[644].

Table 6.1 highlights some of the considerations from *Chapters 1* to *5*.

Table 6.1 Highlights of considerations for system-wide transformation methods from *Chapters 1* to *5*

Section	Summary
1.1	The 2030 Sustainable Development Goals were enacted in 2015, but guidance on methods has been limited.
1.2.1	Complex adaptive systems (CAS) have specific properties (*Table 1.1*).
1.2.2	A system-wide transformation is a grand challenge with specific properties (*Table 1.2*).
1.3.1	Systems thinking is necessary to understand system-wide transformation (*Table 1.4*).
1.4	Transdisciplinary research (TDR) addresses criticisms of Soft Systems Thinking (SST), Hard Systems Thinking (HST), and Critical Systems Thinking (CST) (*Section 1.3.2*).
Box 1-2	Global diplomacy describe a broad range of topics that converge around interaction, the process whereby individuals mutually influence each other and, in so doing, create,

---

[644] See *Section 3.2.3*.

	maintain, change, or terminate a pattern of joint action. Interactions play a pivotal role in constructing, maintaining, and altering our society.
2.2, 2.3, 2.4	Transdisciplinary Systems Research (TSR) has specific ontological (boundaries), epistemological (procedures for examining evidence), and axiological (valuation) considerations.
2.4.3	Intervening early before a conflict breaks out through preventive diplomacy is desirable.
4.1	The contemporary global governance network is a relatively new phenomenon following the end of the Cold War, and the role of non-state actors in global governance has expanded since.
Box 4-1	System-wide transformation methods necessitate the rejection of historical determinism and pessimistic fatalism.
4.2.1	The model of global change processes within the contemporary global governance network in this publication identifies five key actor groups (*Table 4.1*) and their roles (*Table 4.2*).
4.2.2	The current priorities and concepts that are gaining traction within the contemporary global governance network include the 2030 Sustainable Development Goals, the Annual UN Climate Change Conference (COP), the 2024 Summit of the Future, as well as Global Commons and Global Public Goods.
4.2.3	While each of the key actor groups plays different roles in institutional change, there are some commonalities: (1) the importance of organizing to change formal constraints, and (2) the possibility to alter informal constraints by mobilizing culture as symbolic boundaries, frames, narratives, repertoires, and cultural capital. Injustice i.e. group-based inequality or deprivation, catalyzes collective action.
4.2.4	Box 1-2 described global diplomacy as a set of topics that converge around interactions. The synthesis in this chapter shows the importance of interactions to the emergence of informal constraints — they allow stakeholders to contest norms' interpretations and adapt new meanings. Two types of interactions are of particular importance: (1) focused social interactions (i.e. dialogue with a mutual focus of attention, and a mutual appreciation of each other as unique individuals beyond social roles) and sustained and iterative engagements (i.e. repeated dialogue between organizations and stakeholders

that demonstrate reciprocity, which is a condition for knowledge co-creation.)

The lack of enforcement mechanisms at a global level means the global governance network depends on informal (i.e. cultural) constraints to function. Closing the compliance gap will rely on *culture as infrastructure*: describes the culture and cultural organizations that allow stakeholders to contest norms' interpretations and adapt informal constraints in line with the goals of the global community given the absence of enforcement mechanisms at a global level for formal constraints (i.e. laws and policies). Common arguments for culture at a global level, such as creativity, diversity, and heritage, fail to take into account the significance of culture as critical infrastructure for accountability to close the compliance gap in international laws and agreements. In this sense, culture ought to be considered a global public good alongside digital and information.

5.1, 5.2	The global stakeholder consultation process highlighted the importance of: (1) incorporating cultural practices to make an enduring impact in nature-related initiatives, (2) including artists as well as designers in making futures studies accessible, (3) designing a global data compact that considers the connection between data and identity, (3) mutual learning in community engagement, (4) advancing Health for All, (5) supporting cross-sectoral partnerships to evaluate the likely under-reporting of mental health disorders in Africa, (6) establishing intergenerational partnerships, (7) rethinking siloed funding portfolios, (8) studying Artificial General Intelligence (AGI), (9) pre-print first publication models, and (10) examining and communicating how the burden of risks from disasters will be distributed within the population (See *Table 5.1*)

6.2   Defining a Solution Space

While considerations from *Chapters 1* to *5* have narrowed the solution space significantly, there is still a range of viable alternative solutions conjecture that may be applicable to the current context. Transdisciplinary Systems Guidance (TSG) is informed by theory but cannot be determined by theory alone. This is in part because every wicked problem is essentially unique[645], so guidance has to address unique and specific challenges. This publication presents guidance at different levels of specificity to open up the knowledge production process and increase the overall publication's resilience, as guidance becomes more context-dependent as it increases in specificity. This can be understood intuitively: guidance to adopt a specific technology to advance circular economy is far more time sensitive than the more general guidance to adopt circular economic models — another technology may be a better fit in one or two years.

Transdisciplinary Systems Guidance (TSG)

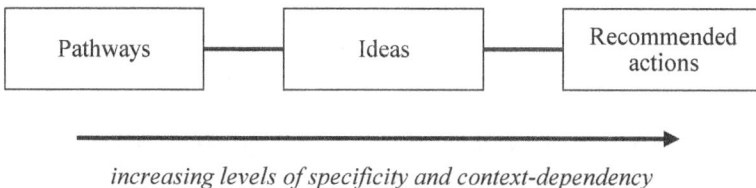

increasing levels of specificity and context-dependency

Figure 6.1 Increasing levels of specificity in Transdisciplinary Systems Guidance (TSG)

---

[645] See *Table 1.2.*

Figure 6.1 defines the different levels of specificity at which this publication offers guidance:

- *Guidance* in TSG refers broadly to advice that is grounded in implementation knowledge, and formulated to help stakeholders achieve shared goals
- *Pathways* in TSG identify viable alternative solutions conjectures based on a narrowed-down solution space with the support of Transdisciplinary Systems Research (TSR), and they serve as mutable boundaries for knowledge co-creation with stakeholders on *guidance*
- *Ideas* in TSG identify high-likelihood, high-impact *pathways*, based on a highly context-dependent assessment of their potential, and they serve as blueprints for redesigning institutions[646]
- *Recommended actions* (or *actionable recommendations*) in TSG specifies how *ideas* might be implemented within a target timeframe by stakeholder groups with due consideration to their goals[647]

Similar to the co-evolution of problem and solution space[648], guidance at different levels of specificity are iterated upon, and it is not necessary to work only in one direction at increasing levels of specificity. For example, a highly promising pathway may not be included in the final written output, if there does not appear to be a satisfactory recommended action within the particular context of the project.

This publication adopts the theory and practice of global diplomacy to guide the construction of a framework of pathways. *Global diplomacy* is the set of principles, methods, and actions to achieve the common goals of the global community within the contemporary global governance network[649]. This publication has considered each of the aspects in sequence. *Part 1* broadly corresponds to principles through considerations of boundaries, procedures to examine evidence, and valuation lenses. *Part 2* discusses the methods to achieve a system-wide transformation by examining the global change mechanisms. *Part 3*, this last chapter of the book, focuses on recommended actions.

As discussed in *Box 1-2*, global diplomacy describes a broad range of topics that converge around *interaction* (i.e. the process whereby individuals mutually influence each other and, in so doing, create,

---

[646] See *Section 4.2.3.*
[647] See *Section 1.2.3.*
[648] See *Section 3.2.3.*
[649] Sergeyev, Yuriy. "Sergeyev's Letter," November 9, 2021. p. 1.

maintain, change, or terminate a pattern of joint action). The synthesis in *Chapter 4* clarified the interactions necessary to facilitate a system-wide transformation. These include: (1) *focused social interactions* (i.e. dialogues with a mutual focus of attention, and a mutual appreciation of each other as unique individuals beyond social roles), and (2) *sustained and iterative engagements* (i.e. repeated dialogue between organizations and stakeholders that demonstrate reciprocity, which is a condition for knowledge co-creation)[650].

There are four areas of diplomacy in particular that emphasizes the types of interactions conducive to a system-wide transformation: (1) cultural diplomacy, (2) science diplomacy, (3) preventive diplomacy, and (4) knowledge diplomacy. These are also extensions from previous discussions on preventive diplomacy[651], culture[652], knowledge diplomacy[653], and climate change[654]. *Table 6.2* identifies 20 pathways in total, 5 for each of the areas of diplomacy. It articulates the solution space for a system-wide transformation. An earlier iteration of *Table 6.2* was available to the public as part of the Global Stakeholder Consultation Process. The final framework reflects the outcome of deliberations over the pathways' potential between the short (up to 1 year) and medium terms (up to 3 years). At this time, longer-term planning is unlikely to be realistic given on-going crises.

The pathways in *Table 6.2* have achieved different degrees of recognition. Of the 20 pathways, there are a few that have achieved recognition within their communities but have not received as much attention at a global level. This includes most of what falls under cultural diplomacy, transdisciplinary research (Pathway 6), community engagement (Pathway 15), discovery research (Pathway 16), and international law education (Pathway 20). I would also like to draw attention to Health for All (Pathway 10). While Health for All has maintained a priority within the WHO, I argue that it deserves further attention: the global nature of the 2030 Sustainable Development Goals feels distant and abstract to individuals. Framing sustainable development in terms of advancing individual health outcomes is highly likely to facilitate a system-wide transformation.

---

[650] See *Section 4.2.4*.
[651] See *Sections 2.4.3.* and *2.4.4*.
[652] See *Section 4.2.3*.
[653] See *Section 4.2.3*.
[654] See *Section 4.2.2* and *Table 5.1*.

Table 6.2 *Solution space*: a framework of pathways from global diplomacy

Pathway	Description
A.	**Cultural diplomacy**: the exchange of ideas, information, art, language and other cultural artifacts to foster mutual understanding
1	Art and design
2	Music
3	Language, literature, and poetry
4	Film, photography, and media
5	Games and sports
B.	**Science diplomacy**: the exchange of scientific ideas to advance sustainable development, facilitate international scientific collaborations, and inform decision-making
6	Transdisciplinary research
7	Climate literacy
8	Responsible technology
9	Media and information literacy
10	Health for All
C.	**Preventive diplomacy**: action taken to prevent disputes from escalating into conflicts and to limit their spread when they occur
11	Mental health
12	Youth leadership
13	Strategic foresight
14	Disaster risk reduction

15	Community engagement

D. **Knowledge diplomacy**: the process of building and strengthening relations through education, research, and innovation

16	Discovery research
17	Circular economy
18	Girls' and women's education
19	Children's education
20	International law education

Sources: UNESCO, "Cutting Edge | From Standing out to Reaching out: Cultural Diplomacy for Sustainable Development | UNESCO," 2022, https://www.unesco.org/en/articles/cutting-edge-standing-out-reaching-out-cultural-diplomacy-sustainable-development; UNESCO, "Arts and Artists," UNESCO, May 14, 2013, https://en.unesco.org/themes/arts-and-artists; DESA, "2021 SDGs in Action Film Festival Programme" (United Nations Department for Economic and Social Affairs (DESA), 2021); WHO, "Health for All - Transforming Economies to Deliver What Matters: Final Report of the WHO Council on the Economics of Health for All" (World Health Organization, 2023); UNESCO, *Not Just Hot Air: Putting Climate Change Education into Practice* (UNESCO, 2015). p. 5; UNOCIT, "Ethical Technology," United Nations Office of Information and Communications Technology (OCIT), 2023, https://unite.un.org/content/ethical-technology; UNDP, "Integrating Mental Health and Psychosocial Support into Peacebuilding," UNDP, 2022, https://www.undp.org/publications/integrating-mental-health-and-psychosocial-support-peacebuilding; United Nations Youth Strategy, "Youth 2030: Working with and for Young People" (United Nations, 2018). p. 4; UN Futures Lab, "UN Futures Lab - Home," UN Futures Lab, accessed March 14, 2024, https://un-futureslab.org/; United Nations Peacebuilding, "United Nations Community Engagement Guidelines on Peacebuilding and Sustaining Peace" (The Peacebuilding Support Office of the UN Department of Political and Peacebuilding Affairs, 2020). Foreword; UN DPPA, "Innovation," UN Department of Political and Peacebuilding Affairs, 2020, https://dppa.un.org/en/innovation; UNDP, "Circular Economy," UNDP, 2024, https://www.undp.org/chemicals-waste/our-work/circular-economy; UNITAR, "Strategic Framework 2022-2025" (United Nations Institute for Training and Research, 2020).

6.3   5 Ideas from Global Diplomacy

Ideas in Transdisciplinary Systems Guidance (TSG) identify high-likelihood, high-impact *pathways*, based on a highly context-dependent assessment of their potential, and they serve as blueprints for redesigning institutions[655]. This publication identifies 5 ideas from global diplomacy and a package of 9 interconnected *recommended actions*[656] that target the short (up to 1 year) to medium (up to 3 years) term horizons. This section will elaborate on the ideas and recommended actions. The 5 ideas are:
1. *Health for All*: increase coherence in private sector initiatives by conducting social impact measurement through health outcomes
2. *Culture as infrastructure*: empower individuals to build the culture and cultural organizations that allow stakeholders to contest norms' interpretations and adapt informal constraints in line with the goals of the global community given the absence of enforcement mechanisms at a global level for formal constraints (i.e. laws and policies)
3. *Discovery research fund approach*: provide grants for exploration and participation
4. *Transdisciplinary research*: encourage higher education institutions to support mutual learning and engage local communities in recognition of the institutions' roles in issue definition
5. *Futures studies*: offer *everyone* the opportunity to see themselves as part of our collective future on the rapidly changing Earth

To offer an example of where context-dependency has influenced the guidance of this publication, consider a Global Data Compact[657]. It is an incredibly important undertaking, but public consultations are already in progress at the United Nations and the potential impact of this publication on the agreement is relatively low. There are many other ideas within the framework of methods that would have been invaluable. It is important to remember that there is no exhaustive list of solutions in grand challenges[658], and anyone can support these ideas

---

[655] See *Section 6.2.*
[656] *ibid.*
[657] See *Section 5.2.9.*
[658] See *Table 1.2.*

or implement solutions even if they lie beyond the guidance of this publication. *The list of final ideas and recommended actions reflect the outcome of this context-dependent assessment at this time and is not exhaustive.*

Box 6-1: Q&A, Can the ideas be implemented locally and globally?

This was a question from an activist. Yes, all of the methods identified can be independently implemented at a local level. Part of the challenge in writing recommended actions is finding a balance between guidance that is specific enough to be meaningful, but leaves room for local adaptations. Future research can study recommended actions for regional, country, and community-levels further. While I believe the United Nations and other institutions possess unique and critical infrastructure, I understand people's experiences may vary. *Chapter 4* has demonstrated the importance of working together, and I encourage people to engage with platforms they trust. Implement the methods locally and independently if that is more comfortable to you – your contributions are just as valued.

6.3.1 Health for All

In 2023, the WHO Council on the Economics of Health for All recognized that:

- "Climate and health are deeply interlinked: transitioning to clean energy, more sustainable food systems and cleaner transportation systems has the potential to generate massive public health benefits in the coming years."[659]
- "Human health relies on a healthy planet. Human and planetary health, in turn, are critical to the resilience and stability of economies worldwide."[660]
- "It is evident that the three great crises of our time – health, inequality and the climate emergency – are profoundly interconnected, and none respect national borders."[661]

Recommendation 1:

- **Conduct social impact measurement for impact investment through health outcomes**. To quote the WHO Council on the Economics of Health for All, "Placing health and wellbeing at the centre of conceptions of purpose, value and economic growth is fundamental for societies that are just, inclusive, equitable and sustainable."[662] Almost all of the 2030 Sustainable Development Goals have a direct or indirect impact on health[663]. *Health for All presents (1) a viable common target for social impact measurement in impact investment that brings cohesion to the currently fragmented measurement landscape[664], (2) a satisfactory measure of an initiative's outcome despite challenges of wicked problems, and (3) measures at an appropriate scale[665] that is easily understandable to funders, collaborators, and local communities. This publication recommends drawing from*

---

[659] WHO Council on the Economics of Health for All, *Health for All - Transforming Economies to Deliver What Matters* (World Health Organization, 2023). p. 6.
[660] *ibid.* p. 7.
[661] *ibid.*
[662] *ibid.* p. 6.
[663] Annebeth Roor and Karen Maas, "Do Impact Investors Live up to Their Promise? A Systematic Literature Review on (Im)Proving Investments' Impacts," *Business Strategy and the Environment*, January 23, 2024, bse.3644, https://doi.org/10.1002/bse.3644. p. 2.
[664] *ibid.* Abstract.
[665] See *Section 5.1.4.*

well-established and robust methods of program evaluation in public health to inform social impact measurement for impact investment. Targeting human health outcomes will likely provide a pathway towards incorporating planetary health outcomes as a standard in the future.

6.3.2 Culture as Infrastructure

The lack of enforcement mechanisms at a global level means the global governance network depends on informal (i.e. cultural) constraints to function. Closing the compliance gap will rely on *culture as infrastructure*: spaces that allow stakeholders to contest norms' interpretations and adapt informal constraints in line with the goals of the global community[666]. This publication identifies support for *culture as infrastructure* through health initiatives. Researchers have recognized arts, culture, and nature as social drivers of health[667]. *Arts on prescription* is "any program in which health and social care providers are enabled to prescribe arts, culture, or nature experiences to patients or clients in order to support their health and well-being"[668].

The 2019 WHO Health Evidence Network synthesis report on the role of the arts in improving health and well-being identifies five broad categories within the arts:
1. performing arts (e.g. music, dance, theatre, singing, and film)
2. visual arts, design and craft (e.g. painting, photography, textiles)
3. literature (e.g. writing, reading, and attending literary festivals)
4. culture (e.g. going to museums, galleries, the theatre, community events, cultural festivals)
5. online, digital and electronic arts (e.g. animations, computer graphics)[669]

---

[666] See *Section 4.2.4*.
[667] Tasha L. Golden et al., "Arts on Prescription: A Field Guide for US Communities" (Mass Cultural Council / University of Florida Center for Arts in Medicine, 2023). p. 9.
[668] Golden et al., "Arts on Prescription: A Field Guide for US Communities." p. 8.
[669] Daisy Fancourt and Saoirse Finn, "Health Evidence Network Synthesis Report: What Is the Evidence on the Role of the Arts in Improving Health and Well-Being? A Scoping Review" (World Health Organization, 2019). p. 1.

The National Health Service (NHS) England's work on *green social prescribing* describes "the practice of supporting people to engage in nature-based interventions and activities to improve their mental and physical health"[670]. It includes what is known as green and blue activities e.g. community gardening projects, and outdoor cultural activities[671].

Research on arts on prescription and green social prescribing show a variety of positive health and social impacts. The 2019 WHO Health Evidence Network synthesis report found that the arts can "help to reduce ethnic tensions and improve interethnic relations and cultural competence"[672]. They are also "contributing to core determinants of health; playing a critical role in health promotion; helping to prevent the onset of mental illness and age-related physical decline; supporting the treatment or management of mental illness, noncommunicable diseases and neurological disorders; and assisting in acute and end-of-life-care"[673]. The National Academy for Social Prescribing and the UK Department of Health and Social Care reviewed the evidence on green social prescribing in 2022. Benefits include lower levels of cardiovascular and respiratory problems, reduced risk of obesity, reduced social isolation, and happiness[674].

---

[670] NHS, "NHS England » Green Social Prescribing," accessed March 17, 2024, https://www.england.nhs.uk/personalisedcare/social-prescribing/green-social-prescribing/.

[671] *ibid.*

[672] Fancourt and Finn, "Health Evidence Network Synthesis Report: What Is the Evidence on the Role of the Arts in Improving Health and Well-Being? A Scoping Review." p. 9-10.

[673] *ibid.* p. 57.

[674] National Academy for Social Prescribing, "Evidence Briefing, Social Prescribing: The Natural Environment" (National Academy for Social Prescribing, 2022). p. 1.

Recommendation 2

- ▪ **Increase pilot programs in arts on prescription and green social prescribing globally to support culture as infrastructure**. Closing the compliance gap to advance the 2030 Sustainable Development Goals will depend on *culture as infrastructure*: spaces that allow stakeholders to contest norms' interpretations and adapt informal constraints in line with the goals of the global community[675]. *Arts on prescription and green social prescribing are programs in which health and social care providers are enabled to prescribe arts, culture, or nature experiences to patients or clients in order to support their health and well-being. This can facilitate a system-wide transformation through: (1) cross-sectoral partnerships[676] that offer a support network for local arts, health, culture, and nature organizations, (2) the potential to integrate thoughtful cultural practices into nature-related initiatives and deliver a longer term impact[677], (3) social support for community members after traumatic events e.g. climate and weather related disasters as well as forced displacement, which are increasing in frequency and severity globally[678].* In a review of 19 studies on social prescribing in the UK by the National Academy for Social Prescribing, researchers found social programs can: (1) deliver between £2.14 and £8.56 for every £1 invested, and (2) reduce pressure on the National Health Service (NHS) through reduced GP appointments, reduced hospital admissions, and reduced Accident and Emergency visits[679]. *This publication recommends cross-sectoral partnerships to fund and develop arts on prescription and green social prescribing.* Organizations leading in this area include the International Arts + Mind Lab at Johns Hopkins Medicine, and the Jameel Arts & Health Lab established by the WHO Regional Office for Europe, and Steinhard School at NYU, alongside others.

---

[675] See *Section 4.2.4.*

[676] See *Section 5.2.3.*

[677] See *Section 5.1.1.*

[678] Fancourt and Finn, "Health Evidence Network Synthesis Report: What Is the Evidence on the Role of the Arts in Improving Health and Well-Being? A Scoping Review." p. 9-10.

[679] National Academy for Social Prescribing, "Economic Evidence," NASP, accessed March 18, 2024, https://socialprescribingacademy.org.uk/read-the-evidence/building-the-economic-case-for-social-prescribing/.

6.3.3 Discovery Research Fund Approach

Financing a system-wide transformation towards the 2030 Sustainable Development Goals has been a persistent challenge. At a time when many funders are moving away from supporting curiosity-based discovery, and towards projects with a nearer-term impact, it is critical that researchers from diverse backgrounds are provided with the resources to look around corners and deliver innovative solutions that can advance sustainable development.

This project identifies two major funding gaps:
1. *Funding for systems research that advances sustainable development*: This issue was raised in another similar systems research initiative for global problems, the Pivot Project. Although their team developed and presented proposals to G20 and COP26, funding streams for collaboration, mobilization, systems thinking, and capacity building were lacking[680]. This project has come to a similar conclusion[681]. Emma Leiken (Chief of Program, Omidyar Network) expressed a similar idea: "Youth communities are much more likely to view technology, education, mental health, climate, economic, and social policy issues as intertwined and interdependent. […] In contrast to the intersectionality youth groups often bring to issues adjacent to technology, funders almost unanimously view these issues as distinct, carving out separate funding portfolios for education, healthcare, civic engagement, and technology policy."[682]
2. *Funding for participation and collaboration*: This issue was raised by numerous historically underrepresented people and communities I have interacted with during the Global Stakeholder Consultation Process. Meaningful participation and an organized response are not possible without some form of dedicated funding[683].

---

[680] See *Section 3.3.2.*
[681] See *Section 3.3.3.*
[682] See *Section 5.2.5.*
[683] See *Section 3.3.4.*

Wellcome Trust is a foundation based in London, United Kingdom, that offers a discovery research program. It defines *discovery research* as studies across a breadth of disciplines that lead to new knowledge and insights into life, health and wellbeing. Based on a survey of more than 4,000 researchers in the UK and globally and nearly 100 in-depth interviews of UK researchers, the Wellcome Trust found that 75% of researchers believe their creativity is being stifled[684]. The Trust's discovery research program is designed to help researchers take on big questions and overcome barriers to progress[685]. It identifies three tiers of funding, including (1) Wellcome Early-Career Awards to help researchers establish their independence and research trajectory, (2) Wellcome Career-Development Awards for mid-career researchers who are ready to achieve international standing, and (3) Wellcome Discovery Awards for established researchers[686].

Recommendation 3

- **Champion a discovery research fund approach towards financing innovation for sustainable development.** *Inspired by Wellcome Trust's discovery research awards, this publication recommends providing small grants of $500 to $2500 USD for exploratory research, collaborations, and participation in consultation processes.* Deliverables can include a theory of change, research papers, policy recommendations, new ventures or programs, public-access workshops or exhibitions, or a summary of findings. *This recommendation can be implemented by current funders e.g. foundations, NGOs, and INGOs, or MNCs that are looking to increase their sustainable development innovation pipeline. The lower entry requirements for funders also open up the possibility for individual funders or networks of individuals, similar to an angel network in venture capital, to participate in financing for sustainable development.*

---

[684] Wellcome, "What Researchers Think about the Culture They Work In," January 15, 2020, https://wellcome.org/reports/what-researchers-think-about-research-culture.
[685] Wellcome, "Discovery Research | What We Do," October 4, 2023, https://wellcome.org/what-we-do/discovery-research.
[686] *ibid.*

6.3.4 Transdisciplinary Research

Transdisciplinary research (TDR) is when researchers work jointly with non-academic stakeholders across disciplinary boundaries towards a problem-solving, common-good oriented, mutual-learning, and comprehensive approach to complex sustainable development problems[687]. By bridging theory and practice, TDR has the potential to advance both simultaneously and facilitate a system-wide transformation[688]. Different academic programs have sought to engage non-academic stakeholders in knowledge production. One of the notable programs is Transdisciplinary Insights (TDI) at KU Leuven Institute for the Future in Belgium, where undergraduate and graduate students from different disciplines can work together with stakeholders to address specific complex problems under the supervision of faculty members[689].

Recommendation 4

- **Encourage initiatives at higher education institutions where the research agenda reflects local communities' priorities.** *Digital open source community engagement platforms such as Pol.is present new opportunities for researchers to respond to the concerns of local communities.* Organizations such as the UNDP[690], the Austrian government[691], the American Assembly (now INCITE) at Columbia University[692], have used Pol.is for research. *Engaging local communities helps (1) increase research's social relevance given the large role academics play in the issue definition phase of norm-setting processes, when*

---

[687] See *Section 1.4.1.*

[688] See *Chapter 1.4.*

[689] Rega Institute KU Leuven, "Transdisciplinary Insights," Page, accessed March 19, 2024, https://rega.kuleuven.be/if/education-training/tdi..

[690] The Computational Democracy Project, "2020 UNDP Case Study," accessed March 18, 2024, https://compdemocracy.org/Case-studies/2020-UNDP-South+S-E-Asia/.

[691] The Computational Democracy Project, "2021 Case Study on the Klimarat in Austria," accessed March 18, 2024, https://compdemocracy.org/Case-studies/2022-Austria-Klimarat/.

[692] Don Sergent, "First-Ever Civic Assembly Gives Residents Chance to Be Heard," Bowling Green Daily News, February 4, 2018, https://www.bgdailynews.com/news/first-ever-civic-assembly-gives-residents-chance-to-be-heard/article_0a17254e-a8bb-5f4f-884f-9d0617ab9c08.html.

*causes and potential solutions are identified[693],
(2) demonstrate the value of research and rebuild trust
amidst rising anti-science sentiment around public health
and climate change issues[694], and (3) empower young
scholars to use their research training to support their
communities and advocate for sustainable development.
This publication recommends new electives or programs at
higher education institutions that: (1) encourage
researchers to define a research agenda in partnership with
local communities, and (2) conduct research based on the
agenda to support local communities.* Existing initiatives
include INCITE at Columbia University, Public Humanities at
Yale University, TdLab at ETH Zürich, Transdisciplinary
Insights at KU Leuven, and others.

Recommendation 5

- **Expand stackable credentials and online degree programs
  while ensuring their affordability**. A system-wide
  transformation can be achieved only when *everyone* takes a
  step forward together. Mutual learning is a core part of
  Transdisciplinary Research (TDR) and it emphasizes the
  importance of access to knowledge. While there are many
  interpretations, *stackable credentials* generally refer to
  certificate programs that can be accumulated over time
  towards a college degree. Researchers from RAND and the
  University of Michigan found that low-income students, and
  students who identify as Asian, Black, or Hispanic are more
  likely to stack degrees in Colorado and Ohio across a sample
  of more than 80,000 students[695]. In Colorado, they were also
  most likely to be women. *This publication recommends
  increasing affordable stackable credentials and online
  degree programs to provide opportunities for access to
  knowledge and mutual learning.* For example, certificate
  programs are offered at Johns Hopkins, Stanford Online, and
  the Oxford Department for Continuing Education.

---

[693] See *Section 4.2.3.*
[694] Naomi Oreskes, "Standing up to Anti-Science," *The Lancet* 402, no. 10407
(September 23, 2023): 1034–35, https://doi.org/10.1016/S0140-6736(23)01966-9.
[695] Lindsay Daugherty et al., "Do Low-Income Students Benefit from Stacking
Credentials?: Descriptive Evidence from Colorado and Ohio" (RAND
Corporation, April 13, 2023),
https://www.rand.org/pubs/research_briefs/RBA2484-2.html.

Recommendation 6

- **Adopt a pre-print first model to disseminate timely research for problem-solving**. Because of the *dynamic*[696] nature of complex adaptive systems (CAS), systems change initiatives are highly time- and context-dependent. In 2021, research by Runde found the median times-to-publication in peer reviewed journals to range from 79 to 323 days[697]. *The significant uncertainty and delay in publishing at peer reviewed journals create a considerable barrier for academics to propose actionable short (up to 1 year) and medium (up to 3 years) term solutions.* A preprint first model can address this challenge. A *preprint* is a complete manuscript published prior to formal peer review, which allows for diverse community feedback[698]. The value of preprint has been recognized. For example: (1) three Nobel Laureates in biology have published preprints in 2016[699], (2) preprints have also been supported by funders such as the Gates Foundation, Howard Hughes Medical Institute, and Wellcome Trust[700], and (3) eLife is a publication that has eliminated "accept/reject" decisions in favor of preprint review and assessment. However, as noted by Stuart RF King (Research Culture Manager, eLife, UK) and Damian Pattinson (Executive Director, eLife, UK), there is still a cultural barrier towards adoption[701]. Researchers have to trust that adopting a preprint first model will not be penalized in terms of their funding and careers[702]. *This publication recommends funders and higher education institutions review incentive structures and ensure that researchers who adopt a preprint first model will not be penalized in terms of their funding and careers.*

---

[696] See *Table 1.1*.
[697] Brendan J. Runde, "Time to Publish? Turnaround Times, Acceptance Rates, and Impact Factors of Journals in Fisheries Science," ed. Charles William Martin, *PLOS ONE* 16, no. 9 (September 23, 2021): e0257841, https://doi.org/10.1371/journal.pone.0257841. Abstract.
[698] PLOS, "Preprints," *PLOS* (blog), accessed March 30, 2024, https://plos.org/open-science/preprints/.
[699] Tricia Serio, "Peer Review Is in Crisis, but Should Be Fixed, Not Abolished," The Conversation, November 15, 2016, http://theconversation.com/peer-review-is-in-crisis-but-should-be-fixed-not-abolished-67972.
[700] See *Section 5.2.10*.
[701] *ibid.*
[702] *ibid.*

Recommendation 7

- **Donate meeting spaces during off-peak business hours to organizations that engage local communities**. As Ivy Kwan Arce (President, Treatment Action Group (TAG)) observed: "The people on the ground need the space and the time to learn, to be able to participate at the table, and then you have to create the table for them to come to you."[703] *For companies that are looking to become more involved with sustainable development, hosting meetings of organizations that engage local communities e.g. non-profit, social enterprises, or research organizations would (1) offer a gentle introduction into the social impact space, (2) create opportunities for mutual learning, and (3) support culture as infrastructure. This publication recommends multinational corporations (MNCs) and companies in general to provide meeting spaces during off-peak business hours to organizations that engage local communities. Companies can begin by pilot testing this with select partnering organizations.*

6.3.5 Futures Studies

Since 2012, UNESCO has championed *Futures Literacy*: "the competency that allows people to better understand the role of the future in what they see and do. [...] Futures Literacy helps people understand why and how we use the future to prepare, plan, and interact with the complexity and novelty of our societies."[704] UNESCO has led over 110 Futures Literacy Laboratories in 44 countries since 2012, and established 37 UNESCO Chairs in Futures Literacy, Futures Studies and Anticipation from 31 countries across all regions since 2014[705].

---

[703] See *Section 5.1.5.*
[704] UNESCO, "Futures Literacy," accessed March 18, 2024, https://www.unesco.org/en/futures-literacy.
[705] *ibid.*

Recommendation 8

- **<u>Empower initiatives that explore the future of humanity at art, design, and architecture schools globally</u>**. To quote UNESCO, "Futures Literacy helps people understand why and how we use the future to prepare, plan, and interact with the complexity and novelty of our societies"[706]. Given increasing disruptions from conflicts and climate change, art, design, and architecture schools can play a role in helping local communities imagine, visualize, and participate in change. These initiatives can range from highly creative graphic narratives that engage the collective imagination about the future, to science-based video games on climate scenarios. They have the opportunity to (1) mobilize local interests, (2) enable critical discussions around pathways to change, and (3) support *culture as infrastructure* to close the compliance gap. *This publication recommends art, design, and architecture schools to: (1) offer electives where students can engage local communities on narratives about the future and science-based visualizations, and (2) partner with schools in STEM to communicate the impact of climate change on local communities. Graphics, narratives, video games, science-based visualizations, and other artistic outputs provide everyone, including youth and historically underrepresented populations, with the opportunity to see themselves in the future[707].*

---

[706] UNESCO, "Futures Literacy."
[707] See *Section 5.1.4.*

Recommendation 9

- **<u>Support board apprenticeship programs for young leaders</u>**. Board apprenticeship programs provide learning, development, leadership, and placement opportunities for young leaders to join private sector and not-for-profit boards. One such program is the UK Boardroom Apprentice supported by the UK Department for Levelling Up Housing and Communities[708]. *These programs give voice to future leaders, support intergenerational partnerships[709], help organizations adapt, and increase their talent pipeline. This publication recommends supporting board apprenticeship programs by (1) offering financial support for apprentices to participate, and (2) hosting apprentices at boards.*

---

[708] Boardroom Apprentice, "Get On Board," accessed March 30, 2024, https://boardroomapprentice.com/uk/.
[709] See *Section 5.2.5.*

6.4 Reflection on Transdisciplinary Systems Guidance (TSG)

This reflection looks back at the grand challenge framing and discusses the limitations of the recommendations in this publication. Recall: a system-wide transformation is a type of particularly challenging problem known as grand challenges (GC). GC's properties include (1) global scope, (2) high significance, (3) potential to be solvable, and (4) "wickedness"[710]. *Table 6.3* reflects on the recommendations with reference to the properties of wicked problems.

Table 6.3 Reflection on the recommendations in *Chapter 6* with reference to the properties of wicked problems

Property	Revised description
1. No definitive formulation	Although there are no definitive formulations, this publication has developed the novel approach of Transdisciplinary Systems Research (TSR) in order to more fully account for the properties of complex adaptive systems (CAS) and grand challenges (GC). Through TSR, the publication synthesized global governance theory and institutional theory to arrive at system-wide transformation methods. This is the most coherent and cutting-edge approach as of the time of writing.
2. No stopping rule	*Section 6.2* explicitly recognized that the final recommendations are highly contingent upon a context-dependent assessment of the likelihood of success and potential impact at the time of writing. Recommendations will have to be updated continuously in the future.
3. No true-or-false solutions	Every effort has been made during the TSR process, including through the engagement of historically underrepresented individuals and communities, to

---

[710] Wojciech Czakon, "Grand Challenges: A Way Out of the Ivory Tower for Management Academic Discipline," *Management Issues* 17, no. 4 (October 17, 2019), https://doi.org/10.7172/1644-9584.84.1. p. 12-13.

	understand and minimize potential adverse effects based on the information available.
4. No immediate tests	While there are no immediate tests, these recommendations have been drawn from extensive research and an understanding of past initiatives. Where necessary, it would be helpful to first conduct pilot studies to understand how the recommendations unfold within specific local contexts.
5. No redo-s	No redo-s recognize the time- and context-dependent nature of the recommendations.
6. No exhaustive list of solutions or permissible operations	This publication uses Maher and Poon's model of the co-evolution of problem space and solution-space model in 1996 (See *Section 3.2.3*) to narrow down the list of viable alternative solution conjectures. While there is indeed no way to prove that all solutions and permissible operations have been identified, the approach has been structured and rigorous.
7. Every wicked problem is essentially unique	This publication presents recommendations at increasing levels of specificity to increase the overall publication's resilience, as the context-dependency of the recommendation increases with the degree of specificity.
8. Every wicked problem is a symptom of another problem	*Section 6.2.1* recommends using health outcomes as a way to increase coherence and address this particular property of wicked problems.
9. Conflicting theories	*Section 4.2* discussed this more extensively: TSR contributes towards understanding the credibility, stability, and precision of mechanisms.
10. Real world consequences	Where necessary, it would be helpful to first conduct pilot studies to understand how the recommendations unfold within specific local contexts.

Note: see revised properties of wicked problems in *Table 1.2*.

6.5 Conclusion / Executive Summary

Amidst escalating global crises and growing climate anxiety, *5 Ideas from Global Diplomacy* offers actionable recommendations to deliver a *system-wide transformation* (i.e. large scale, longer term changes to close the compliance gap between political commitment and action, and advance the 2030 Sustainable Development Goals). The publication journeys beyond sustainability which is typically associated with climate action, and towards sustainable development which includes a critical peace component. It leverages a systems thinking approach to step back and address the contemporary global governance network in which we all participate, rather than target one Goal.

To deliver actionable recommendations, this publication develops a novel approach known as Transdisciplinary Systems Research (TSR). TSR has been formulated to solve grand challenges by combining transdisciplinary research and systems thinking, with a dedicated research philosophy that includes a theory on boundaries (ontology), procedures for examining evidence (epistemology), and valuation lenses (axiology). A key feature of TSR is it sets as boundaries the properties of complex adaptive systems (CAS) and the properties of grand challenges including those of wicked problems. Within this boundary, the publication gathers knowledge to hone in on a solution space by iteratively narrowing down the range of alternative solution conjectures.

This publication gathers four types of knowledge identified by Transdisciplinary Systems Research (TSR).
1. *Systems knowledge*: by framing a system-wide transformation as a grand challenge through systems research.
2. *Transformation knowledge*: by constructing a model of global change processes with reference to the compliance gap within the contemporary global governance network through global governance theory, neo-institutionalist theory, and intentional systems theory. Expert judgment and collaborative research processes from TSR contribute towards understanding the credibility, stability, and precision of mechanisms.
3. *Target knowledge*: by examining emerging perspectives on the 2030 Sustainable Development Goals through sustainable development and participatory action research (SDPAR).
4. *Implementation knowledge*: through the theory and practice of global diplomacy.

In so doing, this publication offers clarity on *system-wide transformation methods*, the means to navigate and alter the formal (i.e. laws and policies) and informal (i.e. cultural) constraints that limit progress towards closing the compliance gap and advancing the 2030 Sustainable Development Goals. At a macro-level, actors can navigate and alter formal constraints through issue definition, adoption, emergence, advocacy, campaigning, and norm-setting phases across a network of private and public organizations. At a micro-level, actors can reinterpret and apply new rules and norms within an organization. Further, this publication shows that actors can alter informal constraints by mobilizing culture as symbolic boundaries, frames, narratives, repertoires, and cultural capital. At both macro and micro levels, interactions among individuals, as well as those among individuals and organizations are critical. Two types of interactions are of particular importance: (1) *focused social interactions* (i.e. dialogue with a mutual focus of attention, and a mutual appreciation of each other as unique individuals beyond social roles) and *sustained and iterative engagements* (i.e. repeated dialogue between organizations and stakeholders that demonstrate reciprocity, which is a condition for knowledge co-creation). Consequently, global diplomacy, with an emphasis on interactions, emerges as the overarching theory for a system-wide transformation.

Through the co-evolution of the problem and solution space, the publication identifies 5 ideas from global diplomacy. *Global diplomacy* describes the set of principles, methods, and actions to achieve the common goals of the global community within the contemporary global governance network. *Ideas* refer to high-likelihood, high-impact pathways, based on a highly context-dependent assessment of their potential, and they serve as blueprints for redesigning institutions. The 5 ideas are:

1. *Health for All*: conduct social impact measurement for impact investment through health outcomes to increase coherence
2. *Culture as infrastructure*: empower individuals to build the culture and cultural organizations that allow stakeholders to contest norms' interpretations and adapt informal constraints in line with the goals of the global community given the absence of enforcement mechanisms at a global level for formal constraints (i.e. laws and policies)
3. *Discovery research fund approach*: provide small grants for exploratory research, collaborations, and participation in consultation processes
4. *Transdisciplinary research*: encourage higher education institutions to engage local communities and support mutual

learning in recognition of the institutions' roles in issue definition
5. *Futures studies*: offer everyone the opportunity to see themselves as part of our collective future on the rapidly changing Earth

Table 6.4 offers a summary of the interconnected and actionable recommendations that target the short (up to 1 year) to medium (up to 3 years) term horizon.

Table 6.4 Table of recommended actions

Recommendation	Action
1. Conduct social impact measurement for impact investment through health outcomes	This publication recommends drawing from well-established and robust methods of program evaluation in public health to inform social impact measurement for impact investment. Health for All presents a viable common target for social impact measurement that brings cohesion to the currently fragmented measurement landscape and measures at an appropriate scale that is easily understandable to funders, collaborators, and local communities.
2. Increase pilot programs in arts on prescription and green social prescribing globally to support culture as infrastructure	This publication recommends cross-sectoral partnerships to fund and develop arts on prescription and green social prescribing. Arts on prescription and green social prescribing are programs in which health and social care providers are enabled to prescribe arts, culture, or nature experiences to patients or clients in order to support their health and well-being. They can offer a support network for local arts, health, culture, and nature organizations, and social support for community members after traumatic events e.g. climate and weather related disasters as well as forced displacement, which are increasing in frequency and severity globally.
3. Champion a discovery research fund approach towards financing innovation for sustainable development	This publication recommends providing small grants of $500 to $2500 USD for exploratory research, collaborations, and participation in consultation processes. This recommendation can be implemented by current funders that are

	looking to increase their sustainable development innovation pipeline. The lower entry requirements for funders also open up the possibility for individual funders or networks of individuals, similar to an angel network in venture capital, to participate in financing for sustainable development.
4. Encourage initiatives at higher education institutions where the research agenda reflects local communities' priorities	This publication recommends new electives or programs at higher education institutions that: (1) encourage researchers to define a research agenda in partnership with local communities, and (2) conduct research based on the agenda to support local communities. Engaging local communities helps (1) increase research's social relevance given the large role academics play in the issue definition phase of norm-setting processes, when causes and potential solutions are identified, (2) demonstrate the value of research and rebuild trust amidst rising anti-science sentiment around public health and climate change issues, and (3) empower young scholars to use their research training to support their communities and advocate for sustainable development. Digital open source community engagement platforms such as Pol.is present new opportunities for researchers to respond to the concerns of local communities.
5. Expand stackable credentials and online degree programs while ensuring their affordability	This publication recommends increasing affordable stackable credentials and online degree programs to provide opportunities for access to knowledge and mutual learning. Effective collaborations, engagements, and consultation processes rely on a time and space where stakeholders can learn to engage.
6. Adopt a pre-print first model to disseminate timely research for problem-solving	This publication recommends funders and higher education institutions review incentive structures and ensure that researchers who adopt a pre-print first model will not be penalized in terms of their funding and careers. The significant uncertainty and delay in publishing at peer reviewed journals create a considerable barrier for academics to propose actionable short (up to 1 year) and medium (up to 3 years) term solutions.

7. Donate meeting spaces during off-peak business hours to organizations that engage local communities	This publication recommends multinational corporations (MNCs) and companies in general to provide meeting spaces during off-peak business hours to organizations that engage local communities. For companies that are looking to become more involved with sustainable development, hosting meetings of organizations that engage local communities e.g. non-profit, social enterprises, or research organizations would (1) offer a gentle introduction into the social impact space, (2) create opportunities for mutual learning, and (3) support culture as infrastructure. Companies can begin by pilot testing this with select partnering organizations.
8. Empower initiatives that explore the future of humanity at art, design, and architecture schools globally	This publication recommends art, design, and architecture schools to: (1) offer electives where students can engage local communities on narratives about the future and science-based visualizations, and (2) partner with schools in STEM to communicate the impact of climate change on local communities. Graphics, narratives, video games, science-based visualizations, and other artistic outputs provide everyone, including youth and historically underrepresented populations, with the opportunity to see themselves in the future.
9. Support board apprenticeship programs for young leaders	This publication recommends supporting board apprenticeship programs by (1) offering financial support for apprentices to participate, and (2) hosting apprentices at boards. These programs give voice to future leaders, support intergenerational partnerships, help organizations adapt, and increase their talent pipeline.

Note: see *Section 6.2*

Although the final recommendations will have to be updated due to the dynamic nature of complex adaptive systems, an enduring principle will hold: *a system-wide transformation can be achieved only when everyone takes a step forward together, like a puzzle that will be solved only when we turn all the keys at the same time.*

6.6 References

Appelo, Jurgen. "The Persona Protocol." In *Startup, Scaleup, Screwup*. Wiley, 2019. https://learning.oreilly.com/library/view/startup-scaleup-screwup/9781119526858/c04.xhtml.

Boardroom Apprentice. "Get On Board." Accessed March 30, 2024. https://boardroomapprentice.com/uk/.

Czakon, Wojciech. "Grand Challenges: A Way Out of the Ivory Tower for Management Academic Discipline." *Management Issues* 17, no. 4 (October 17, 2019). https://doi.org/10.7172/1644-9584.84.1.

Daugherty, Lindsay, Peter Riley Bahr, Peter Nguyen, Jennifer May-Trifiletti, Rooney Columbus, and Jonah Kushner. "Do Low-Income Students Benefit from Stacking Credentials?: Descriptive Evidence from Colorado and Ohio." RAND Corporation, April 13, 2023. https://www.rand.org/pubs/research_briefs/RBA2484-2.html.

Fancourt, Daisy, and Saoirse Finn. "Health Evidence Network Synthesis Report: What Is the Evidence on the Role of the Arts in Improving Health and Well-Being? A Scoping Review." World Health Organization, 2019.

Golden, Tasha L., Amy Bantham, Keely Mason, Jill Sonke, Käthe Swaback, Maria Nagae Kuge, Alyson Maier Lokuta, et al. "Arts on Prescription: A Field Guide for US Communities." Mass Cultural Council / University of Florida Center for Arts in Medicine, 2023.

National Academy for Social Prescribing. "Economic Evidence." NASP. Accessed March 18, 2024. https://socialprescribingacademy.org.uk/read-the-evidence/building-the-economic-case-for-social-prescribing/.

———. "Evidence Briefing, Social Prescribing: The Natural Environment." National Academy for Social Prescribing, 2022.

NHS. "NHS England » Green Social Prescribing." Accessed March 17, 2024. https://www.england.nhs.uk/personalisedcare/social-prescribing/green-social-prescribing/.

Oreskes, Naomi. "Standing up to Anti-Science." *The Lancet* 402, no. 10407 (September 23, 2023): 1034–35. https://doi.org/10.1016/S0140-6736(23)01966-9.

PLOS. "Preprints." *PLOS* (blog). Accessed March 30, 2024. https://plos.org/open-science/preprints/.

Rega Institute KU Leuven. "Transdisciplinary Insights." Page. Accessed March 19, 2024. https://rega.kuleuven.be/if/education-training/tdi.

Roor, Annebeth, and Karen Maas. "Do Impact Investors Live up to Their Promise? A Systematic Literature Review on (Im)Proving Investments' Impacts." *Business Strategy and the Environment*, January 23, 2024, bse.3644. https://doi.org/10.1002/bse.3644.

Runde, Brendan J. "Time to Publish? Turnaround Times, Acceptance Rates, and Impact Factors of Journals in Fisheries Science." Edited by Charles

William Martin. *PLOS ONE* 16, no. 9 (September 23, 2021): e0257841. https://doi.org/10.1371/journal.pone.0257841.

Sergent, Don. "First-Ever Civic Assembly Gives Residents Chance to Be Heard." Bowling Green Daily News, February 4, 2018. https://www.bgdailynews.com/news/first-ever-civic-assembly-gives-residents-chance-to-be-heard/article_0a17254e-a8bb-5f4f-884f-9d0617ab9c08.html.

Serio, Tricia. "Peer Review Is in Crisis, but Should Be Fixed, Not Abolished." The Conversation, November 15, 2016. http://theconversation.com/peer-review-is-in-crisis-but-should-be-fixed-not-abolished-67972.

The Computational Democracy Project. "2020 UNDP Case Study." Accessed March 18, 2024. https://compdemocracy.org/Case-studies/2020-UNDP-South+S-E-Asia/.

———. "2021 Case Study on the Klimarat in Austria." Accessed March 18, 2024. https://compdemocracy.org/Case-studies/2022-Austria-Klimarat/.

UN DPPA. "Innovation." UN Department of Political and Peacebuilding Affairs, 2020. https://dppa.un.org/en/innovation.

UN Futures Lab. "UN Futures Lab - Home." UN Futures Lab. Accessed March 14, 2024. https://un-futureslab.org/.

UNDP. "Circular Economy." UNDP, 2024. https://www.undp.org/chemicals-waste/our-work/circular-economy.

———. "Integrating Mental Health and Psychosocial Support into Peacebuilding." UNDP, 2022. https://www.undp.org/publications/integrating-mental-health-and-psychosocial-support-peacebuilding.

UNESCO. "Arts and Artists." UNESCO, May 14, 2013. https://en.unesco.org/themes/arts-and-artists.

———. "Cutting Edge | From Standing out to Reaching out: Cultural Diplomacy for Sustainable Development | UNESCO," 2022. https://www.unesco.org/en/articles/cutting-edge-standing-out-reaching-out-cultural-diplomacy-sustainable-development.

———. "Futures Literacy." Accessed March 18, 2024. https://www.unesco.org/en/futures-literacy.

———. *Not Just Hot Air: Putting Climate Change Education into Practice*. UNESCO, 2015.

UNITAR. "Strategic Framework 2022-2025." United Nations Institute for Training and Research, 2020.

United Nations Peacebuilding. "United Nations Community Engagement Guidelines on Peacebuilding and Sustaining Peace." The Peacebuilding Support Office of the UN Department of Political and Peacebuilding Affairs, 2020.

United Nations Youth Strategy. "Youth 2030: Working with and for Young People." United Nations, 2018.

UNOCIT. "Ethical Technology." United Nations Office of Information and Communications Technology (OCIT), 2023. https://unite.un.org/content/ethical-technology.

Wellcome. "Discovery Research | What We Do," October 4, 2023. https://wellcome.org/what-we-do/discovery-research.

————. "What Researchers Think about the Culture They Work In," January 15, 2020. https://wellcome.org/reports/what-researchers-think-about-research-culture.

WHO. "Health for All - Transforming Economies to Deliver What Matters: Final Report of the WHO Council on the Economics of Health for All." World Health Organization, 2023.

WHO Council on the Economics of Health for All. *Health for All - Transforming Economies to Deliver What Matters*. World Health Organization, 2023.

Closing Thoughts

This project was a tremendous undertaking. It would not be possible without the support of reviewers and readers like you. I hope this book inspired you to think differently about the methods to advance sustainable development. Thank you again to everyone who came on this journey with me. And thank you for reading this publication.

If you would like to support my work, you can:
- recommend my book on social media
- leave a review on Goodreads
- gift a copy of the book to a friend or colleague
- email me a 1-2 sentence endorsement for the book

I am also very open to feedback or collaborations, and I enjoy advising. Please feel free to reach out.

Marvin Cheung

Marvin@UnbuiltLabs.com

Index

A system-wide
transformation for all

Visit the official book webpage to join our *List of Readers*.
Access supplementary materials, events, and more:
https://unbuiltlabs.com/5-ideas-from-global-diplomacy

www.ingramcontent.com/pod-product-compliance
Lightning Source LLC
Chambersburg PA
CBHW070057030426
42335CB00016B/1927